DONALD V. NIGHTINGALE is a member of the School of Business at Queen's University.

This book begins with a historical review of how authority in the Canadian workplace has changed over the past century. It proceeds to outline a theory of organization which provides a broad conceptual framework for the empirical analysis which follows. This theory is based on five concepts: the values of organization members; the administrative structure of the organization; interpersonal and intergroup processes; the reactions and adjustments of organization members; the social, political, economic, and cultural environments of the organization.

A sample of 20 industrial organizations was selected to examine the effects of significant employee participation and to test the theory. They are matched pairs: ten permit some form of participation, and ten – similar in size, location, industry, union/non-union status, and work technology – follow conventional hierarchical design.

The resulting data demonstrate that greater productivity results from employee participation in decisions relating to their work, in productivity bonuses, and in profit sharing and employee share-ownership plans.

MAX CLARKSON of the Faculty of Management Studies, University of Toronto, has contributed a foreword to this important study.

DONALD V. NIGHTINGALE

Workplace Democracy:
An inquiry into
employee participation in
Canadian work organizations

Foreword by Max B.E. Clarkson

UNIVERSITY OF TORONTO PRESS
Toronto Buffalo London

658.315
N68w

© University of Toronto Press 1982
Toronto   Buffalo   London
Printed in Canada

ISBN 0-8020-5574-5 (cloth)
ISBN 0-8020-6471-1 (paper)

Canadian Cataloguing in Publication Data

m.R.

Nightingale, Donald V.
Workplace democracy
Includes index.
ISBN 0-8020-5574-5 (bound) ISBN 0-8020-6471-1 (pbk.)
1. Employees' representation in management –
Canada. 2. Employees' representation in management
– Canada – Case studies. 3. Employees' representa-
tion in management. I. Title.
HD5660.C3N55   658.3′152′0971   C81-095043-X

To my father, A. Victor Nightingale

Contents

Foreword

This important book shows how ten different enterprises have responded to the challenge of introducing democratic principles into the decision-making processes of the workplace. The underlying assumption governing the different approaches in these organizations has been that workers have a moral right to participate in the decisions which affect them in their jobs, just as they have a moral right to participate in the political decision-making processes which affect them in their lives away from the workplace.

Different processes, structures, and institutions have been developed in different democracies to enable citizens to participate in decision-making at various levels of government and public administration. In the United States and France, as in Canada, human and moral values of the highest order are made explicit in such statements of national purpose as 'life, liberty and the pursuit of happiness,' 'liberté, égalité, fraternité,' and 'peace, order and good government.' The average citizen may become frustrated in his pursuit of these ideals and discouraged by the inability of elected governments to make substantive progress towards their attainment, but he is free to voice his discouragement and to attempt to improve the system.

But we find a very different picture when we look at the workplace, whether in the public or the private sectors. Work organizations rarely state their purpose in terms of moral or human values. It is more likely, if there is any statement at all, to be phrased in terms of technological or bureaucratic efficiency, of maximizing profits for anonymous shareholders. The values of technology and of 'the bottom line,' of bureaucracy and control, have taken priority in organizational life over the human and moral values which are the foundations of our democratic way of life. The principles by which we manage our work organizations are very different from those which we espouse in our daily lives, at home or in our communities. Professor Nightingale has summarized these differences in the following table.

The contrasting principles of democratic society and the modern work organization

The principles of democratic society	The principles of the modern work organization
1 Accountability of leadership to the governed	1 Accountability of leadership to higher authority (owners, superiors in the hierarchy of authority)
2 Citizen participation or consultation in decisions; right to be informed	2 Decision-making made at highest levels of the hierarchy
3 Leaders chosen by the governed	3 Leaders chosen by higher authority
4 Right to question leaders	4 Leaders' judgments and decisions not subject to review by subordinates
5 Right to dissent, free speech	5 Uniformity, compliance with directives demanded
6 Freedom of movement, association, liberty, individual expression	6 Activities, interactions closely defined and circumscribed
7 Informed and knowledgeable constituency	7 Information limited to immediate task requirements

Professor Nightingale identifies these differences in principle as the underlying reason for the widely held beliefs 'that something is wrong at the workplace ... [and] that authoritarian practices at the workplace are no longer necessary or appropriate.' Perceptively he points out that a 'significant component of the mounting problems in the workplace is the contradiction between the values celebrated in the larger society and the values underpinning the workplace. The young Canadian worker – native-born, socialized in the anti-authoritarian ideology of contemporary Canadian society, and raised on a philosophy of equality, freedom, and the inherent dignity of the individual – cannot fail to be disappointed by the workplace. In the modern work organization, the employee's freedom is suspended in many important respects, justice is limited, obedience to superiors is demanded, and the workplace is permeated with the symbols of authority, deference, and subordination. The worker experiences a vague and imperfectly articulated sense that a contradiction exists between our social values of individual expression, freedom, and initiative and the values of obedience and subordination in the workplace' (6).

Values act as guides to action and have been defined by Milton Rokeach as 'enduring beliefs that specific modes of conduct or end states of existence are personally or socially preferable to other modes of conduct or end states of existence.' Values, Rokeach maintains, are then organized into a hierarchy of relative importance, which becomes the value system of a particular individual. When issues arise or decisions about conduct and behaviour are made, the relative importance of one value compared with others will have a significant influence on the decisions and on the behavioural outcome. Values, obviously, can be in conflict. Behaving both honestly and lovingly can sometimes be difficult, and choices must be made. The choices which we make in our daily lives may well result in behaviour which is not consistent with our stated value system. We say one thing but do another, a phenomenon of the human condition to which children often draw our attention.

The difference is often great between what Argyris has called the 'espoused' system of values and actual behaviour. This difference becomes most marked in the work organization, where often we are required to hang up our personal value system with our coat as we enter the workplace and wear instead the value system of the work organization. If there is a poor fit, we shall be uncomfortable.

If the organization's value system has placed the highest priority on technological efficiency and maximizing profits in the short term, we can be reasonably certain that obedient behaviour will be rewarded, while independence and honesty may not be appreciated. When the conflict between the individual's value system and that of the work organization becomes serious, alienation and lack of commitment will result, with inevitably negative consequences in terms of behaviour, performance, and productivity. When the technical systems of a work organization have not been integrated with the social and value systems of the people working in that organization, there will be difficulties with motivation, productivity, and commitment.

A social system in a work organization which depends, for the achievement of its objectives, on the authority of hierarchical rank and coercive power exemplifies a value system dominated by obedience. Obedience, together with politeness and cleanliness, used to be an important value in the social systems of the western world. Obeying orders, knowing your own place, doing the job, doing your duty, and postponing gratification were all precepts of a value system which was espoused and instilled at home, in the church, and at school until well into the twentieth century. But this is no longer the case.

The diminution of serious expectations about the evolutionary nature of the life hereafter coupled with the loss of faith in the present value of religious salvation has led to concentration on the here-and-now and to rising expectations about self-improvement, self-respect, and self-development.

The development of human potential has become a central concern of the educational system from kindergarten onwards. Regardless of our opinions about contemporary educational methods and results, the values of freedom or independence and 'doing your own thing' have been instilled on a widespread basis. The values of independence and obedience are difficult to reconcile. There is no social premium placed on obedience today, except in the context of 'the law' and of the behaviour of the very young and very old. Independence or freedom and their corollary, choice, have become values of great importance in contemporary society.

Work organizations have been adjusting to this change in the relative importance of values for some time. The present concern with the management of human resources, the historical development of which is clearly outlined in this book, is an attempt to deal constructively with the fundamental change in the relative importance of the values of independence and obedience which has occurred in Canada and the United States in the period following the Second World War.

The coercive and authoritarian uses of power result in loss of independence and choice for those who must obey. When choice and independence are lost, people feel powerless. The essence of powerlessness is to have no choice. Feelings of powerlessness cause anger, frustration, and destructive behaviour. It makes little sense, therefore, in the workplace, to construct systems of management and decision-making which rely on hierarchical rank and authoritarian power in order to try and achieve the organization's objectives. If we are educating people across Canada to place a high value on freedom, independence, and choice, we should be creating management systems which capitalize on the importance of these values to people, rather than ignoring these values or, worse still, denying their existence.

If as a society we are still pursuing the democratic ideal of responsible, free people making informed choices, then as managers we have a responsibility to create in our work organizations management systems which are morally compatible with democratic ideals. Democracy has been defined as 'a moral process for resolving conflict in a pluralistic society.' Conflict, as Professor Nightingale discusses fully, is inescapable in work organizations. We cannot avoid conflict and disagreement on the job. But we do have a choice about how we deal with it. We can choose the authoritarian, coercive way, or we can choose the democratic, participative way. In making the choice, we should be sure that we are well-informed. Valid and appropriate information is the essence of sound decision-making and of learning.

Managers of profit-making organizations usually learn quickly. If they do not, their organizations become bankrupt or their survival is seriously threatened. In the 1950s and 1960s the 'learning' of managers was focused on the internal organization of the enterprise. The manager's main function was to achieve control of the different elements of the business and learn how to respond to the principal challenge of that long period of economic expansion in the Canadian and world economies. This challenge was the management of growth and of the accompanying large bureaucratic structures. This meant learning how to cope with the problems of finance, accounting and control, production and inventory control, marketing and personnel. But now it is becoming clear that organizations cannot implement their plans and strategies without paying serious attention to the larger environment of which they are a part. The successful management of the internal functions of an organization is no longer sufficient, because the socio-economic setting in which organizations now operate is increasingly uncertain, complex, and political. Management now faces the challenge of learning from and understanding the multitude of signals being received from this rapidly changing environment and of developing positive strategies, rather than reacting in a negative manner to changes imposed by external pressures or forces.

This important book is about the strategies, based on the values of participation and choice, which have been developed in ten different Canadian organizations in order to manage more constructively the multiple and complex relationships between workers and other stakeholders in the enterprise. Of particular interest is the unique way in which Professor Nightingale has compared these organizations with other organizations of similar characteristics, except that their management styles and structures are hierarchical and autocratic, based on the value of obedience. The conclusions drawn from these comparisons should be of great interest to practising managers, as well as to academics. Participation in decision-making does not result in all the nightmarish permissive anarchy predicted by the authoritarian manager. McGregor's Theory Y assumptions about human nature can be incorporated into the management philosophy and practices of productive and profitable enterprises. It is not necessary to subordinate the consideration of human values to the values of technology and 'the bottom line.' It is possible for enterprises to serve moral purposes and provide products and services for society at a profit in a manner which obtains the commitment of the employees.

These are important conclusions, based upon careful and thorough research, which should be taken seriously by all those interested in the development of productive Canadians in a democratic and prosperous Canada.

MAX B.E. CLARKSON
Faculty of Management Studies
University of Toronto

Preface

This book is about employee participation in decision-making. The form of participation examined in this book, however, is not commonly found in work organizations in the industrialized western nations. 'Workplace democracy' is a form of participation which gives employees at all levels in the organization the right to participate in decisions which affect them.

This inquiry will lead us to questions of fact as well as to questions of value. In addressing questions of fact we shall examine a sample of innovative Canadian firms which have gone far beyond conventional practice in broadening opportunities for employee participation in decision-making. Data from 1,000 respondents in twenty companies have been collected through standardized instruments and through extensive interviews with managers and trade union officials.

As we explore the effects of workplace democracy on the well-being of organization members, we shall be addressing implicitly the question of how other organizations in our society might be altered to allow greater sharing of decision-making responsibilities among organization members at all levels.

This research on workplace democracy is founded on my belief that the effectiveness of the modern work organization should be measured in terms of the well-being of its members as well as in terms of its economic success. This exploration is also guided by a belief that employees can and should have significant influence – subject to certain limitations – in their work lives; that employees should be treated as responsible and contributing members of the organization; and that the workplace should provide opportunities for friendship, achievement, and personal fulfilment.

I also believe that a more humane and democratic work environment is most likely to be achieved in the democratic western industrialized nations, and that workplace democracy is entirely consistent with private ownership of property, an open, pluralist, democratic political system, and a market economy.

The relative power of labour and capital will always be a source of contention in a democratic society. The rights of labour and capital – as this book demonstrates – have been subject to continuing review in the industrialized western nations for the past 100 years. The rights of labour and capital will be subject to scrutiny and review in any dynamic society.

This book is an exploration of one means of accommodating the interests of labour and the interests of capital, and this sample of organizations demonstrates that there are creative and resourceful solutions to the timeless problem of accommodating the diverse interests represented within a work organization.

Workplace democracy is both an end and a means. As an end it is a form of organization which reconciles economic imperatives with the psychological requirements of its members. As a means it is a way to a better future. Workplace democracy unleashes creative resources, motivation, and commitment, which are currently held in check by the inhospitable conditions in the modern work organization.

The problems of today's workplace challenge fundamental management and union practices – practices which were developed in an earlier era to meet different conditions. This book examines an alternative which may lead us towards a new era of labour-management co-operation.

D.V.N.
Kingston, Ontario

Acknowledgments

Many people have contributed to this book – some in indirect ways through shaping my interests and perspective and some in direct ways through assisting with data collection, analysis, and interpretation. Among those who first kindled my interest in employee participation are Arnold Tannenbaum, Stanley Seashore, Daniel Katz, and Rensis Likert. This remarkable group of scholars at the University of Michigan deeply influenced my views of workplace democracy.

The data collection and analysis are the product of a large team of persons. I am particularly indebted to Pierre D'Aragon and Gilbert Tarrab of the Université du Québec à Montréal for their assistance with data collection in Quebec. This study would not have been possible without their assistance.

The questionnaire administration, interviews, and field observations were handled by Maureen Doyle, Mary-Jane Dundas, and John Rudan. They were assisted by Ann Cameron, Vivian Aronson, Mary Zurick, Madeleine Murphy, Robert Schnurr, and Louis O'Brien. The data analysis was conducted by Carol Peterson, Carolyn Farquhar, Peter Lawton, Les Kearney, and Dave Brining. Carolyn Farquhar also assisted with the literature review and the assembling of the manuscript. Rose-Marie Baird transcribed the manuscript from tape and Connie Raymond typed the final version.

The manuscript was greatly strengthened by the perceptive reviews of several colleagues. Among these are Arnold Tannenbaum of the University of Michigan, Harvey Kolodny of the University of Toronto, and Alan Clarke of St Lawrence College. Finally, I am indebted to my wife, Maureen, who accepted without complaint my absence during the data collection and preparation of this book. Pat Collom prepared the index and the bibliography and assisted with editing the final manuscript. Special thanks goes to Joan

Homer of Durham College whose substantive and editorial comments significantly improved the manuscript and whose encouragement is much appreciated. Finally, Alan Whitehorn of the Royal Military College offered many valuable comments on the manuscript.

Funding for this study comes from many sources. The pilot grants which allowed a preliminary assessment of the field sites were provided by the Associates' Workshop in Business Research of the School of Business Administration of the University of Western Ontario; the Canada Council supported the data collection in the twenty organizations; at Queen's the McLeod Endowment of the School of Business provided research assistants for data analysis and the Computing Centre provided funds for data analysis; Labour Canada provided a grant through its university research fund for the preparation of the case disciplines in appendix I; and the Ontario ministry of industry and tourism provided funds for part of the analysis of profit-sharing and employee ownership.

This book has been published with the help of a grant from the Social Science Federation of Canada, using funds provided by the Social Sciences and Humanities Research Council of Canada, and a grant from the Andrew W. Mellon Foundation to the University of Toronto Press.

This book, of course, would not have been possible without the support and co-operation of those people who took time from their working day to participate in this study. To all of them I extend my warmest appreciation.

WORKPLACE DEMOCRACY:
AN INQUIRY INTO EMPLOYEE PARTICIPATION IN
CANADIAN WORK ORGANIZATIONS

1

Workplace democracy: issues and challenges

There is a growing conviction among Canadian working people of every description and circumstance that something is wrong at the workplace. Despite substantial and continuing improvements in wages, benefits, and working conditions, there is a widespread perception among Canadian working people that the work organization does not operate to their advantage.

In the face of mounting employee alienation and labour unrest, there is a search – not only in this country, but across the industrialized world – for new and effective means of fulfilling employee expectations while enhancing the productive capability of the work organization. More than at any other time in the past, we seek new forms and patterns of work.

Among these new forms of work organization is an alternative which evokes both strong support and strong condemnation. This alternative has been hailed by some as a strategy for the revitalization of the modern industrial organization, and denounced by others as a dangerous and disruptive intrusion into the rights and prerogatives of managers and shareholders. This alternative is 'workplace democracy.'

Although widely adopted in western Europe, 'workplace democracy' (or 'industrial democracy' as it is also called) is almost unknown in Canada and has remained largely outside the mainstream of management practice and trade union goals in this country. Nevertheless, the principle that working people should have a voice in matters which materially affect them at the workplace is more widely accepted today than in the past. It is unclear precisely how deeply the concept of 'workplace democracy' has penetrated the public's consciousness in this country. It is clear, however, that frequent references to the term 'industrial democracy' in the popular press and the growing dissatisfaction – among managers and workers alike – with the 'command-and-obey' system reflect the general belief that authoritarian practices at the workplace are no longer necessary or appropriate.

Much of the confusion and apprehension about the concept of 'workplace democracy' arises from the absence of a precise and established definition. Both technical and popular presses abound with a profusion of terms: 'co-determination,' 'industrial democracy,' 'self-management,' 'co-management,' 'worker control,' 'humanization of the workplace,' 'formal participation,' 'quality of work life,' to name a few. Each of these terms varies in ideological depth and each is embraced by groups with differing political and economic interests. Nevertheless, common to all terms is a substantial reallocation of power over major organizational decisions to employees at lower hierarchical levels.

The effects of this redistribution of power on the modern work organization will be explored in this book. The exploration will focus on the philosophical underpinnings of this concept as well as on the climate of attitudes and opinion in organizations which permit significant employee participation in decision-making. Inevitably, this analysis will draw us into a discussion of the effects of workplace democracy on society and its institutions. Political democracy, trade unionism, the rights of capital and labour, and the responsibilities of government for enhancing employee welfare at the workplace will be examined. Before turning to these issues, however, we shall explore the forces in Canadian society which have placed workplace democracy on the political agenda.

THE 'SPREADING PSYCHOLOGY OF ENTITLEMENT'

Although the labour relations problems of this country arise from many factors, perhaps the most fundamental is the 'spreading psychology of entitlement.' The prosperity of the post-war period has created – particularly among young employees – a belief that working people are entitled to a meaningful job, a rising standard of living, and a voice in decisions which affect their work lives as a matter of social right.

This generation of workers is the first not raised in the shadow of the great depression. No more than 10 per cent of Canadians currently in the labour force actually held a job or looked for a job during the 1930–35 period. The deprivation of that period has nearly faded from the consciousness of the Canadian worker.

These expectations of entitlement are not likely to change. The impact of the great depression on the attitudes and expectations of those who lived through it is understandable. However, it lasted only five to ten years in

most regions of Canada. When the impact of the depression on the expectations of working people is compared to the impact of the thirty years of
uninterrupted prosperity which have shaped the expectations of most
young employees, it is clear that these expectations of entitlement are firmly
anchored in the minds of young workers, and nothing is likely to reverse
them.

Increasingly, institutions in Canadian society can no longer assume the
unearned loyalty of their members. The willingness of people to immerse
their lives in the organization, to be loyal to the organization, and to seek
fulfilment for themselves at work is slowly eroding. Perhaps this trend is
healthy – self-fulfilment should be available through cultural, spiritual, and
family pursuits as well as through work activities. However, the workplace
touches virtually every aspect of our lives and profoundly shapes our personalities, self-concepts, and social relationships. Our life-styles, the nature
and quality of our family relations (how often and when we see our children, how domestic chores are allocated), and the amount of leisure time we
enjoy are patterned by our work lives. The well-being and fulfilment of
Canadians are deeply influenced by the work organization.

However, the affluence and prosperity of the Canadian economy in the
post-war period is only partly responsible for the lengthening list of entitlements. The rising educational attainment of the Canadian worker is also in
part responsible. The Canadian work-force is the youngest and fastest growing in the western world. Because of the low average education of retirees
and the high average education of new entrants, the average educational
level of the work-force is rising dramatically. The demands of a more educated labour force for challenging and autonomous work cannot be ignored.
William and Margaret Westley point out: 'rising levels of education have
produced more people who are potentially better able and more willing to
participate in democratic processes, whether in the union, the factory, or the
nation. Fortunately or unfortunately, this does not necessarily mean more
peaceful industrial or political relations.'[1]

In addition, pressures on the work organization will mount as the roles
and responsibilities of women change. The accelerating participation rates
of women in the work-force over the past two decades has exerted a
depressing effect on employee demands for improved conditions of work
and for a greater voice in decision-making. Surveys find that women expect
less from their jobs than men, and they tend to be more satisfied than men
with existing organizational conditions. However, as more women view

1 Westley and Westley 1971, 41

their work as a career and as more expect to spend their careers at work, their tolerance for authoritarian practices will diminish.

A significant component of the increasing problems in the workplace is the contradiction between the values celebrated in the larger society and the values underpinning the workplace. The young Canadian worker – native-born, socialized in the anti-authoritarian ideology of contemporary Canadian society, and raised on a philosophy of equality, freedom, and the inherent dignity of the individual – cannot fail to be disappointed by the workplace. In the modern work organization the employee's freedom is suspended in many important respects, justice is limited, obedience to superiors is demanded, and the workplace is permeated with symbols of authority, deference, and subordination.

The worker experiences a vague and imperfectly articulated sense that a contradiction exists between our social values of individual expression, freedom, and initiative and the values of obedience and subordination in the workplace. Too much of the working person's time and energy is devoted to the job to permit indifference to this contradiction. Demands for changes in the manner in which authority is exercised in the workplace have been muted in the past by the pursuit of more immediate and pressing needs – union recognition, seniority and due process protection, and control over the more obvious shortcomings of the workplace – yet the demands for a stronger voice in decision-making will assume greater urgency in the future.

CHANGES IN EMPLOYEE ATTITUDES AND EXPECTATIONS

Changes in employee expectations and job satisfaction have been of interest to survey researchers for over forty years. The interpretation of worker survey results is currently the subject of considerable controversy. Some social scientists[2] argue that job satisfaction is not decreasing, as popularly believed, but rather is increasing and has been increasing for the past forty years. They argue that recent unfavourable changes in absenteeism and quit rates are attributable to standard economic variables such as changes in hours of work, in the unemployment rate, and in the occupational and demographic composition of the work-force.

Other social scientists, however, argue that job satisfaction is declining at an alarming rate. A synthesis of twenty-five years of survey research on employee attitudes shows that employee dissatisfaction is increasing and is becoming manifest in ways which have major implications for the manner

2 Strauss 1974; Flanagan, Strauss, and Ulman 1974

in which authority is exercised in the workplace.[3] There is mounting evidence from major workplace surveys[4] as well as case studies[5] and anecdotal evidence from trade union and management officials that employee reaction to the workplace is increasingly negative.

These studies indicate a disconcerting trend: most employees feel that their company is not as good a place to work as it once was; hourly and clerical workers increasingly expect intrinsic satisfaction from work (respect, achievement, challenge, recognition), yet they find these opportunities lacking; there is a downward trend in feelings of equity, perceptions of company concern for employee problems, beliefs that the workplace provides opportunities for achievement, and perceptions of company responsiveness to employee concerns.

Although management practices have been evolving over the past twenty-five years in a direction which addresses employee concerns, employee expectations have been evolving at an even faster pace. Human relations training for supervisors does not appear to help.[6] The sources of discontent reach far deeper, and more significant initiatives are required.

THE EROSION OF CONSENT

The modern work organization can never gain the moral commitment of those whose lives it rules without itself embodying a moral purpose. Unfortunately, many of the practices of the modern work organization are without moral justification; the legitimacy of these practices rests solely on economic and productive efficiency. The rights that management enjoys in any democratic society depend ultimately on the consent of the larger society. This consent, and the legitimacy it confers on managerial authority, is eroding at an increasing rate, and as the consent disappears a new set of challenges faces work organizations and those who manage them.

The interactions among organization members can be understood only by reference to the shared definitions held by organization members. The erosion of the perception of common purpose underlies many of the human relations problems in the modern work organization. Any human collectivity operates on consent – that is, the willingness of members to

3 Reported by Cooper, Morgan, Foley, and Kaplan 1979
4 Fenn and Yankelovich 1972; Sheppard and Herrick 1972; *Work in America* 1973; Economic Council of Canada, 1976
5 Schrank 1978; Terkel 1972. A detailed discussion of the job satisfaction figures is found in chapter 6.
6 Cooper et al. 1979

co-operate in the pursuit of the collectivity's objectives. Historically, this consent has been secured in work organizations by the exercise of threat and punitive sanctions.

More and more, however, work organizations are unable to obtain the consent of their members through use of threat or coercion. Willing contributions were easy to obtain from employees for whom unemployment and a long period of deprivation were the alternatives to compliance with managerial directives. Working spouses, due process clauses in collective agreements, statutory regulations governing unjust dismissal, unemployment insurance, and a society which offers many employment alternatives have substantially undermined the authority of managers. Employee identification with the organization and internalization of its norms and objectives are far beyond the reach of most managers and, increasingly, even the grudging compliance of employees is difficult to obtain.

DECLINE OF CONFIDENCE IN INSTITUTIONS

The major institutions in Canadian society – government, business, trade unions, the professions, the church, the educational system, the judicial system, to name a few – have suffered a decline in the public's confidence in recent years. There is widespread questioning of the ability of these institutions to fulfil the public's expectations. Their responsiveness to new challenges and their willingness to pursue the common good have also been questioned. The business community has been slow to recognize that it has new responsibilities to employees as well as to consumers, the environment, and the community. Trade union leaders have largely misunderstood and continue to underestimate public anger at strikes which disrupt the daily lives of citizens.

Demands for greater accountability to broader constituencies and demands for more diverse input to decision-making will affect all institutions in Canadian society. The workplace can no longer remain sheltered from these forces.

THE INDIVIDUAL AS CITIZEN AND EMPLOYEE

It is in the area of basic democratic freedoms that the discrepancy between the individual as citizen and the individual as employee is most apparent. In a democracy an individual cannot forfeit or sell his freedom to another and cannot, within limits, deprive others of their freedom. Individuals possess rights of freedom by virtue of citizenship and by virtue of unstated and inviolable human values which stand above the employment contract. An individual may make available to another his time, energy, and skills, under carefully delimited circumstances and under conditions which permit him to negotiate freely with the other. The boundary between the rights of every employee as citizen in a democracy and those the employee is permitted to suspend or alter in an employment contract is shifting.

The practices of the Ford Motor Company early in this century contrast sharply with the prevailing practices of today. Henry Ford was considered to be an enlightened employer in his era. When he opened the Dearborn plant in 1919, he paid his workers a salary of $5 a day, an extraordinary sum for that period. By so doing Ford ensured that his employees were well housed, clothed, and fed.

However, Henry Ford exercised a degree of control over his employees which is unimaginable by today's standards. Ford created a group within the company to which he gave the quaint name Sociology Department. This department was staffed by thirty social workers and investigators who were responsible for ferreting out immoral and undesirable behaviour on the part of Ford employees. Infractions ranging from inappropriate dress to non-attendance at church, swearing, visiting a pool hall, and being shaved in a barber shop were punished by pay-roll deductions. Records show that very few of Henry Ford's employees earned their full pay. 'No one discerned anything improper in investigators' knocking on the door of workers' homes to check that the beds were made up, in demanding to see savings account passbooks, or in requiring an itemization of household debts. Fellow workers, neighbors, wives, children and even the doctors of workers were interviewed.'[7]

The work organization cannot stand outside the realm of values, principles, and practices followed in other areas of society. Indeed, the workplace should reinforce the values of society – that is, broaden and deepen democratic principles, and reinforce practices and beliefs about fair play, due process, and human equality. Regrettably, most managers have been slow to accept this challenge.

Democratic practices have not proceeded as far in the workplace as they have in other areas of our society. The economic enterprise, the government agency, the trade union, the political party, the church, are all essentially undemocratic in their decision-making practices. Few organizations in our society make any pretence of being democratic, and those which do – universities, trade unions, political parties – are in practice rarely democratic.

7 Conot 1974, 176

THE PLURALIST PERSPECTIVE

Any organization is composed of individuals with differing interests and perspectives. It is a complex of competing claims which must be reconciled or 'managed' if the perception of common interest is to govern the manner in which these divergent interests are accommodated.

Conflict is inevitable in any organization by virtue of its diverse membership and by virtue of the inevitable coalitions of members pursuing divergent interests. This inevitable conflict should not be viewed as pathological or as symptomatic of breakdown; nor should it be viewed as something to be suppressed or smoothed over.

This 'pluralist' view of organization is not generally advocated by proponents of workplace democracy. The view that a normal workplace is characterized by unity of purpose and harmonious relations is one of the greatest weaknesses of the North American perspective on workplace democracy. The pluralist perspective on the modern work organization is based on the following principles.

1 The parties do not question the right of the other to exist; nor do they question the basis of their relationship; all parties subscribe to the survival of the relationship and the survival of other parties.[8]
2 The parties accept the right of others to pursue their self-interests within a broad framework of mutual rights and obligations.
3 The claims of each party fall within the other's range of acceptability.
4 The values and beliefs of the parties are not so divergent that mutually acceptable solutions are unattainable.
5 Neither party can unilaterally impose its will on the other.
6 The parties are morally committed to their joint decisions.

In the work organization there can never be complete consensus on all matters affecting the lives of organization members. If there were, any one organization member would make the same decision as any other, and democratic procedures would be unnecessary. The very existence of differences makes democratic decision-making desirable. However, democratic decision-making practices are disruptive in the absence of consensus on fundamental goals.

8 The term 'party' will be used to identify interest groups within the organization; for example, labour and management, white-collar and blue-collar, direct labour and indirect labour.

Many Marxist observers would argue that conflicting interests are usually reconciled in a manner which does not give equal say to all parties. Alan Fox, in a thoughtful analysis of relations between employer and employee, observes: 'Overwhelmingly the greater part of the collaborative structure and its mode of operation is settled already; settled on terms and principles which discriminate in every important respect in favour of its owners and controllers, and which the rank and file do not contest ... the discussion may be about marginal adjustments in hierarchical rewards, but not the principle of hierarchical rewards; about certain practical issues connected with the prevailing extreme subdivision of labour, but not the principle of extreme subdivision of labour.'[9]

From the Marxist perspective, the work organization in capitalist society is not a voluntary and spontaneous association of free and independent participants. Consent rests on false consciousness; workers have been indoctrinated by the larger society to accept the class, power, and status system without question. This cultural conditioning leads to submission, and an unconditional acceptance of what would otherwise be intolerable conditions.

The idealism of Marxist commentators is admirable, but this idealism must be reconciled with practical necessity. The analysis and commentary in this book are guided by ideals, but inevitably this idealism must be tempered in light of economic and political realities. The great challenge lying before us is the achievement of a more humane and democratic workplace while avoiding easy appeals to simplistic and doctrinaire panaceas. The protection and enhancement of personal liberties and freedoms, the emphasis on growth opportunities, and the enhancement of self are not antithetical to private ownership, rewards based on merit, or the pursuit of economic efficiency.

PROGRESS WILL BE SLOW

The spread of participative management practices in Canadian work organizations has been slow in the past, and the diffusion of these practices will very likely continue at a slow pace in the future. The absence of enthusiasm for the concept of workplace democracy in Canada is surprising in light of the widespread adoption of democratic practices in European workplaces. The failure to explore innovative forms of work organization (which according to European experience reduce labour strife and improve the

9 Fox 1974, 285–6

loyalty and commitment of the work-force) results primarily from the incompatibility of democratic forms of work organization with the ideologies of Canadian managers and trade unionists.

Canadian managers and trade union leaders are captives of an outdated ideology. Most trade union leaders in Canada rose to power by challenging unilateral management authority and most trade unionists remain in power by effectively representing their members' interests. These union leaders now face the difficult challenge of moving from an adversarial relationship, in which all matters are subject to negotiation, to a relationship based on substantial commonality of interest. The union's role as the sole protector of workers' rights is undermined when the worker is drawn into management ranks. If workplace democracy makes workers partners with management, rather than adversaries of management, the role of some trade unions is jeopardized.

Unlike their European counterparts, Canadian trade unions continue to struggle for recognition and security. In Canada, while union membership as a percentage of the labour force continues to grow, there is little growth in the industrial sector.[10] Trade union officials find it difficult (except in a few local cases) to collaborate with management on the introduction of new forms of decision-making in organizations while their right to exist continues to be threatened.

Changes in workplace democracy will come slowly in organizations in which management is preoccupied with the protection of its prerogatives. The rationale underlying these prerogatives rests on two principles: (1) the logic of efficient organization and (2) the right of control over private property. Managers fear that sharing power with employees who lack technical knowledge may jeopardize the viability of the enterprise. The need for quick response to turbulent and changing market conditions, they argue, precludes power-sharing with the rank and file.

Management's long-standing opposition to encroachments upon 'residual rights' reflects its preference to direct the enterprise by means of unilateral and unchecked authority rather than from a position where decisions are open to debate and discussion. Furthermore, many argue that the rights of the owners of capital will be abrogated by arrangements which involve employees as partners in making important decisions at the workplace.

Many managers fear that increased participation in decision-making will lead to demands for higher wages. They feel that workers will argue that since they are contributing more to the organization through participation

10 See *Current Economic and Industrial Relations Indicators* 1979.

and heightened responsibility, they should be paid more. Some managers who are willing to share power with workers balk at the prospect of paying higher wages. Presumably, these managers do not believe that employee participation will improve the performance of the organization; they introduce workplace democracy in the belief that participation in decision-making is sufficiently rewarding in itself.

Lower- and middle-level managers also oppose workplace democracy. They stand to lose many of their prerogatives; changes in decision-making on the shop-floor threaten the personal and occupational security of supervisors who manage in the traditional way. New roles will have to be learned; relationships remade; perspectives, beliefs, and values changed.

The difficulties of changing supervisory styles from authoritarian and hierarchical to consultative and participative should not be underestimated. In fact, opposition from first-line supervision represents the most serious obstacle to the spread of shop-floor democracy in Canada. Senior management may enthusiastically embrace changes in the authority structure on the shop-floor; but they remain less enthusiastic about changes in decision-making at higher organizational levels.

The 'sport' of adversarial relations is enjoyed by an unfortunately large number of managers and trade unionists. The move to more collaborative and participative forms of decision-making will require new relationships. The established practices, the ideology underlying these practices, and the personalities will continue as they have in the past. Change will inevitably proceed slowly.

However, the values celebrated in the larger society – freedom, autonomy, self-determination – must inevitably be reflected in organizational practices. If they are not, these societal values cannot survive. In the long run a society cannot embrace democracy as a central principle while denying its introduction to the workplace.

THE RESEARCH PERSPECTIVE

In North America research on participation in the workplace has been dominated by the 'human relations' perspective. From its beginnings[11] to its current interpretations[12] human relations has focused on a form of participation which takes place within and is consistent with the conventional hierarchical structure of the work organization. Human relations has endeavoured to

11 Mayo 1931, 1945; Roethlisberger and Dickson 1939
12 Likert 1961, 1967

soften the effects of the command-and-obey system without requiring fundamental change to this system. In recent years, however, there have emerged growing demands for forms of participation based on a substantial redistribution of power to organization members at lower hierarchical levels. Human relations has been unable to answer these demands.

Participation in the human relations tradition is based on a supervisory style characterized by supportiveness, informality, openness, and trust. Supervisors and managers are under no obligation to share decision-making power with their subordinates, and the participation, for the most part, concerns matters on the shop floor, not matters of organization policy. Participation in the human relations tradition is not codified in organizational documents. In other words, supervisors are free to be autocratic or democratic and are not obliged to share decision-making authority with their subordinates.

Research in the human relations tradition suffers from many ideological, conceptual and methodological problems, and many of its conclusions have been called into question.[13] The growing interest in workplace democracy in North America reflects a desire to move beyond the informal, subjective, and largely personal preoccupations of human relations and a desire to explore forms of participation which significantly alter the relationship between superior and subordinate.

Recent research on workplace democracy is based on power-sharing which is organization-wide and extends decision-making rights to members at lower levels of the organization's hierarchy. These rights are documented, commonly agreed upon, and have legal standing. They may be codified and sanctioned by legal arrangements outside the organization, as in Yugoslavia and the Federal Republic of Germany,[14] or they may be codified in the organization's charter or collective agreement.

This distinction between 'workplace democracy' and 'human relations' is similar to the 'formal' and 'informal' participation of Tannenbaum (1974) and Dachler and Wilpert (1978). This distinction is also similar to several others in the literature, including Walker's (1974) 'structure' and 'living' participation; French's (1964) 'objective' and 'psychological' participation; Roy's (1973) 'institutional' and 'interpersonal' participation; Emery and Thorsrud's (1969) 'real' and 'apparent' participation; and Bass and Shackelton's (1979) 'industrial democracy' and 'participative management.'

13 Perrow 1979; Strauss 1963; Strauss and Rosenstein 1970
14 Tannenbaum et al. 1974

This study of workplace democracy in Canada is guided by a theoretical framework based on the following concepts:

1 The value system of organization members.
2 The administrative structure of the organization, including spans of control, job descriptions, the codification of rules and procedures, the emphasis on the hierarchical chain of command, and administrative controls.
3 Interpersonal and intergroup processes within the organization, including conflict between persons and groups, conflict resolution modes, the amount and accuracy of communication among organization members, and the nature of day-to-day relations between superiors and subordinates.
4 Individual outcomes, including job-related satisfactions, physical and mental health, attitudes towards management, and loyalty and commitment to the firm.

In this conceptual framework power is the central concept. The sources of power, the manner in which power is exercised, and its effects on organization members are explored in a matched sample of highly participative and hierarchically structured organizations. Of particular interest is the degree of 'congruence' among the four concepts in the two types of organization.

The theory of organization proposed here is intended to bridge two currently disparate themes or paradigms in organizational research. Contemporary research on organizations is conducted within one of two perspectives – the 'macro' and the 'micro' perspectives. Pondy and Boje (1976) refer to these two perspectives as the 'social facts' and the 'social behavior' paradigms respectively. This empirical analysis is based on the belief that these conflicting paradigms can be reconciled in broadly based theories of organization.

ISSUES TO BE ADDRESSED

This book is concerned with forms of participation in the workplace which go significantly beyond conventional North American practice in giving considerable power to rank and file employees. This inquiry must inevitably lead to questions of value as well as to questions of fact. To address issues of fact, – that is, the nature and extent of differences in employee welfare in democratically and hierarchically managed organizations – questionnaire, interview, and field observation data will be examined from a sample of

1,000 working people (including senior managers and rank and file workers) in twenty industrial organizations. In this sample are ten firms which have gone far beyond conventional practice in broadening opportunities for employee participation in decision-making and ten firms of conventional hierarchical design which are matched with each of the democratic firms. This analysis will focus on a systematic comparison of the democratic and hierarchical organizations on the dimensions of values, administrative structure, interpersonal and intergroup processes and outcomes such as employee satisfaction, loyalty, commitment, and mental health.

Questions of value include the desirability of introducing workplace democracy more widely in work organizations, the role of unions in co-managing the workplace, the rights of capital and labour, and the role of the modern work organization in promoting employee well-being and guaranteeing the rights enjoyed by all citizens in our society.

One of the more curious aspects of the debate over workplace democracy is that the concept is embraced by elements of both the left and right of the political spectrum. Some members of the political left view workplace democracy as a step in the collective appropriation of the means of production, as a way of redistributing wealth, reducing social injustice, and tempering some of the harsher effects of the free enterprise system. Elements of the political right regard workplace democracy as an adjustment to the current system, as possibly capitalism's only hope of survival with any semblance of private ownership and market discipline.

While the explicit focus of this book is the workplace, issues of broader import will also be addressed. Among these issues are the following. Can European forms of industrial democracy be introduced in Canada, with its unique labour-management traditions and political, social, and cultural conditions? Are there organizational designs and strategies which are appropriate in our own culture but not in others?

What role will trade unions play in workplace democracy? Is trade unionism a more viable form of workplace democracy than forms which operate independently of trade unions or in which trade unions are not an integral part? Can workplace democracy be introduced without trade union co-operation? And if trade union co-operation is essential, how can it be secured?

How can managers and supervisors be encouraged to make the transition from authoritarian styles of leadership to the more participative, supportive and collaborative forms of leadership required in contemporary work organizations?

Can changes be made in the decision-making structure of the organization without altering the nature of the work itself? To what extent do technological and economic constraints limit opportunities to redesign work to permit greater employee participation in decision-making?

Will employees who are given the right to make decisions demand that the work itself be altered? Will employees who are able to set their own wages and to determine their hours of work and their working conditions, manage the organization any differently than their managerial counterparts?

Are wages and benefits more evenly distributed in the democratic than in the hierarchical organizations?

Are employees in the democratic organizations able to grasp the technical matters of finance, marketing, and economics and thereby understand and participate fully in policy level decision-making in the firm?

Are forms of workplace democracy which are more consultative in nature and which are limited to issues on the shop-floor able to produce the same loyalty, satisfaction and commitment as forms of workplace democracy which provide employees with opportunities to participate fully in policy-level decisions?

Are there some limited forms of employee participation and consultation which permit management and labour to work in a collaborative manner, lead to high employee motivation and satisfaction, yet allow management to retain control over the workplace?

Is the democratic work organization as profitable as its hierarchically managed counterpart?

Before turning to the comparisons of democratic and hierarchical organizations, we shall define and examine in detail the central theoretical concepts of this book: 'power,' 'authority,' 'consent,' and 'democracy.' The application of these concepts in Canadian workplaces over this century will then be outlined in chapter 3. This historical perspective will illustrate how current thinking about workplace democracy has evolved and how significantly it departs from conventional practice. In chapter 4 a theory of organization will be outlined. This theory will serve as the conceptual foundation for the empirical comparisons to be reported in chapter 5. Subsequently, the effects of work on employee well-being will be explored and the nature of work in the democratic and hierarchical organizations compared. In chapter 7 the roles of trade unions in workplace democracy will be examined, and two models of trade union participation in organizational decision-making will be proposed and evaluated. Profit-sharing, a neglected dimension of workplace democracy will then be described and evaluated. Particular attention will be directed towards the similarity of the philosophical underpinnings of profit-sharing and workplace democracy. In the final chapter the implications of the theory and data on workplace democracy will be explored and public policy options evaluated. Details of the forms of workplace democracy studied here are found in appendix I.

This work was inspired in part by the seminal studies of Arnold Tannenbaum at the University of Michigan. Tannenbaum, who was one of the first to study workplace democracy in the European context, concludes, 'Participation *can* work. This is not to assert (or deny) that participation *will* work under any and all circumstances or that it is inevitably a more successful system than are non participative alternatives. Nonetheless, successful examples can be cited, and these, it would seem, demonstrate a principle and a possibility.'[15]

The human and social problems at the workplace will be resolved when the gap between popular expectation and attainable reality becomes manageable. This book is an exploration of one means of reconciling expectation with reality.

15 Tannenbaum 1974, 102–3

2

Power and consent

'In the entire lexicon of sociological concepts none is more troublesome than the concept of power ... we all know perfectly well what it is – until some-one asks us.'[1] Although power has been a preoccupation of the disciplines of political science, law, philosophy, and sociology, few organizational theo-rists consider power as a central concept in their theories. There is not a single reference to power in the extensive index of Marvin Dunnette's (1976) compendium, *Handbook of Industrial and Organizational Psychology.*

In this chapter the concepts 'power,' 'authority,' and 'participation' will be defined and their relationships with the concept 'democracy' explored. From these concepts the 'stakeholder theory' of workplace democracy will be developed. This theory provides a rationale for broadened employee partici-pation in decision-making.

POWER

The definition of power is deceptively simple. One party has power over another to the extent that he can determine the behaviour of the other party. Consider two parties, A and B. A and B may be persons, groups, or organiza-tions. A has power over B to the extent that A can get B to do something that B would not otherwise have done.

Power is a property of the relationship between A and B; it is not an attribute of A or B. In Eric Hoffer's colourful phrase, 'Power doesn't come in cans.' A's power over B is a function of characteristics of A and B, as well as of the relationship between A and B. Any relationship between parties must

1 Bierstedt 1950, 730

involve power, even when this relationship is not direct or face-to-face. For example, A may modify B's social or physical environment for the purpose of changing B's behaviour ('ecological power').

The power relationship between parties is typically asymmetrical, although it is not necessarily so. A and B may have equal power over one another or may control different types of the other's behaviour, or may exercise power over the other in a different manner.

The power one party exercises over another is defined by four dimensions:[2] (1) degree, the extent to which one party influences another party; (2) domain, the parties subject to the influence of another party; (3) scope, the issues or behaviours subject to influence; (4) source, the bases on which the influence of one party over another rest.

Degree The degree of power is defined as the magnitude of the change in probability that B will do as A desires. To put it another way, the degree of power is the net increase in the probability of B's behaving in a particular manner after A has intervened, compared to the probability of B's behaving in a particular manner in the absence of A's intervention.

Domain The domain of power identifies the number of Bs subject to A's power. Traffic policemen, doctors, and company presidents enjoy a rather large domain of power, while first-line supervisors have a more limited domain of power. Rank and file workers – according to the formal design of the organization – have no domain of power, but informally the domain may include immediate supervisors as well as fellow workers.

Scope The power of one party over another is typically limited to a set of issues or behaviours at the workplace. Supervisors exercise power over subordinates on matters pertaining largely to work; they do not generally exercise power over matters which fall beyond the purview of the workplace. Even at the workplace a supervisor's power is limited in scope. In many provincial jurisdictions the decision to refuse hazardous work rests with the subordinate, not with the superior. A central theme of this book is that the scope of power of organizational officials is dwindling, and changes must therefore be made in organizational decision-making. In democratic workplaces the scope of issues subject to participation is increased significantly beyond that of hierarchically managed organizations.

Source Following the model of French and Raven (1960), there are five sources (bases) of power: (1) expert power; B obeys A because B respects A's knowledge; (2) reward power, B obeys A because A can reward B; (3)

---

2 Two of these dimensions – degree and scope – are used in chapter 5 to operationalize the concept, 'workplace democracy.'

coercive power, B obeys A because A can punish or otherwise disadvantage B; (4) referent power, B obeys A because B likes A and wishes to develop or maintain a positive interpersonal relationship with A; (5) legitimate power, B obeys A because a rule requires that B obey A. Menachem Rosner adds a sixth source of power: 'law of the situation.'[3] This term, taken from Mary Parker Follett,[4] describes A's power over B in situations where B's obedience is necessary if the organization is to function properly. This source of power is frequently employed in kibbutz organizations.

AUTHORITY

Power is the ability to affect the behaviour of others. When this power is organizationally sanctioned, it is called 'authority.' Authority resides not in a person, but in an organizational role. Authority is defined precisely in terms of weight, domain, scope, and source.[5]

Authority is pervasive in the modern work organization. Obedience to superiors is one of the fundamental commandments of organizational life, although this requirement is rarely made explicit and rarely appears in the subordinate's job description. Despite the subliminal character of authority, failure to obey a superior evokes the full weight of organizational sanction. Failure to obey authority, more than any other action, threatens the very foundations of the organization.

Authority ultimately rests on what Dornbusch and Scott (1975) call the 'normative order,' a set of social norms and values which are regarded as binding on organization members. The extent to which subordinates acknowledge the existence of a normative order is defined as the 'validity' of authority. The validity of authority is ascertained by asking subordinates 'Does A have the right to exercise power over you?'

The extent to which subordinates approve of the normative order is the 'propriety' of authority. Propriety is determined by asking 'Should A have the right to exercise power over you?'

Power which is not supported by commonly shared values or norms inevitably leads to conflict between the more and the less powerful. Power which is not regulated by norms defining the manner and occasions in

---

3 Rosner in Tannenbaum et al. 1974, 74–6

4 Fox and Urwick 1973

5 Authority is occasionally defined as 'legitimate power' (i.e., the source of the superior's power is legitimacy). According to the definition of this book, however, authority is not conferred by those below. Authority is conferred by persons at upper hierarchical levels and reflects their judgment of what the incumbent of a particular role has a right to do.

which it may legitimately be exercised remains simply power, not authority. Bierstedt observes that when values govern the exercise of power in the organization, 'power is dissolved without residue into authority.'[6]

The institutions of the larger society as well as the leadership of the organization support and defend a particular distribution of power as morally proper. Belief systems supporting institutional arrangements vary from culture to culture and from era to era within any society, as Bendix (1956) has pointed out. The problem with authority in contemporary Canadian work organizations is that while its validity continues to be accepted, its propriety is not.

PARTICIPATION

Participation in decision-making includes those forms of B's power over A which are accepted as legitimate by both A and B. Participation is the 'upward' exertion of power by subordinates over superiors. According to this definition coercion by subordinates of reluctant and unwilling superiors is not participation. Threats, intimidation, and harassment are forms of power but are not forms of participation. Participation in decision-making reduces the imbalance of power between superior and subordinate. In the terminology of Arnold Tannenbaum subordinate participation in decision-making affects both the slope and height of the control curve.

There are many varieties of participation in decision-making found in Canadian workplaces. Participation may include direct, face-to-face interaction between superior and subordinate, or it may occur through the delegation of responsibility to the subordinate. Consultation is a form of participation which involves direct, face-to-face contact between superior and subordinate. Consultation implies that the superior retains the right of final decision, but subordinates influence the decision by expressing their opinions.

POWER AND OBEDIENCE

Power is a valued commodity. It is sought for purely *pragmatic* reasons because it can be instrumental in fulfilling personal needs or ambitions. But power is also sought for its *symbolic* value.

Those who have power command greater respect than those who do not. Mauk Mulder, a Dutch psychologist who has spent a lifetime studying power and its effects on superiors and subordinates, likens power to a hard

6 Bierstedt 1950, 734

drug. Power has a compulsive and addictive character; those who have it want more; those who don't have it are less interested in acquiring it.

Authority – who has it, how and over whom it is exercised – concerns everyone. To date attention has focused primarily on those who wield authority (and those who abuse authority) rather than on the acquiescence of those who are subjected to it. The exercise of authority rests fundamentally on the willingness of subordinates to accede to this authority. While the reluctance of subordinates to obey directives from their superiors is a major problem in the modern work organization, reflex obedience to authority figures is equally disquieting.

Mulder's (1971) laboratory studies of power have uncovered some disturbing and subtle dimensions of the relationship between the powerful and the less powerful. For example, the powerful are admired by the less powerful, even when the powerful abuse their power, use it for narrow personal gain, or use it to pursue illegitimate or reprehensible objectives. The public display of admiration for the powerful by the less powerful is understandable, but Mulder finds that the less powerful express their admiration for the powerful in private and under circumstances when there is no opportunity for personal advantage.

The pioneering studies of obedience conducted by Milgram (1965) raise an even more disturbing spectre: blind, reflex obedience to authority, regardless of harm to third parties. Milgram requested volunteers through a local newspaper to participate in a psychological experiment. The study was ostensibly conducted to test the effects of punishment on an individual's memory. The subject was instructed to administer an electric shock to another subject whenever that person failed to recall correctly a paired associate in a series of nonsense syllables. The subject was instructed to administer shocks which increased in magnitude until the level was harmful. The individuals receiving the shock were collaborators of the experimenter and they were not actually given shocks.

Fully 65 per cent of subjects continued to administer shock to the hapless subject, even when the subject begged to be unstrapped from the apparatus. The study demonstrates that many individuals will harm others when they are instructed to do so by an authority figure.

However, there is encouraging evidence from subsequent (and rarely cited) modifications of the Milgram experiment. When the subject was placed in the presence of three others who were instructed to refuse to obey the authority figure, only 10 per cent of subjects obeyed the authority figure when the shocks were apparently harming the subject. Social pressure seems to protect persons from the tendency to obey an authority figure.

THE MORAL LEGITIMACY OF WORKPLACE DEMOCRACY

Political democracy is a fragile institution. From its beginnings in Greece and Rome in the sixth century BC, to the city states in north Italy in the tenth and eleventh centuries, to the flowering of democratic states following the American and French revolutions, political democracies have never been more than a tiny minority among states. Currently, only thirty nations among the world's 150 nation states enjoy any semblance of democratic process.

At the organizational level the democratic process remains virtually untried, even in the western liberal democracies. 'Who says organization, says oligarchy,' concluded Robert Michels (1962), the German sociologist who studied the rise of socialist political parties in Europe during the early years of this century. Michels recognized that without power there could be no organization, and he concluded that power would inevitably concentrate in the hands of a few and would be used to their advantage. Michels regarded this process as inevitable, even in socialist political parties which were founded on egalitarian and democratic principles.

The absence of democracy in the contemporary workplace may be inevitable, as Michels observes. Those who have fought for the control of the work organization have succeeded in a competitive and political struggle. They are unlikely to advocate a new system which may reward different skills and in which their roles, prerogatives, and privileges may be subject to review. Furthermore, for the lower-ranking masses limited information, political skills, and resources make effective challenges to the powerful at higher ranks almost impossible.

The authoritarian character of the modern work organization may be attributed to a temporary and correctable lag in the spread of the democratic ethic throughout our society. Warren Bennis, in a classic analysis of the prospects of the work organization, once proposed that 'democracy is inevitable.'[7]

During his tenure as president of the University of Cincinnati Bennis had many occasions to reflect on his forecast. He describes his experiences with reconciling the diverse interest groups within his university.

In vital decisions I must consider not only our students, faculty members and administrators; I must consider city councilmen and state legislators, the city manager, the governor and the federal government, as well as alumni and parents ...

7 Slater and Bennis 1964

As for the internal environment, we face a new movement of populism – the fragmentation of constituencies. On our campus we have more than 500 governance and interest groups, including a variety of women's groups, a gay lib, black organizations for students and for faculty members, and a faculty council for Jewish affairs ...

I now have some 40 suits pending against the university, naming me as defendant. I can no longer make even a trivial decision without consulting our lawyers.[8]

The crisis of authority in contemporary work organizations (and the mounting pressures for democratic decision-making processes) raises the issue of the moral legitimacy of this authority. In the western democracies this crisis of authority arises not so much from opposition to the actual decisions made by those in authority, but from resistance to the principle that some organization members have unilateral power over other organization members.

Increasingly, authority is exercised without the consent of those over whom it is exercised. The 'propriety' of authority is no longer accepted; it is exercised without moral sanction, and it is replaced by power resting on reward and coercive bases. When the conventional coercive sources of power are limited by legislation (as are some of the reward bases of power under wage and price controls), those who are charged with the responsibility of managing work organizations find themselves without the sanctions or skills necessary to obtain the commitment of their subordinates.

The erosion of the moral legitimacy of authority in the workplace is a serious problem. Employees can be compelled to obey but they cannot be compelled to believe in the superior competence of another. Victor Thompson (1961) coined the term 'dramaturgy' to describe the posturing and histrionics of superiors to ensure the legitimacy of hierarchical power in the face of rising subordinate doubts about their competence and the legitimacy of their power. Superiors emphasize the heroic and charismatic qualities of their roles, while subordinates work hard to create the impression that they are awed by the superior's leadership qualities. Each party has increasingly less respect for the other.

More and more, the claim is made that employees should have the right to participate in decisions which materially affect them. The moral legitimacy of this claim and the consistency of this claim with principles underlying our political democracy are issues to which we now turn.

The moral legitimacy of one employee (A) making decisions which materially affect another employee (B) can be judged by three criteria: (1) the

8 Bennis 1975, 20

criterion of personal choice, (2) the criterion of competence, and (3) the criterion of economy.[9]

Criterion of personal choice

A decision-making process which ensures that decisions made by A are similar to those B would have made if B had had the chance meets the criterion of personal choice. This criterion must be interpreted in light of the diversity of the work organization. Organizations are made up of individuals whose perspectives, goals, and viewpoints will inevitably be incompatible with those of other organization members. Perfect harmony among the diverse interests of organization members is an unattainable ideal; consequently, each member must compromise some of his personal choices. Each organization member's pursuit of unrestrained personal choice results inevitably in anarchy.

The criterion of personal choice cannot mean the right of every individual to do as he pleases – otherwise every form of organization would be undemocratic. A cannot satisfactorily gain his own ends unless B is allowed the opportunity to pursue his ends on an equal basis. Therefore, according to the criterion of personal choice, the decision-making process should give equal weight to the personal choices of all parties.

Criterion of competence

According to the 'criterion of competence,' decisions made by A are morally justifiable when A possesses special competence which B does not possess. Organization members may accept a decision because it is made by persons who are skilled or qualified to render a competent judgment. Competence in decision-making may rest on skills, knowledge, and training or on moral and ethical understanding.

The criterion of competence is fundamentally neither democratic nor undemocratic, but it has been used by authorities from Plato to the contemporary manager to justify undemocratic practices. For example, it can be argued that the increasingly complex management skills and technical training required to manage contemporary work organizations render democratic decision-making practices inefficient. Furthermore, one would not want to be a patient in an operating theatre where decisions were made on the basis of a poll of hospital employees, nor would one entrust his livelihood and economic well-being to an enterprise in which complex financial, marketing, and strategic matters were decided by persons without adequate training.

9 From Dahl 1970

It might be argued, as a matter of principle, that organization members should have the right to participate in decisions which materially affect them. It is not always rational, however, for organization members to insist on participating in decision-making under conditions where their competence is lacking. B may freely choose to defer to the authority of A, when B believes A is more competent to make a particular decision. B may expect to be fully informed, but otherwise B defers to the expertise of A. The fundamental premise underlying the criterion of competence is that B (on the whole) is more competent than anyone else to decide the circumstances under which he will permit A to make decisions on his behalf.

Criterion of economy
This criterion lacks the philosophical appeal of the first two criteria, but it is nevertheless an important principle defining circumstances under which an individual will permit another to make decisions on his behalf. Does A's making a decision affecting B economize time and effort which B could more productively spend in other ways?

A frequently voiced criticism of participative decision-making practices in the management literature centres on the time required to make decisions. However, the essential issue is B's choice. If B is willing to incur the costs of participating in making decisions affecting him, then B should have this right. At a pragmatic level managers often make decisions on their own, because consultation or participation with others demands time. However, they subsequently spend countless hours explaining and justifying their decisions to those who will not co-operate because they were not involved in making the original decision.

The principle 'employees should participate in decisions which materially affect them' is contentious. Much of the debate over the acceptability of this proposition as a general statement of how organizations should operate focuses on the definition of 'materially affected.' An organization member who defines this term broadly might feel that he has a moral right to participate in all decisions. An employee with an acute sense of social justice might justify enlarging his sphere of influence to include major policy decisions which affect human welfare in the larger society. The definition of 'materially affected' is cultural and is constantly shifting. The growing concern of employees and trade unions about corporate responsibility and investment policy of Canadian multinationals is one reflection of the changing public perception of 'materially affected.'

The application of the three criteria to decision-making in work organizations suggests that the case for democratic decision-making is strongest when organization members share a basic understanding of the objectives of the organization and of their respective roles in the pursuit of the organization's objectives; when differences in competence of organization members are minimal; and when organization members are willing to incur the costs entailed in participating in decision-making. Democratic decision-making is least desirable under conditions of fundamental ideological disagreement among members; great differences in competence among members; and unwillingness of organization members to bear the opportunity costs of participating in decision-making.

DEMOCRACY AS PROCESS

The right of B to participate in decision-making on matters which affect him does not ensure that the decisions will be to his liking or his advantage. Workplace democracy is defined in terms of the process of decision-making, not in terms of the outcomes of the process.

Democracy does not mean that power will necessarily be used humanely or with any consideration of the interests of minorities. In fact, democratic decision-making procedures will inevitably lead to outcomes not desired by some members.

The question of what is done with power (substantive actions resulting from the exercise of power) as opposed to how power is exercised (the process of arriving at decisions) has been a long-standing preoccupation of philosophers and political scientists. In Plato's *Republic*, acceptance of the ruler was based on the quality of his decisions, not on how decisions were made.

For Rousseau, however, legitimacy rested on the process, the only legitimate decisions being those obtained through the expression of the general will. Philosophers since Rousseau have generally accepted his definition of democracy as 'process' rather than as 'outcome.' Few organizations and nation states have adopted Rousseau's notions of the general will. Doubts about the wisdom of full Rousseauian democracy have led to a variety of limitations on the power of political leaders – judicial review, separation of powers, clear delineation of the limits of power, and ombudsmen, to name a few.[10]

10 Although the participative companies examined here are among the most participative firms in Canada, only one, The Group at Cox, approaches the Rousseauian ideal of 'one person, one vote.' In fact, most forms of employee participation in decision-making are not democratic, if by democratic is meant 'one person, one vote.' Representation on boards of directors, works councils, and other decision-making or decision-influencing bodies is rarely proportional to number of constituents.

In political theory the 'public interest' is defined in terms of both results and process; that is, the soundness of the decision is based on a judgment of the extent to which the decision meets community needs and the extent to which the public participated in the decision-making process. In the political realm, however, the task of voters is not to decide what their elected representatives should do, but rather to decide who should make the decisions. In the work organization the analogous 'employee interest' is defined solely in terms of the accountability of superiors to their subordinates.

WORKPLACE AND POLITICAL DEMOCRACY COMPARED

In the political sphere the term 'democracy' means government by the many, rather than by the few. The meaning of 'workplace democracy' is consistent with the political definition, but it subsumes a variety of forms of democratic decision-making. Workplace democracy may mean that organization members make decisions (either unilaterally or in collaboration with others); that organization members control the procedures under which decisions are made; or that organization members consent to representatives' making rules and policies on their behalf.

The authoritarian decision-making practices of the modern work organization have prompted frequent editorial comment. The contrast between the principles of democratic society and the principles of the work organization (outlined in table 1) remains one of the greatest anomalies in western society. This contradiction has not seriously penetrated the public consciousness until very recently, since it has been obscured by the traditional values and teachings of the school, church, and family. For those who have been socialized in the anti-authoritarian environment of the last two decades the contradiction is obvious. Unquestionably, however, the practices of work organizations are approaching the democratic ideals of the larger society; the contradiction is too great to continue indefinitely.

The disappointment of social critics and organizational theorists with the discrepancy arises in part from a rather forgiving view of the democratic political process. In practice democratic societies often fall short of the ideal. Political democracy does not live up to its billing for many reasons: representation is not proportional to numbers; the poor, the uneducated, the uninformed and the deliberately misinformed cannot always exercise their franchise; the selection of candidates by party officials rather than by direct popular nominating procedures limits choice of leaders; franchise is limited to property owners, males, citizens, and individuals above the age of majority; and elected officials (especially in countries with frequent elections) cannot influence an entrenched and powerful public service.

TABLE 1
The contrasting principles of democratic society and the modern work organization

The principles of democratic society	The principles of the modern work organization
1 Accountability of leadership to the governed	1 Accountability of leadership to higher authority (owners, superiors in the hierarchy of authority)
2 Citizen participation or consultation in decisions; right to be informed	2 Decision-making at highest levels of the hierarchy
3 Leaders chosen by the governed	3 Leaders chosen by higher authority
4 Right to question leaders	4 Leaders' judgments and decisions not subject to review by subordinates
5 Right to dissent, free speech	5 Uniformity, compliance with directives demanded
6 Freedom of movement, association liberty, individual expression	6 Activities, interactions closely defined and circumscribed
7 Informed and knowledgeable constituency	7 Information limited to immediate task requirements

CONSENT OF THE GOVERNED

The co-ordination, order, and regularity central to organizational life do not occur spontaneously, but must be created and maintained. The authority of organizational officials which is essential to this order ultimately rests on the consent of the governed.

Organizations could not exist without many uncounted acts of co-operation. If subordinates did not consent to authority or did not consent to function far beyond the demands of their role prescriptions, work organizations would be enormously inefficient. For some organizational theorists authority and consent are inseparable. Herbert Simon, for example, observes that 'a subordinate is said to accept authority whenever he permits his behavior to be guided by the decision of a superior, without independently examining the merits of that decision.'[11] Without the subordinate's consent, a superior's authority may be 'valid,' but not 'proper.' The subordinate's consent is a collective consent and is not entirely subject to individual interpretation. This collective judgment is subject to change; and it is both culture and time bound.

11 Simon 1957, 11–12

Work organizations contain a mixture of common and conflicting interests. The relative balance between commonalities and differences varies from organization to organization. A system of authority, a hierarchy of offices, and an array of sanctions have evolved in organizations to manage and reconcile these multiple and conflicting goals of organization members. A means of reconciling conflicting interests is an inevitable part of organization. Unanimity of purpose and organizational harmony cannot be attained simply by eliminating autocratic leadership.

In any organization there are groups with legitimate and conflicting interests which compete for advantage. Since organizational goals can be defined in a variety of ways, the fundamental question of organization is not how to design the organization to achieve these goals, but rather whose preferences and interests will be served by the organization.

However, continuing and irreconcilable conflict over fundamental issues is in no one's interest (with the exception of organizations in a monopoly position, such as the Canadian Post Office, where each side can pursue a single-minded strategy of subduing its opponent without jeopardizing the survival of the organization).

THE 'SOCIAL CONTRACT'

The consent of the governed is a familiar theme in political science. Despite manifest differences in viewpoint, political philosophers such as Hobbes (1651), Locke (1948), and Rousseau (1762) did agree that power is a trust and that the governed voluntarily submit to this power. According to this notion civil society originates from a contract. This contract may be either implicit or explicit and is consented to by each individual. This contract supports a government guided by law, impartial justice, and civil morality.

The concept of social contract has deeply influenced western political thought. Kendall (1968) observes that central to this concept is a belief that only those societies or governments resting on consent are legitimate and that people can be bound only by their own consent.

Similar concepts have been proposed in the behavioural sciences. Bruyn and Nicolaou-Smokovitis (1977) propose the term 'psycho-social contract' to describe the complex of obligations, expectations, responsibilities, rights, and privileges which exists between the individual, the organization, and the society. These obligations and expectations are not officially recorded in a formal agreement, but they operate powerfully to determine the behaviour of organization members. This concept combines the psychological con-

TABLE 2
Consent and the distribution of power

Consent of subordinates	Distribution of power	
	Democratic	Hierarchical
High	2	1
Low	3	4

tract of Schein (1965) and Argyris (1962) with the 'social contract' of Hobbes, Locke, and Rousseau.

CONSENT AND THE DISTRIBUTION OF POWER

Consent of the governed is obtained through a decision-making process which is regarded as fair and proper by contemporary standards. A decision-making process which is participative is not necessarily more effective than a centralized decision-making process. Effective distributions of power depend upon the degree of value consensus among organization members. The greater the consensus on the terms of the relationship (that is, the greater the acceptance of pluralist principles)[12] the more effective will be the participative decision-making process. Conversely, the less the consensus of fundamental issues, the more effective is the centralized decision-making process. Combinations of consent and power are presented in table 2.

Effective distributions of power are found in cells 2 and 4; that is, in cells where there is congruence between the distribution of power and value consensus. Organizations in cell 3 cannot survive in their present form. Political struggles among individuals and coalitions will ensure a move to either cell 2 or cell 4. Organizations in cell 1 are 'overmanaged.'

STAKEHOLDER THEORY OF WORKPLACE DEMOCRACY

Organizations consist of competing groups and individuals who pursue their respective self-interests. Interest groups take many forms in organizations. They may be small, informal groups limited to certain hierarchical strata, or they may be larger, formal associations. Some interest groups are weak, others strong; some are temporary, others relatively enduring; some muster

12 See chapter 1.

the support of limited numbers of employees, others have allies external to the organization; some match functional or administrative lines, others cut across these jurisdictions.

Power struggles among competing interest groups are generally interpreted as problems of communication, incentives, organization design, or training and recruitment practices. However, conflict among competing interests is an integral part of organizational life. Any theory of organizational decision-making should recognize that consensus on organizational matters is a chimerical ideal. The question is: whose interests *should* be served when decisions are made?

This question is perplexing because it is subject to numerous interpretations. A general principle, the stakeholder theory, is proposed here to define persons and groups with a legitimate right to participate in organizational decision-making. Such persons and groups are called 'stakeholders.' Stakeholders who have a legitimate right to participate in organizational decision-making are identified by the principle of 'long-standing interest.' Stakeholders with long-term, continuing, and intensive interactions with others in the organization have a more legitimate claim to shape the activities and direction of the organization than do stakeholders whose interactions may be less frequent, more transient, and more casual. A continuing commitment can be defined in terms of financial investment or in terms of the investment of one's career in the organization. For example, a customer who purchases an automobile from General Motors may be considered a stakeholder, but this customer has less right to participate in decision-making than employees who devote their careers to the company (and less right to participate than a customer who purchases a fleet of cars from the company).

A consumer of a public utility, however, may well have a legitimate claim to participate with others in decisions made by the utility. The consumer is a 'captive' of the utility, and has a continuing interest in the policies of the utility. In addition, members of the community who may be adversely affected by pollution from the organization or by the firm's hiring or wage policy also have a legitimate claim to participate in decision-making.

The interests of suppliers, customers, former employees, and environmentalists may well not coincide with the interests of management or other full-time employees. The extent of participation permitted by various stakeholder groups should be determined by the extent of the groups' commitment to the organization. An entrepreneur who risks his financial future and the financial future of his family by beginning an economic enterprise might be expected to have a greater say over organizational decision-making than employees newly recruited to the organization. However, the claim that employees of large corporations such as General Motors should be excluded from shaping the decisions of these organizations because shareholder interests might be compromised is less persuasive.

Friedlander and Pickle (1968) in a classic study of organizational shareholders examined the effectiveness of ninety-six small businesses in the United States from the perspective of the owners, employees, customers, suppliers, creditors, and local and federal governments. They found widely differing assessments of the performance of the businesses by representatives of the seven groups. The authors conclude that an organization cannot satisfy all stakeholders at once and cannot satisfy all equally well. Definitions of success vary according to one's position and relation to the organization. Consensus is neither possible nor desirable, although consensus on fundamental issues is critical to the survival of work organizations.

CONCLUSION

The crisis of the modern work organization is a crisis of authority and consent. Canadian work organizations historically have relied on the values and socialization practices of the larger society to ensure that organization members obey the directives of their superiors. In the past new recruits could be assumed to hold values about authority and deference which had a transcendental character. However, as Katz and Georgopoulos (1971) point out, the very growth of bureaucratic systems contributed to the decline of values which gave the organization its legitimacy. In the modern work organization pragmatism has replaced tradition. Criteria of success centre on results and achievement, not on moral principle. Rules and laws are instruments for the purpose of achieving goals (which are largely economic in character) and they can be changed at will if they become ineffective. This process has undermined the traditional and moral basis of authority, and the contemporary work organization can no longer rely upon moral commitment of subordinates to its directives.

The decline of the moral legitimacy of organizational power over the past century will now be explored. This historical analysis of power and authority in the workplace will put in perspective the contemporary crisis of authority and will identify the source of mounting social and legal sanctions against the unilateral exercise of power in the workplace.

3

A historical perspective on authority in the workplace

Over this century the ideology underlying managerial authority has been substantially transformed. Early in the century management practice was justified by a Spencerian doctrine of natural superiority, while more recently, management practice is justified in terms of its stewardship of the resources of the organization and its role in accommodating the diverse interests of organizational stakeholders.

This chapter will trace the evolution of ideology and practice over this century, with particular emphasis on ideological appeals directed towards subordinates for the purpose of securing their compliance with managerial directives. This analysis will show how deeply and significantly ideology affects (and is affected by) management practice. Furthermore, it will identify the intellectual traditions from which workplace democracy has emerged and will demonstrate that contemporary interest in workplace democracy is a natural evolution of concerns which were first raised over one hundred years ago.

The term 'ideology' may not be the most appropriate term to describe the doctrines underlying management practice. Clark Kerr proposes the term 'shared understanding' to describe fundamental perspectives which grow out of common experience rather than a common philosophy.[1] The term 'ideology' will be used here, but it is taken to include both carefully constructed and reasoned philosophies as well as mixtures of ad hoc and self-serving justifications.

The nature and style of managerial authority in the workplace is subject to many and competing pressures from the larger society, and these pressures have not always been mutually reinforcing. The managerial practices

---

1 In Bendix 1956

in any era have been influenced by the ideologies and practices of earlier eras. Further, since the 1920s, the ideology underlying organization theory has been more 'progressive' than management ideology and practice. Consequently, the evolution of managerial authority over the past century is not easily divided into discrete and successive stages. Nevertheless, there are five distinguishable perspectives in workplace authority which have arisen over the past century. Each represented a break with the perspective prevailing in its era, and each has significantly shaped subsequent management practice. The six perspectives are: (1) the early factory system (1880–1910), (2) the rise of bureaucracy (1920–40), (3) scientific management (1900–45), (4) human relations (1930–60), (5) human resources (1960–80), and (6) workplace democracy 1965 through the 1980s. The dates associated with each perspective identify the period of growth, intellectual excitement, and productive advances.

THE EARLY FACTORY SYSTEM (1880–1910)

The period 1880–1910 was an era of unprecedented economic growth in North America; the industrial revolution was just beginning in 1880, and the new industrial enterprises were struggling with the complex problems of managing and co-ordinating large numbers of workers. By 1880 industrialization was well underway in England, France, and Germany. In England social reform movements designed to mitigate some of the untoward effects of the industrial revolution were gaining momentum in the 1860s and 1870s. The first trade unions had appeared, and reform of factory conditions was on the political agenda.

In North America opposition to the conditions and practices of the factory were weak and ineffectual. A strident Spencerian ideology provided those who owned the means of production with a moral basis for unlimited and unilateral control over their property, including employees. According to this ideology, the success of the few and the powerful was a reflection of personal virtue and natural superiority. Poverty, subordination, and dependence were the natural and inevitable fate of the unfit. In the era of the early factory system employers enjoyed a pre-eminent place in the social hierarchy.

The stability of the social order was believed to rest on the unchecked control of the employer over his property. The will of the employer was absolute; his judgments on work as well as on personal matters were final. The inferior were enjoined by this ideology to obey those whose success in the competitive struggle entitled them to command. The management practices of this era could be characterized by despotism (in both its benevolent and its tyrannical forms), cruel exploitation, arbitrary use of power, and subjective and capricious treatment of subordinates. Decisions concerning wages, hours of work, and discipline were based on personal loyalties and friendships. Employees who were abused or who felt aggrieved had no legal recourse.

The employee, like the servant, was regarded as the chattel of the master. In fact, under Anglo-Saxon law the employment relationship is modelled after the master-servant relationship. A court judgment in the *Payne v. Western & A.R.R.* decision illustrates this perspective: 'May I not refuse to trade with anyone? May I not forbid my family to trade with anyone? May I not dismiss my domestic servant for dealing, or even visiting, when I forbid? And if my domestic, why not my farm-hand, or my mechanic, or teamster?'[2]

In the early 1900s trade unions began to challenge in earnest the employer's right to manage his 'own' plant with absolute authority. Employers in the early part of the century were unalterably opposed to negotiating with workers or their representatives. They owned the business; they were responsible for its success; and they determined the manner in which their property would be used. The brutal practices of this era – arbitrary and instant dismissal for any infraction, forced employment in dangerous and unhealthy conditions, discharge of injured workers without compensation – led to savage battles between organized labour and management.

The violent reaction prompted by the trade union challenge is difficult to comprehend in a modern context. The temper of the times is illustrated by the editorial response of the *Journal of Commerce* to the rioting following an industrial dispute in Valleyfield, Quebec in 1900:

The proprietors of the Valleyfield mills are capitalists to whom Canada is under deep obligations for their enterprise in establishing and maintaining a great national industry ... It will be a sorry day for Canada when those who venture their fortunes in manufacturing enterprises can be intimidated and their property and their business interests jeopardized by rioters without the miscreants receiving the due reward of their crime against law and order. The non-service of warrants issued against the ringleaders shows lamentable weakness somewhere. Is it possible that there is a district of this law-abiding Colony where the Queen's writ does not run?[3]

The issue was power. Trade unions endeavoured to counter the unilateral control of the employer over the workplace. The intensity of the feeling is illustrated in the words of an owner of a Galt iron foundry during the strike

2 Reported by Blades 1967, 1416
3 *Journal of Commerce*, 2 Nov. 1900, 1194–5

of 1889: 'There is my factory. It is a large one, it is built of brick and stone. You might begin to take it away piecemeal – one brick at a time, one stone at a time – carrying the particles on your own shoulder over into the next county, going as slowly and deliberately as you please, and then, when all has been taken away, I will be no nearer to yielding the management of my business to your trade union than I am now. I will never do it.'[4]

While the response of most employers to the stirrings of organized labour was implacably hostile, there was some sympathy for the problems of the working man as well as expressions of concern and outrage at the more glaring injustices of the period. Many employers of the era voluntarily endeavoured to improve the conditions of their employees. Programs of 'welfare work' and 'industrial betterment' were early signs that employer attitudes towards the working person were beginning to change.

The challenges facing supervision in the new factory system were overwhelming. Supervisors were usually illiterate workmen promoted through the ranks because of their superior technical skills. Most were paid only slightly more than workers and most were attracted to the job because it gave the incumbent the power to hire wives and children to work in the factory. These supervisors were left on their own to work out their own management style. The style adopted by most was authoritarian.

The new factories were faced with the problem of attracting labourers from rural to urban life. The migration of farm labourers to the factories broke the traditional family ties of the worker and exposed him to the alien urban culture. In response to the conditions of factory life – regular working hours, mechanical pacing of the work, rigid discipline, and subordination – many workers became restless, truculent, and unco-operative. The autocratic practices of the era were in part necessitated by a reluctant and unwilling work-force.

The view of labour as chattel and the belief that the subordinate owes the superior absolute obedience could not continue in face of mounting social and political pressures. The ruthless practices of this era could not be justified – even in the pursuit of national progress. What emerged was a form of authority which was more rational, impersonal, limited, and was based on rules and laws rather than on personal fiat.

THE RISE OF BUREAUCRACY (1920–40)

The bureaucratic form of work organization is generally, but incorrectly, attributed to Max Weber. Weber's seminal work on the theory of bureau-

4 Bliss 1974, 86–7

cracy was not translated into English and hence was not available to managers or social scientists in this country until 1948. Although Weber's work has profoundly influenced modern organizational sociology, the bureaucratic form of work organization which appeared in the early part of this century was the product of resourceful and innovative management rather than of the organizational theorist.

From the experiences of these managers (and consultants who eagerly embraced the new bureaucratic principles) there emerged the principles of bureaucracy which were ultimately to transform both the ideology underlying managerial authority and the manner in which authority was exercised in the workplace. Among the major contributors are Henri Fayol (1916), J.D. Mooney and A.C. Reiley (1931; 1939), Oliver Sheldon (1923), Luther Gulick (1937), and Lyndall Urwick (1938; 1944). From this perspective came a rational model for the co-ordination of activities in the organization. Much of this work was concerned with the elaboration of 'principles' defining the best way of managing.

Many of these principles concerned the exercise of authority. The 'scalar principle,' for example, stipulated that authority and responsibility should flow in a clear and unbroken line from upper to lower hierarchical levels. The 'unity of command principle' stated that no member of an organization should receive orders from more than one superior. According to the 'exception principle,' routine problems should be referred to subordinates, and important, non-recurring problems should be referred to superiors. The span of control of the superior should be limited to roughly five or six subordinates, so that each subordinate could be directly supervised.

These bureaucratic principles severely limited the power the employer was able to exercise over subordinates. Under the bureaucratic form of organization, the employer's power over the subordinate was limited to the subordinate's conduct of his work, and was bound by a defined set of rules. As long as the subordinate performed in accordance with the rules, the superior could not act in a subjective manner. The superior's power was vested in his role, not in his person, and this power was recognized as so vested by the person over whom it was wielded.

The depersonalization of authority was a major preoccupation of this era. According to the bureaucratic model organizational officials were to deal in an impersonal manner with their subordinates, to disregard all personal considerations, and to maintain complete emotional detachment from their subordinates. Superiors had specified spheres of authority, and administrative acts, decisions, and rules which govern the relationship between superiors and subordinates were formulated and recorded in writing. Obedience was now rendered not to the person but to a set of impersonal principles.

Although the bureaucratic form of organization is often regarded as inhumane and insensitive to individual needs, it nevertheless represented a significant advance over the practices of the early factory system. Rules served to limit the discretion of superiors over subordinates and for the first time provided the subordinate with protection from the whim of the superior. The problems of the earlier age – particularism, favouritism, corruption, nepotism, patronage, subjectivity, and inefficiency – were to be eliminated in this new form of organization.

The next perspective on workplace authority – scientific management – provided, for the first time, a coherent rationale for the union of employer and employee in a common endeavour.

SCIENTIFIC MANAGEMENT (1900–45)

While the bureaucratic model focused primarily on the administrative component of the organization, there emerged at about the same time a concern with efficient methods of production on the shop floor and with the relationship between the first-line supervisor and the worker. This perspective was called 'scientific management' by its first proponent, Frederick Winslow Taylor.[5]

The authoritarian work environment of the early factory system was the product of an ideology which supported the owner's right of absolute control over his property. Scientific management further strengthened the hierarchical character of the workplace by adding a second element: obedience to the laws of science. Scientific management reinforced the authoritarian practices of the era and subordinated the worker to the objective and rational principles of industrial engineering. The principles of scientific management reinforced the perception of the worker as an instrument, to be purchased by management for the performance of a specific task.

It is important to note, however, that scientific management was, in an important sense, a challenge to the arbitrary power of management. The personal and subjective exercise of authority on the shop-floor would be replaced by scientific and impartial inquiry. From this moment on the employer could not rule over the workplace by appealing to an ideology extolling and upholding his natural abilities and superiority. The principles of scientific management were generally available to and readily understandable by the layman, and the doctrine of mystical superiority no longer commanded the obedience of subordinates.

---

5 Recent evidence suggests that many of the principles of scientific management were not Taylor's, although he presented the principles as his own. See Wrege and Stotka 1978.

Taylor argued that scientific management would bring harmony to the workplace. Scientific management would remove the old-fashioned, dictatorial methods and replace them with rational judgment. Standards of work and wages would now be subject to rational scientific calculation and would be removed from the realm of subjective determination or traditional practices – both of which inevitably lead to conflict.

Giving testimony before the Special Committee of the House of Representatives to Investigate the Taylor and other Systems of Shop Management under authority of House Resolution 90 in 1912, Taylor observed,

under scientific management arbitrary power, arbitrary dictation ceases; every single subject, large and small, becomes the question for scientific investigation, for reduction to law ...[6]

The man at the head of the business under scientific management is governed by rules and laws which have been developed through hundreds of experiments just as much as the working man is, and the standards which have been developed are equitable ... those questions which are under other systems subject to arbitrary judgment and are therefore open to disagreement have under scientific management, been the subject of the most minute and careful study in which both the workman and the management have taken part, and they have been settled to the satisfaction of both sides.[7]

Taylor pursued his ideas with tactless zeal. Throughout his work are references to the worker as an 'intelligent gorilla,' and an 'ox.' These and other epithets reveal Taylor's contempt for the worker: 'Now, one of the very first requirements for a man who is fit to handle pig iron ... is that he shall be so stupid and so phlegmatic that he more nearly resembles ... the ox than any other type ... he must consequently be trained by a man more intelligent than himself.'[8]

Reference to Schmidt, an immigrant Dutch labourer, provides further insight into Taylor's view of the worker. Schmidt was not an aberration or an unfortunate by-product of the new methods, but rather a necessary and desirable component: an unthinking, dependent, obedient worker. David Jenkins states,

scientific management strengthened the authoritarian structure, further, raised the principle of unthinking obedience to the status of an iron law, restricted even fur-

6 Taylor 1947, 212
7 Ibid., 189
8 Taylor 1911, 59

ther the worker's freedom to 'exert his understanding,' and tightly locked him into a process in which his every movement was controlled.

[Scientific management] has lent additional force to the notion that employees, and not only low-level production employees, need to be told precisely what to do and how to do it; that independent thinking is dangerous and unpermissible; that the planning of the work needs to be separated from its actual execution; and that the only motivation is money.[9]

Taylor's ideas were opposed by many employers. Scientific management was regarded by many as an unwarranted intrusion into the domain of managerial prerogative. Managers objected to the substitution of scientific technique for judgment and discretion. Taylor once observed that nine-tenths of his trouble in implementing scientific management came from managers, and one-tenth from the workers.

In many respects the principles of scientific management reinforced those of classical bureaucratic theory. The employee is an automaton to be guided by financial incentives, the application of sound engineering principles, and firm and directive leadership. Predictably, scientific management did not reconcile the interests of labour and management. In fact, scientific management has come to be seen as a management tool to be used against the worker.

An investigation of Taylor's practices and other systems of 'shop management' was called for by the U.S. Commission on Industrial Relations in 1914. Robert Hoxie, the chairman of this commission, prepared a report critical of scientific management. He characterized Taylor's philosophy as a 'Utopian ideal.' According to Hoxie's report the actual practices of scientific management departed significantly from Taylor's ideal. 'In practice, Scientific Management must, therefore, be declared autocratic; in tendency, a reversion to industrial autocracy, which forces the worker to depend on the employer's conception of fairness, and limits the democratic safeguards of the worker.'[10]

Taylor's disciples elaborated and extended his techniques. One of these students, Frank Gilbreth, became one of the pioneers of scientific management. The following anecdote, reported by two of Gilbreth's children, aptly summarizes the 'mind set' of Gilbreth and others who worked in this tradition.

Dad took moving pictures of us children washing dishes, so that he could figure out how we could reduce our motions and thus hurry through the task. Your regular

9 Jenkins 1973, 30–1
10 Hoxie 1915, 112

jobs, such as painting the back porch or removing a stump from the front lawn, were awarded on a low-bid basis. Each child who wanted extra pocket money submitted a sealed bid saying what he would do the job for. The lowest bidder got the contract ...

Yes, at home or on the job, Dad was always the efficiency expert. He buttoned his vest from the bottom up, instead of from the top down, because the bottom-to-top process took him only three seconds while the top-to-bottom took seven. He even used two shaving brushes to lather his face, because he found that by so doing he could cut seventeen seconds off his shaving time. For a while he tried shaving with two razors, but he finally gave that up.

'Can save 44 seconds' he grumbled, 'but I wasted 2 minutes this morning putting this bandage on my throat.'

It wasn't the slashed throat that bothered him. It was the two minutes.[11]

From this account, Gilbreth appears to be somewhat eccentric; and the image of the hapless children generally evokes bemused sympathy. However, generations of workers have been subjected to similar treatment and rarely is much sympathy evoked for their plight. Such is our view of the worker and the workplace.

The new field of experimental psychology and the growing influence of experimental and industrial psychologists in the military and in industry reinforced the principles of scientific management and provided it with an intellectual base. In the 1930s immigrant labour willing to work for almost any wage became increasingly scarce. Shortages of skilled labour, the rising influence of trade unions and a growing public awareness of the externalities of authoritarian practices prompted a concern with social and psychological factors in the workplace. The worker would soon be seen as a person with emotions, feelings, and needs. In addition, the increasing complexities of the work organization – staff and committee work, delegation of authority, specialization and the lengthening of the chain of command and the chains of communication – stimulated the emergence of the next and in many ways the most influential perspective on authority in the workplace.

HUMAN RELATIONS (1930–60)

The human relations perspective is commonly identified with Elton Mayo.[12] It is not an understatement to say that Mayo's work led to a reinterpretation of managerial authority. Bendix (1956) observes that while Mayo may not

---

11 Gilbreth and Carey 1948, 2–3
12 Mayo 1931; 1945, Roethlisberger and Dickson 1939

have had much effect on actual managerial practices, he did have a profound effect on managerial values.

For Mayo the work organization was a unitary and integrated structure. The work group was the vehicle through which management's directives could be supported and enforced. The work group was the basic social unit for integrating the interests of the individual and the interests of organization. Mayo viewed trade unions as destructive of co-operation and mutual commitment of labour and management.

Mayo did not envision fundamental change in the work organization. The division of labour, the power and status of employees, and the relationship between superior and subordinate were to remain the same. However, through supportive and participative supervision, the employee could be made more compliant in the pursuit of organizational goals.

The answer to preparing leaders for the new human relations role was training at all levels to learn skills in human understanding of logical and non logical behavior, understanding the sentiments of the worker through listening and communications skills, and developing the ability to maintain an equilibrium between the economic needs of the formal organization and the social needs of the informal organization ... Through the social structure, workers obtained the recognition, security, and satisfactions which made them willing to cooperate and contribute their services toward the attainment of the organization's objectives.[13]

Much of Mayo's work is concerned with means for attaining the 'spontaneous cooperation' of employees. Mayo decried the loss of solidarity and sense of community in the work organization and sought to replace the impersonality of relations at work with more supportive human contact. Mayo firmly opposed the fragmentation he observed in modern society. He believed that the divisions in modern society were the product of 'the rabble hypothesis' (society consists of a horde of unorganized individuals; every individual acts in a manner calculated to secure his self interest; and every individual thinks logically in the pursuit of his self-interest).

Mayo regarded conflict as pathological and sought its eradication from the industrial organization. For Mayo, conflict was irrational. He did not recognize that there could be legitimate conflicts of interest between labour and management. This yearning for a co-operative workplace, on management's terms, represents one of the fundamental weaknesses in Mayo's work.

Mayo (like Taylor before him) felt that the worker could be integrated into the organization without any substantial change in the distribution of power and authority. Programs such as supervisory training and employee interviews would be sufficient to secure the consent and commitment of employees. Mayo was a strong advocate of programs of employee interviews and introduced a program of regular employee interviews at Western Electric. The interviews were to allow employees to talk through their problems and thereby to gain insight into the reasons behind their 'undesirable' behaviour. The interviewers would simply sit and listen; they had no power to change conditions identified by employees.

Critics of the human relations perspective point out that human relations presents 'the friendly face' of organizations while leaving unchanged the conditions giving rise to employee complaints.[14] Many feel that human relations is manipulative – that is, it aims to obtain employee commitment through supportive supervisory practices – while the authoritarian character of the organization remains unchanged.

The human relations perspective dealt yet another blow to the infallibility of the employer. Success and virtue were now associated with human relations skills. Leaders of men were no longer born and no longer moved inexorably to positions of authority. They could now be trained in human relations skills and could learn how to elicit the consent of subordinates.

The emerging concern with the worker and his feelings was also an important theme in the work of Mary Parker Follett and Chester Barnard, although they are not commonly identified with the human relations movement. Barnard was both an academic and an executive (president of New Jersey Bell Telephone and director of the Emergency Relief in New Jersey during the early days of the depression). Barnard has exerted a profound influence on modern behavioural science. His major work, The Functions of the Executive (1938) presents a theory of organization which posits that organizations by their very nature are co-operative systems. That is, members voluntarily join organizations and co-operate with others in the pursuit of common goals. Barnard understood that conflict existed and often persisted in organizations, but this situation was seen as a result of a failure to establish a common purpose and to inculcate a sense of common endeavour in the minds of employees.

For Barnard communication was the means of improving co-operative effort. He did not envision a participative process as a means of attaining co-operation; understandably, any such suggestion would have been inappropriate for the era (the post-depression years). There emerged in the work of Barnard the belief that the power of managers can survive only if it is legiti-

14 The term 'cow sociologists' was used in 1949 in the UAW publication *Ammunition* to describe Mayo and his colleagues.

mate, and legitimacy is conferred by the broader society. Without legitimacy organizational power has no moral base and the retort that power is essential for efficiency is a recognition that there is no longer a higher purpose which justifies the subordination of one person to another.

Barnard was the first to propose that the source of authority did not reside in those who exercised authority, but rather in subordinates. While Mayo endeavoured to 'soften' formal authority through supportive and participative interpersonal relations (and Mary Parker Follett sought to depersonalize authority through the 'law of the situation'), Barnard emphasized the consent of subordinates as the ultimate source of authority. For Barnard the 'authority of leadership' was derived from the subordinate's respect for the superior's competence, judgment, and personal abilities, not from his rank or position.

Mary Parker Follett also eloquently expressed many of the concerns of the human relations perspective, although she predated Mayo's work by a decade or so.[15] Many of her observations on labour-management relations, conflict in organizations, and power and authority are deeply insightful, and she has profoundly influenced many contemporary organizational theorists.

Follett's writings are dominated by the themes of developing effective leadership, achieving the co-ordination of the diverse interests or organization members, defining authority and responsibility, and creating an 'integrative unity' of labour and management. The unity of effort of all organization members, she argued, was undermined by the artificial distinction between those who manage and those who are managed. She deplored collective bargaining because of the tendency for both sides to lose sight of their common interests. Further, beyond the level of the firm, she believed that all employees should recognize the integrative unity of the firm and its environment – customers, shareholders, and competitors.

The existence of a management hierarchy and the roles of superior and subordinate creates the perception of divergent interests and inevitably leads to conflict. She argued that superiors should exercise 'power with' subordinates, rather than 'power over' subordinates. For Follett authority resides in the situation not in the person or the position. 'One person should not give orders to another person, but both should agree to take their orders from the situation. If orders are simply part of the situation, the question of someone giving and someone receiving does not come up.'[16]

Follett emphasized that when people were motivated to fulfil their common purposes, personal control of superiors over subordinates was unneces-

15 Fox and Urwick 1973; Metcalf and Urwick 1942
16 Metcalf and Urwick 1942, 59

sary. The leader should 'make his co-workers see that it is not *his* purpose which is to be achieved, but a common purpose, born of the issues and activities of the group. The best leader does not ask people to serve him, but the common end. The best leader has not followers, but men and women working with him.'[17]

The human relations perspective has generated more research on work organizations than any other perspective, and it has generated a good deal of controversy as well. From the time of the pioneering work of Roethlisberger and Dickson (1939), research on participative management has been the subject of controversy and varying interpretations, and has sparked what Landsberger (1958) calls a 'spectacular academic battle.'

Certainly many of the seminal studies on participation in the human relations tradition are seriously flawed by lack of controls, subtle experimenter effects, over-interpretation of small samples of single work-groups, and by a manifest ideological bias favouring participative management. Nevertheless, human relations theory and research have become an important part of contemporary management thinking and have significantly affected modern organization theory. The compelling logic of the research and the consistency of this perspective with democratic and cultural values help explain the popularity of human relations theory.

It is clear that the human relations perspective no longer enjoys the pre-eminent status it once did.[18] The recent and growing interest in workplace democracy reflects an attempt to move beyond the informal, subjective and largely personal preoccupations of the human relations perspective and to explore forms of participation involving more significant sharing of power.

The growing body of empirical evidence and the increasing sophistication of behavioural science led to a recognition that the world was not as Mayo described it or as he hoped it might be. A subtle yet significant change in the perception of behavioural scientists emerged in the early 1960s. This shift was first identified by Raymond Miles (1965).

HUMAN RESOURCES (1960–80)

The 1960s and 1970s were years of ferment and excitement in both management practice and organization theory. Sensitivity training, human resource development, organization development, human potential, and humaniza-

---

17 Ibid., 333
18 The critiques of Perrow (1979), Strauss (1963), Strauss and Rosenstein (1970), and others have identified ideological, conceptual, and methodological problems which call many of the conclusions of the human relations perspective into question.

FIGURE 1 The human relations and human resources perspectives

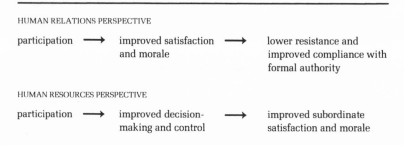

tion of work are some of the themes and techniques of these years. The human relations perspective of the earlier era was replaced by a more sophisticated, empirically based, and less manifestly normative perspective, which Raymond Miles labelled 'human resources.' Miles discovered in the writings of Douglas McGregor, Rensis Likert, and Abraham Maslow an emerging and incompletely developed theme which departed dramatically from traditional management theory and practice. According to this theme employees were considered to have the capacity for self-direction and self-control, and participative management was the key to releasing the productive capability of the employee.

Although both the human relations and the human resources perspectives emphasized participative decision-making, the rationale for participation differs significantly in the two perspectives. This difference is illustrated in figure 1.

Under human relations, the manager shares information, consults with subordinates, and encourages self-direction solely to improve subordinate satisfaction and morale. According to the human resources perspective the manager allows subordinate participation because more effective decisions are made by those directly involved in and affected by the decisions. This perspective proposes that morale and satisfaction are related to participation, but they result from the climate of creative problem-solving generated by participative management.

The most significant contributions to human resources theory were two books by Rensis Likert. The books – New Patterns of Management published in 1961 and The Human Organization published in 1967 – outline a theory of organization centred on the concept of participation.[19]

19 The theory presented in chapter 4 owes much to Likert's perspective on the work organization.

While the human resources perspective is based on the premise that participation permits the more effective use of the knowledge and skills of subordinates, no proponent of the human resources perspective envisioned a significant change in the distribution of power and authority at the workplace. Participation was to be limited to the immediate work group and to matters which under the conventional hierarchical design fell within the domain of the work group. The participation envisioned by Likert was to be 'informal,' that is, it was to be practised by the enlightened supervisor, but was not a formal component of the decision-making structure of the organization.

Nevertheless, the human resources perspective has been an important link between human relations and the perspective on workplace democracy taken in this book. Participation was no longer practised because it improved satisfaction and morale. Rather, it was practised because it produced better decisions and more effectively utilized the human resources of the organization.

The political left is deeply critical of the human resources perspective. Greenberg (1975) dismisses this perspective (which he calls 'the management school') as more expedient than humanitarian. He argues that its advocates – business leaders, some academics, and government officials – are concerned primarily with productivity and the under-utilization of human resources in an environment where traditional management prerogatives are limited by statute and collective agreement. Greenberg argues that the techniques preferred by this perspective include job enlargement, job enrichment, and limited shop-floor participation which entails no alteration of traditional managerial authority and prerogative. Its goal, in face of the threat of legislation giving broader participation rights to employees, is to institute limited reforms as necessary to raise morale, lower absenteeism, and increase the worker's commitment to the enterprise.

WORKPLACE DEMOCRACY (1965 THROUGH THE 1980s)

The final perspective in this historical view of systems of authority in the workplace is 'workplace democracy.' This perspective on authority has emerged from the work of Carole Pateman (1970), Paul Blumberg (1968), Arnold Tannenbaum and his colleagues (1974; 1974), Gerry Hunnius et al. (1973), and Jacques Grand'Maison (1975). Dahl's (1970) theory of the democratic process, Vanek's (1971) theory of democratic market socialism, and Trist and Bamforth's (1953) socio-technical systems theory are supporting themes. The major tenet of this perspective – that labour as a legitimate stakeholder in the enterprise has a moral right to play a role in the management of the enterprise – may never become widespread in this country; nevertheless, these principles will be assimilated in one form or another into management ideology and practice of the future.

'Workplace democracy' is a generic term which subsumes a variety of specific forms. This perspective will define and shape the debate about employee rights and authority at the workplace in the coming decade. The debate promises to be as heated and acrimonious as the battles over trade union recognition were in the era of the early factory system. Two important themes in this perspective are the 'participatory left' and the 'humanist school.'[20] The participatory left covers a spectrum of viewpoints which are united in a desire for a decentralist, non-bureaucratic socialism (Czechoslovakia under Dubcek, the plant seizures in France in May 1968, and the Yugoslav system of self-management).

G.D.H. Cole (1920), Gramsci[21] and Gorz (1967; 1973) see the spread of participation at the workplace as part of a larger revolutionary struggle. They envision the management of organizations through worker-controlled works councils. Through these works councils, workers would control the production process and would learn the skills and confidence required to rule society. These works councils would create a revolutionary consciousness and would overcome the false consciousness of capitalism.

The 'participatory left' has not been particularly influential in Canada, although proponents of this perspective have offered some suggestions for enhancing rank and file control over the workplace.[22] The Regina manifesto of the CCF in 1933 contained a blueprint for industrial democracy. Through 'collective agreements and participation in works councils, the workers can achieve fair working rules and share in the control of the industry and profession; and their organization will be indispensible elements in a system of genuine industrial democracy.'[23]

This theme emerged many years later in the Waffle Manifesto of 1969. The 'central objective of Canadian socialists must be to further the democratic process in industry ... Those who work must have effective control in the determination of working conditions, and substantial power in determining the nature of the product, prices, and so on ... The struggle for worker participation in industrial decision making and against management "rights" is such a move toward economic and social democracy.'[24]

20 Greenberg 1975
21 See Cammett, 1967.
22 See Hunnius et al. 1973; Wilson 1974; Finn 1973; and Trower 1973.
23 Zakuta 1964, 164–5, as quoted in Antonides 1980
24 Godfrey and Watkins 1970, 106–7, as quoted in Antonides 1980

The 'humanist school' is animated by a vision of what people could be, given the opportunity. According to this perspective the modern work organization stunts human potential, degrades the human spirit, and produces passive and incomplete individuals.

Although the proponents of this viewpoint[25] did not view participative management as central to ameliorating the conditions which prevail at the workplace, participative practices are nevertheless an important part of their thinking. The imperatives of the modern work organization (designed according to Weberian and Taylorist principles of rigid hierarchical control, work specialization, defined channels of communication, and strict subordination) are precisely those which prevent the development of the mature personality. The industrial worker is expected to be no more expert, mature, or fully developed the day he retires than the day he began work. The importance of this perspective lies in recognizing that the structure of human personality and character is in part dependent on the nature of the workplace and the manner in which authority is exercised in the workplace.

An important variant of the human relations model comes from the work of Eric Trist and his colleagues at the Tavistock Institute in London, England.[26] They were concerned with the relationship between social and human factors at the workplace and the work technology. They argued that attempts to maximize productive efficiency of a work system by concentrating solely on the work technology while ignoring the social and human components of the work system would lead to 'sub-optimal' solutions.

This perspective, which later became known as 'socio-technical systems' theory, continues as a dominant theme of the quality of work life movement. Although socio-technical systems theory does not address directly the issue of authority and superior-subordinate relations, it does have important implications for the exercise of authority in the workplace. Through appropriate design of the work, the employee becomes self-directing and self-regulating. The worker is allowed to control the work through his own initiative and discretion; the superior becomes a facilitator and an educator and undertakes more consequential planning for the work group.

SUMMARY

The six perspectives on authority in the workplace are summarized in table 3. Each view of authority is based on a unique set of propositions about the nature, conditions, causes, and consequences of authority. Each view also

25 Argyris 1964; Maslow 1954; and Rogers 1961
26 Trist and Bamforth 1951

TABLE 3
A historical perspective on systems of authority in the Canadian workplace

Practice	Supporting theory	View of authority	View of subordinate	View of superior
Early factory system (1880–1910)	– social Darwinism (Spencer) – market capitalism (Ricardo, Smith)	– unilateral, absolute, subjective	– morally and intellectually inferior to the superior – unfit, shiftless, uncooperative – subordinate is chattel and bound by contract to obey directives of superiors	– the 'fittest' in competitive struggle – superior virtue and ability confers right to demand abject obedience
Bureaucracy (1920–40)	– administrative management theory (Faylo, Urwick, Sheldon, Mooney)	– unilateral, limited, rational, impersonal, based on rules	– in need of direction – bound by contract to obey directives of superiors	– technical and administrative skills qualify superiors to lead
Scientific management (1900–45)	– industrial engineering (Taylor) – experimental and industrial psychology (Munsterberg)	– authority based on rational judgment and impartial inquiry	– unproductive and uncooperative, except when guided by economic incentives	– no longer infallible – guided and constrained by principles of scientific management
Human relations (1930–60)	– group dynamics (Roethlisberger and Dickson, Lewin) – social theory of Mayo	– directive, but with supportive interpersonal skills – subordinates should be 'treated as human beings'	– co-operative and productive when needs for social interaction and recognition are met at the workplace	– leadership a higher calling – leadership sensitive to subordinates

Human resources (1960–80)	– interaction-influence theory (Likert)	– 'informal' participation enhances authority of superior	– energy, commitment, skills of subordinates liberated through participation	– responsible for co-ordination and enhancement of human effort
Workplace democracy (1965–80s)	– political theory (Dahl) – European social democratic theory – organizational sociology (Blumberg, Tannenbaum, Pateman) – democratic market socialism (Vanek) – socio-technical systems theory (Trist and Bamforth)	– without consent of subordinates, authority of superior is ineffective	– subordinates are legitimate stakeholders in the organization – subordinates are creative and responsible contributors to the organization – subordinates have a moral right and legitimate role to play in managing the organization	– accountable to all stakeholders, including subordinates

presents a different set of criteria for judging the success or failure of participative management.

Over this period of time management has adapted to significant restrictions on its freedoms, rights, and prerogatives, while the rights the employee
enjoys in the workplace have been broadened and deepened substantially.
The changes from period to period have been incremental, but cumula-
tively, they have been revolutionary. Although they have evolved in an
unstructured way, they have outpaced the capacity of many managers to
adapt.

Changes in the larger society have also been far-reaching. Among the more
significant changes has been a move from a powerless and unorganized
labour force to an increasingly educated, demanding, and powerful work
force; a move from control by the owner-entrepreneur to shareholder control to professional management control; a waning of the work ethic and the
promotion of individual freedom, self-realization, and self-gratification; a
loss of respect for authority; a move away from authoritarian relationships
and rigid codes of conduct; and a rise in the absolute level of wealth, a
declining marginal utility of each addition to this wealth, and consequently
a decline in the power of those who allocate wealth.

The changing ideology underlying authority and changes in the rights of
those subjected to authority have been bitterly opposed by those who have
held power. They have claimed and continue to claim that the erosion of
their rights and prerogatives presages the demise of our economic system.
Any infringement on these rights represents, according to this argument, a
violation of natural law.

Each change in perspective has precipitated a crisis of management. Each
change has prompted a search for an explicit rationale for the role of
management. The search has sought to identify the sources and limits of
managerial authority and the nature of the rights and responsibilities associated with this authority.

The justification for the unilateral management control today is very
different than it was fifty years ago. In the earlier era limits on the
employer's freedom of decision-making were believed to lead inevitably to
the loss of freedom for others. If the entrepreneur could be deprived of
rights to use his property as he wished, then no man's freedom was secure.
Today, however, the justification for unilateral management control rests on
the pressures from the market-place. Demands for flexibility, new markets,
products, and processes require rapid adjustment and technical and professional skills beyond the capability of the average employee.

The current system of workplace authority in Canada is a combination of themes from the previous perspectives. The uneven pace of development in different sectors of the economy and in different parts of the country makes it difficult to define a unitary contemporary perspective. Practice often lags behind the rhetoric and vocabulary of the day, although the rhetoric provides a vision towards which practice inevitably moves.

4

Congruence theory: a framework for the study of workplace democracy

The field of organizational studies is splintered by multiple and competing theories or 'paradigms.' This variety of theories is a natural result of the complexity of modern organizations. Organizations are diverse and complex mixtures of the rational and the irrational; they have legal, political, social, psychological, and technological dimensions which are not easily captured by any single theory of organization.

Stogdill (1966) identifies no less than eighteen approaches to the study of organizations in the organizational theory literature. Organizations have been viewed as input-output systems, as collections of individual members, as summations of member characteristics, as subgroups in interaction, as systems of structure and function, as exchange agents with the environment, as socio-technical systems, and as biological systems.

Taking Ritzer's (1975) definition of paradigm as 'a fundamental image of the subject matter within the science' (which defines topics to be studied, questions to be asked, and methods to be employed), Pondy and Boje (1976) point out that contemporary research on organizations falls into one of two paradigms: the 'social facts' paradigm encompasses research on macro-level concepts and the 'social behavior' paradigm encompasses research on individual-level concepts.

Although there is considerable disagreement over the likely resolution of the current state of unconnected and unintegrated theories and paradigms, there is some opinion that theories bridging the psychological and sociological perspectives on organizations can and should be unified into more broadly based theories.[1]

---

1 Child 1973; Indik 1972; Nightingale and Toulouse 1977; Rousseau 1977; 1978

The theory proposed here integrates concepts from the 'social facts' and 'social behavior' paradigms. This theory provides a 'mid-range' perspective on organizations and avoids the loss of precision and explicitness of all-embracing theories while avoiding the fragmentation and narrow purview of single-theme theories. The purpose of this theory is to provide a conceptual and propositional integration of concepts relevant to the study of democratic work organizations.

This chapter will begin with a definition of organization and then define and discuss five concepts – values, structure, process, outcomes, and environment – which will be linked in a theory of organization. This theory is based on the congruence of these concepts.[2] The dynamics of this theory will be described and two ideal types of organization proposed: the 'democratic organization' and the 'hierarchical organization.'

THE DEFINITION OF ORGANIZATION

The term 'organization' is used in common parlance to mean many things: a legal entity, a physical plant, a group of people. This 'public language' is convenient but imprecise; a more abstract definition is required for the theory to be developed in this chapter.

'Organization' is defined here as a system of relatively enduring and patterned interactions among individuals.[3] The interactions among organization members follow predictable patterns. Organization member interactions, in general, are stable, continuous over time, and predictable. These interactions typically involve a mixture of collaboration and forced compliance. Random or non-recurring interactions among individuals do not constitute organization. The interactions among organization members are made stable and predictable by an authority structure. The authority structure is justified by an ideology which encourages interactions of a particular character.

The organization prescribes acceptable forms of behaviour for those who elect to become members. The authority structure establishes acceptable

---

2 Congruence theory is proposed and examined empirically by Nightingale and Toulouse 1977.
3 This definition is similar to several others in the organization theory literature. Barnard (1938) defines organization as a system of consciously coordinated personal activities; Stogdill (1966) defines an organization as a structured system of behaviour with role prescriptions defining the nature of these behaviours; and Presthus (1958) defines organization as a system of structured interpersonal relations.

patterns of interaction, appropriate beliefs, attitudes and modes of conduct. Many of the interactions defining organization are frequent and intense, others are periodic and casual. Organization members who interact intensively with one another are 'full' members of the organization; members who interact less frequently are 'partially included' members.

'Partially included' members have commitments, loyalties, interactions with, and obligations to groups or organizations outside of the organization in question. Examples include part-time employees, and organization members (such as salesmen) who interact primarily with others outside of the organization. According to this definition organizations can 'expand' or 'contract' by increasing or decreasing the interactions among members. An organization's 'size' depends on the amount of interaction among organization members. Entropy occurs when interaction among members ceases.

The boundary of the organization is defined as the point at which interactions among individuals reach a particular level. The level may be defined in a variety of ways, some stringent, others more liberal. The boundary of an organization is like the boundary of a cloud; it cannot be precisely located. The location of the boundary rests on a definition of 'density' and density does not change in discrete stages, but rather changes in imperceptible steps. Organizational membership can be defined in such a way that customers, suppliers, government authorities and representatives, community leaders and shareholders are members, or the boundary may be defined by more intense interaction among members, in which case, membership is more limited. The definition of membership is not a trivial matter; on p. 000 the rights of individuals to participate in organizational decision-making are defined in terms of membership in the organization.

COMPONENTS OF CONGRUENCE THEORY

The theory proposed here encompasses the values of organization members, the structure of the organization, the nature of interpersonal and intergroup interactions, and the attitudes, reactions, and adjustments of organization members.

Values
Values are abstract and generalized judgments which define appropriate behaviours and beliefs and provide an underlying continuity to behaviours and beliefs.

A 'value system' is an internally consistent constellation of separate judgments. A value system is not a carefully reasoned set of propositions but is all those beliefs, ideas, and perspectives which are taken for granted and, by and large, remain unquestioned and unstated.

The judgments comprising a value system tend to be internally consistent but may not necessarily be so. For example, an individual may hold certain religious values (brotherhood, honesty), but at the same time he may believe that ruthlessness and dishonesty in business dealings are acceptable. The individual may feel no need to justify the internal inconsistency of these values.

Both individuals and social systems have values. Although values are relatively enduring, they are nevertheless subject to change.

Organizations are systems of human interaction. The interaction among organization members raises fundamental issues such as meaning given to the concepts of community, justice, fair play, mutual respect, freedom, dignity, and self-worth.

Perhaps the best-known typology of values was offered by Douglas McGregor (1960). McGregor proposed the theory X–theory Y dichotomy to capture contrasting sets of assumptions about human nature.

Theory X propositions
1 Management is responsible for organizing the elements of productive enterprise – money, materials, equipment, people – in the interest of economic ends.
2 With respect to people, this is a process of directing their efforts, motivating them, controlling their actions, modifying their behaviour to fit the needs of the organization.
3 Without this active intervention by management, people would be passive, even resistant, to organizational needs. They must therefore be persuaded, rewarded, punished, controlled.
4 The average person is by nature indolent: he works as little as possible.
5 The average person lacks ambition, dislikes responsibility, prefers to be led.
6 The average person is inherently self-centred, indifferent to organizational needs.
7 The average person is by nature resistant to change.
8 The average person is gullible, not very bright, the ready dupe of the charlatan and the demagogue.

Theory Y propositions
1 Management is responsible for organizing the elements of productive enterprise – money, materials, equipment, people – in the interest of economic ends.

2 People are not by nature passive or resistant to organizational needs. They have become so as a result of experience in organizations.

3 The motivation, the potential for development, the capacity for assuming responsibility, the readiness to direct behaviour towards organizational goals are all present in people. Management does not put them there. It is a responsibility of management to make it possible for people to recognize and develop these human characteristics for themselves.

4 The essential task of management is to arrange organizational conditions and methods of operation so that people can achieve their own goals best by directing their own efforts towards organizational objectives.

Raymond Miles (1975) has extended the work of McGregor by proposing three 'theories of management': the 'traditional model,' the 'human relations model,' and the 'human resources model.'

Each manager has an implicit theory of management which defines his role as manager, specifies his responsibilities to the technical and social systems, and guides his managerial choices in the areas of reward systems, communications systems, job design, and decision-making practices. The three models are outlined below.

Traditional model
Assumptions
1 Work is inherently distasteful to most people.
2 What workers do is less important than what they earn for doing it.
3 Few want or can handle work which requires creativity, self-direction, or self-control.

Policies
1 The manager's basic task is to closely supervise and control his subordinates.
2 The manager must break tasks down into simple, repetitive, easily learned operations.
3 The manager must establish detailed work routines and procedures and enforce them firmly but fairly.

Expectations
1 People can tolerate work if the pay is decent and the boss is fair.
2 If tasks are simple enough and people are closely controlled they will produce up to standard.

Human relations model
Assumptions
1 People want to feel useful and important.
2 People want to belong and to be recognized as individuals.
3 These needs are more important than money in motivating people to work.

Policies
1 The manager's basic task is to make each worker feel useful and important.
2 The manager should keep his subordinates informed and listen to their objections to his plans.
3 The manager should allow his subordinates to exercise some self-direction and self-control on routine matters.

Expectations
1 Sharing information with subordinates and involving them in routine decisions will satisfy their basic needs to belong and to feel important.
2 Satisfying these needs will improve morale and reduce resistance to formal authority; subordinates will 'willingly cooperate.'

Human resources model
Assumptions
1 Work is not inherently distasteful. People want to contribute to meaningful goals which they have helped to establish.
2 Most people can exercise far more creative, responsible self-direction and self-control than their present jobs demands.

Policies
1 The manager's basic task is to make use of his untapped human resources.
2 He must create an environment in which all members may contribute to the limits of their ability.
3 He must encourage full participation on important matters, continually broadening subordinate self-direction and self-control.

Expectations
1 Expanding subordinate influence, self-direction, and self-control will lead to direct improvements in operating efficiency.
2 Work satisfaction may improve as a 'by-product' of subordinates making full use of their resources.

The three models of management are based on the prevailing theories of different eras of this century. The traditional model is based on social Darwinism: life is a competitive struggle in which the capable survive through the energetic application of their natural abilities. This value system underlies the practice of the early factory system and scientific management.

The human relations model is based on a set of values which have come to be identified with the Hawthorne study of Roethlisberger and Dickson (1939). Elton Mayo (1931; 1945) and Mary Parker Follett (1924) also proposed solutions to industrial problems based on the human relations model. The workplace was harmful to human well-being, and workers required humane treatment, sympathetic understanding, and personal attention. Low morale, resistance to change, and substandard performance could be alleviated by understanding the feelings of workers.

The human resources theory of management is commonly identified with Abraham Maslow (1954), Rensis Likert (1961), and Raymond Miles (1975). This value system holds that people want opportunities at work to develop and apply their abilities and that people are capable of self-direction and self-control. Further, this theory holds that increased organizational effectiveness will result when people are given a significant voice in the conduct and planning of their work.

An individual's value system changes according to his experiences and according to the value systems of others with whom he interacts. Consequently, the human relations theory of management is no more 'correct' than the traditional model, nor is theory X more 'correct' than theory Y.

The relationship between values and behaviour is self-reinforcing – that is, most people behave and interact with others in a manner consistent with their values, or they justify their behaviours and interactions by reference to values. Requiring individuals to behave in certain ways without appropriate changes in values becomes, at best, a superficial alteration.[4]

Senior managers in contemporary work organizations hold the values that they learned from those under whom they trained. Their views of subordi-

4 This proposition is controversial. Some theorists, such as Chris Argyris (1964), feel that skills and behaviours follow values; values rarely follow skills. Other theorists, such as Chapple and Sayles (1961), feel that to obtain lasting change the organizational constraints acting on people must be changed; changing values is impractical and unnecessary. It is easier to change the structure of the workplace (work flow, reporting relationships) than it is to change values. Changes to structure will lead to changes in behaviour and attitude and ultimately to changes in values.

nates come from someone who was trained by someone whose values were acquired in an era in which conditions were very different from those of today. Managerial values, therefore, tend to reflect the influences of past generations, and these values tend to be permanently out of step with the requirements of the present.

Structure
Organization structure is defined as the prescribed and officially sanctioned relationships among organization members. Organization structure includes the concerns of the classical management theorists – spans of control, reporting relationships, the responsibilities and prerogatives of organization members, the codification of rules and procedures, and the decision-making rights of organization members of different rank.

Organization structure renders the interactions among organization members predictable by reducing the variability and spontaneity of member behaviour. In most cases organization structure can be identified through organizational records, handbooks, and collective agreements. In other cases structure can be identified through 'common law' practices which are long-standing and commonly understood by organization members.

Social interaction in organizations follows predictable patterns. This predictability can be obtained in a variety of ways. First, rules and procedures may be emphasized. There is great scope for variation in the frequency, closeness, and punitiveness with which rules are enforced. Because of the diverse interests, incomplete socialization, and partial inclusion of organization members, patterns of behaviour are generally maintained by rules and procedures; structure is imposed on organization members through definitions of authority, communication channels, job descriptions, and evaluation procedures.

Second, peer group enforcement of rules may be used to ensure uniformity of member behaviour. Shared values, ideals, and common perceptions of the organization's mission may make external enforcement of member behaviour unnecessary.

Third, order, regularity, and predictability may be obtained through the work technology. A typewriter, for example, is a technology which provides standardized output and eliminates rules governing the size and spacing of letters.

Fourth, the hiring of professionals or the inculcation of professional norms can be used as a means of obtaining predictability. In this case rules are not externally imposed and enforced but are willingly accepted by organization members. The variability of organization member behaviour and interaction can also be reduced by hiring individuals with uniform abilities, motivation, and interests.

Finally, member variability can be reduced by sealing the organization off from its environment and thereby reducing external environmental influences on members.[5]

Process
Processes are the individual, interpersonal, and intergroup behaviours and relations which take place within the defined structure of the organization. Examples of process include the amount, content, and quality of communication among organization members, the nature and quality of interpersonal relations, intergroup conflict, conflict resolution practices, the manner in which authority is exercised, and relationships between superiors and subordinates.

Structure and process are conceptually rather similar. Structure is inferred from interpersonal and intergroup processes but is formally prescribed and is more enduring than process.[6]

Outcomes
Outcomes include the full spectrum of attitudes, reactions, adjustments, and behaviours of organization members. Attitudinal outcomes include alienation, mental health, work-related satisfactions (including satisfaction with supervision, wages, benefits, co-workers, and conditions of work), trust in management, attitudes towards management, motivation, commitment, loyalty to the organization, and felt responsibility for the attainment of organizational goals. Behavioural outcomes include quality and quantity of

---

5 See discussion of 'total institutions' in this chapter, 73.
6 The distinction between structure and process can be illustrated by Tannenbaum's distinction between 'formal' and 'informal' participation. Tannenbaum et al. (1974) identify organizations such as Israeli kibbutzim and workers council organizations in Yugoslavia as 'formally participative,' since they have codified and officially sanctioned procedures which define the decision-making rights of employees. Other organizations, such as those in the United States, do not give employees a legal or formal right to participate in the management of the enterprise but they do occasionally and informally give employees a voice in the management of the enterprise. These organizations are 'informally participative.' Research on the departures of organizational practice from the formal organizational design is voluminous and addresses the distinction between 'process' and 'structure.' Studies of the actual as contrasted with the formal prescribed distribution of power include Dalton's (1959) study of line and staff officers and Thompson's (1956) study of authority and power in two air force wings.

the individual's output, training to improve job skills, participating in employee association or union activities, tardiness, absenteeism, and frequency of accidents and grievance filing.

By aggregating the outcomes of individual organization members, outcomes can also be considered at the work group or organizational level of analysis. Organizational outcomes include the quality and quantity of output, the competitive position of the organization and its long-term survival, flexibility of the organization and its ability to anticipate and respond to change, rates of absenteeism, turnover and grievance filing, frequency of strikes and lock-outs, accident rates, frequency of disciplinary hearings, and work slow-downs.

The meaning and definition of outcomes will vary according to the level of analysis; a 'positive' outcome at one level might lead to a 'negative' outcome at another level. Improvements in health and safety regulations may reduce profits; a work process which requires that organization members learn multiple skills may impair productivity; high levels of commitment and enthusiasm on the job may lead workers to accept more overtime and may as a result adversely affect family relationships.

The organization's environment
The organization's environment is defined as all conditions external to the organization which influence its behaviour and the behaviour of its members. The modern work organization operates within a matrix of environments of almost endless variety and complexity. There are cultural, social, political, economic, legal, and technological environments. Open systems theory has stressed the importance of these environmental influences on internal organizational dynamics.[7]

The notion that the organization is influenced by its environments is intuitively appealing, and has preoccupied organizational theorists from the time of Burns and Stalker (1961). The relationship between the organization and its environments has proved to be difficult to study empirically, because different environments change at different rates. Some environments are more critical to the organization than others, and organizational environments generally do not produce consistent pressures on the organization; the work technology and competitive economic pressures may, for example, be inconsistent with cultural or political pressures.

The values celebrated by the larger society exert a profound influence on the practices of the work organization. Among these influences are the

7 Katz and Kahn 1966

willingness of the society to experiment with new ideas; the tolerance of the society for diversity; and the history, theology, folklore, and mythology defining the society's institutions. Among the more immediate societal values which influence the nature of power and consent in the workplace are the relative emphasis which the society places on individualism versus collectivism; the democratic-authoritarian traditions of the society; the emphasis on class interests; and prevailing and generally accepted notions of authority, deference, and subordination.

The values embraced by the modern work organization cannot depart substantially from the values of the larger society. Organization members bring their values and ideologies with them into the workplace. Along with the family, the church, and the school, the work organization is a major 'carrier' of society's values. The relationships between the environment and the work organization are reciprocal; that is, society's values are created and reinforced in the work organization. Hammer and Stern (1980) report that support from the larger community for the concept of employee ownership was essential to the survival of the firms they studied. They observe that the successful purchase of a firm by employees was facilitated in all sixteen cases investigated by political, media, and trade union pressure.

However, there are some obvious and surprising discrepancies between the values and practices in work organizations and the values of the larger society. Yugoslavia, for example, is a political dictatorship, yet employees in Yugoslavian work organizations exert considerable influence over the conduct of their enterprises. Through their representatives on the workers' council, workers have the right to hire the chief executive officer and to determine matters of company policy. Conversely, Great Britain, the United States, and Canada have long-standing democratic political traditions, while organizations in these countries remain fundamentaly authoritarian.

Nevertheless, within these countries, there are regions in which democratic work organizations seem to thrive. In Canada the co-operative movement is particularly strong in Saskatchewan and Quebec. In the United States democratic workplaces are found primarily in New England and the Pacific north-west.

In the past the work expectations of organizational members were shaped by the long period of socialization in the schools, the church, and the family. Before entering the work-force, new recruits had generally accepted the legitimacy of hierarchy and authority; they understood the subordination and deference to authority required by the roles they were to assume; and they held the general expectation that they had little right to control their work. The system of authority in work organizations was viewed as morally legitimate both by those who wielded authority and by those who were subjected to it.

The accelerating expectations of entitlement of Canadians have drawn frequent comment. The modern industrial economy, with its slow growth rates and declining real incomes, seems increasingly unable to satisfy the expectations of working people, and tensions in the workplace are certain to grow in the future.

Beyond the failure of the Canadian economy to meet working people's expectations, there is a new source of rising expectations: social legislation guaranteeing economic security and protecting the employee from the arbitrary use of power by the employer. Authoritarian supervision is more difficult to practise when legislation protecting employees from unjust dismissal and subjective treatment, unemployment insurance, and trade union vigilance are part of the organization's environment.

Few people recognize how significant these changes have been over this century. In the early part of the century the owner-entrepreneur exercised unilateral and unchecked authority over those in his employ. The treatment of subordinates was generally subjective and arbitrary, and failure to comply with the superior's directives meant unemployment and privation. High levels of education, the influence of the mass media, widespread affluence, and more liberal child-rearing practices have all contributed to the pressures on managers and supervisors to change their relationship with subordinates and to involve them in decision-making.

It has become rather commonplace to observe the crumbling of authority and the decline of the legitimacy of leadership in many areas of life. The issue of what people accept as given and what they aspire to change is subject to continuing review in any dynamic society. Values regarding authority have changed as dramatically as any values in our society. In part, past abuses and excesses in work organizations have stimulated this change. Although the practices of the contemporary work organization are more consistent with the values of personal dignity, freedom, and self-determination which we celebrate in the larger society than they have been at any time in the past, managers are nevertheless subject to continuing pressure to meet the rising expectations of employees.

The higher educational attainment of new entrants to the labour force is one of the most significant factors affecting the contemporary workplace. Along with higher educational attainment come expectations of freedom from close supervision, the expectation of having an opportunity to exercise self-control at the workplace, and higher expectations regarding challenge, variety, and responsibility at work. Increasingly, the educational system is based on and reflects an anti-authoritarian and egalitarian ideology. Most new recruits find the authoritarianism of the modern workplace to be in sharp contrast with their school experiences and are unable to cope with the discipline, the machine-dominated and closely regulated pace of work.

The greater participation rate of women in the work-force is another environmental change which will affect the practices of the modern work organization. In an era in which women participated for limited periods in the work-force and in which they worked to supplement the family income, undesirable conditions of work could be tolerated, since they were viewed as temporary. More often today, however, women view their work as a career rather than as a supplement to the family income. The work they perform must be well paid, must utilize their skills and reflect their sense of self-worth. Further, larger numbers of women no longer accept the submissive and compliant role of earlier generations, and they demand the same benefits, opportunities and conditions of work as their male counterparts.

The growing prevalence of working spouses also weakens the control that the work organization exerts over the individual. Individuals with working spouses have greater economic freedom to leave work which is not to their satisfaction. The frequency of 'second careers' and 'early retirement' is evidence of the economic security enjoyed by persons with working spouses.

Rather than changing the work or the nature of supervision, many managers in this country have sought new sources of labour willing to accept authoritarian practices. However, the reduced numbers of immigrant workers in this country and the spread of urban / industrial values to rural areas provide diminishing opportunities to avoid either the restructuring of work or the introduction of significant employee participation in decision-making.

The Canadian economy over the post-war period has moved from a goods-producing to a service-oriented economy. Although the modern assembly line has become the prototype of the modern industrial process, less than 5 per cent of the Canadian work-force is employed on assembly line jobs. More and more the weight of economic activity in our society is white collar, and is performed in smaller units. Year by year in Canada fewer individuals work at jobs which are machine-paced and in which output can be strictly controlled and monitored. An increasing proportion of workers earn their livelihoods under conditions where the employer has difficulty setting norms, establishing the pace of work, and exercising close supervision. Under these conditions less authoritarian styles of supervision are desirable, and work organizations unable to make the transition to participative practices will find it more difficult to maintain labour peace.

The prevailing relations between organized labour and management and the nature of the industrial relations climate in the country also substantially affect the manner in which employers respond to the workplace. There are three key dimensions of the Canadian industrial relations system which affect labour-management relations. The first is trade union security. When trade union leaders are defensive about their role and their legitimacy in society, they are unlikely to co-operate with governments or employers in ways that are perceived to weaken rank and file support of the union. The percentage of the work-force which is organized and the rate of growth of trade union membership are measures of trade union security.

The second dimension is the perceived 'rights' of labour and management. Reports from the OECD indicate that countries differ consistently over time in the number and duration of strikes and in the number of man-days lost through strikes and lock-outs each year. In some countries management is concerned with its 'residual rights' and harbours deep suspicions about the motives and good faith of labour leaders. In many of these same countries union leaders espouse an ideology of 'social unionism' (as opposed to 'job unionism'). Trade unions with a larger agenda of social change are not generally welcomed by employers. When the political aims of the trade union movement are revolutionary rather than reformist, the relationship with management is likely to be hostile and adversarial. In some countries, the relationship between the trade union movement and employers is characterized by a modicum of mutual respect for the other party, while in other countries the parties view their interests as unalterably opposed.

The third dimension is the role and power of governments in encouraging labour peace. In some countries government takes a strong leadership role in encouraging positive industrial relations, while in other countries (such as Canada) a more laissez-faire attitude prevails.

The industrial relations climate is not separate from the values, traditions, and practices of the larger society. To the extent that class interests and the class struggle are part of the ideology or folklore of society, industrial relations will be characterized by adversarial relations, and workplace democracy will take a different form than it will in countries without this ideology.

The exercise of authority in work organizations is constrained by the rights afforded to employees as citizens. The public's changing expectations of the business enterprise in the areas of social as well as economic goals will exert considerable pressure on future work organizations. Business and labour leaders increasingly accept the proposition that the corporate enterprise should promote and support social values such as dignity, the worth of the individual, and self-determination, even when the pursuit of economic goals is thereby impeded.

The environmental pressures on an organization do not always point in the same direction. In an open and pluralistic society the work organization will face competing and divergent environmental pressures. For example, it may be that pressures towards increased bureaucratization and technological sophistication will dominate pressures towards more democratically managed organizations.

Conflicting pressures have existed in the past. Milton Derber (1970) points out that the collective bargaining model of 'industrial democracy' triumphed over competing models in the United States (paternalism, representative bodies, syndicalism, producer co-operatives, profit-sharing and socialism), because it was more consistent with national ideology and sentiment. Farm labour movements found little success in urban industrial areas where social and cultural values differed from those which inspired the movement.

A CONGRUENCE THEORY OF ORGANIZATIONS

The five concepts just defined – organizational environment, values, structure, processes, and outcomes – are reciprocally interdependent. Each concept simultaneously influences (and is influenced by) the other concepts. This reciprocal linking of the concepts creates what Harold Leavitt (1972) calls the 'volatile organization' in which everything triggers everything else. A change in one concept will create changes in all the other concepts. The relationships among the five concepts are illustrated in figure 2. To illustrate the mutual effects of the concepts on each other, one set of associations among the many in figure 2 is outlined below.

Consider a value system based on the following beliefs: employees are by nature lazy; employees are untrustworthy and dishonest; people prefer to follow strong and forceful leaders; and the average employee is not capable of assuming responsibility or participating meaningfully in the affairs of the organization. This value system (when held by organization members at upper hierarchical levels) is hypothesized to lead to the following structure: decision-making responsibilities centralized at upper hierarchical levels; relatively little, lower-level, member participation in decision-making; emphasis on formal role prescriptions and job descriptions; emphasis on the hierarchical chain of command; proliferation of rules, procedures, and con-

FIGURE 2 Congruence theory

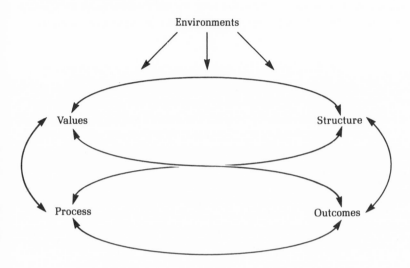

trol mechanisms to monitor employee behaviour; emphasis on vertical communication with no formal allowance for lateral communication; and narrow spans of control.

A structure of this form exerts in turn a profound influence on the nature and quality of interpersonal and intergroup relations in the organization. These relations will be characterized by an unwillingness of subordinates to share information with superiors; high levels of conflict among individuals and groups; less open, friendly, cohesive, and trusting relations among work group members; reliance on the hierarchical chain of command to resolve conflicts and less willingness to employ open confrontation and problem-solving; and less supportive and participative relations between superiors and subordinates.

The individual, interpersonal, and organizational outcomes resulting from the above set of values, structures, and processes are predictable: absence of trust between organization members at different hierarchical levels; low motivation, especially at the rank and file level, to achieve the organization's objectives; absence of loyalty to the firm and commitment to its objectives; dissatisfaction with organizational conditions; high alienation; high frequency of stress-related illnesses; reduced sense of self-worth and self-importance; and poor mental health. At the organizational level of analysis, the organization would suffer from high absenteeism and turnover rates and from periodic work slow-downs and strikes.

From figure 2 it is clear that there are equally important causal connections which flow in the direction opposite to the relationships just outlined: from structure to values, from process to structure, and from outcomes to process. For example, organizations with centralized decision-making will tend to shape the values of members in a manner consistent with this structure. In this case the values would reflect the view that people are basically self-seeking, unmotivated, unco-operative, and incapable of self-direction. Similarly, when rank and file employees evidence poor attitudes towards work and mistrust of their superiors, and when they produce work of substandard quality, those in authority will design the organization so that the behaviour of rank and file employees can be monitored and controlled.[8]

A predictable and congruent pattern emerges from the reciprocal relations among the five concepts. The interactions among organization members follow predictable patterns. These interactions are based on and justified by a value system; they take place within a defined structure and are governed by rules, procedures, and formal communication channels; and they yield a predictable set of attitudes, feelings, reactions, and adjustments.

The degree to which the interactions, values, structure, and attitudes form an internally consistent pattern is called 'congruence.' This phenomenon has also been described as 'equilibrium,' 'steady state,' and 'dynamic homeostasis' and has drawn the attention of many organizational theorists. In fact, the search for systematic relations among technology, structure, attitudes, and values has been a major preoccupation of modern organization theory. Theorists differ in the variables they believe to be critical to defining equili-

8 The dynamics of congruence – the tendency for the dimensions of organization to move toward an internally consistent state – have been identified by 'social comparison theory' (Festinger 1954). The needs and attitudes of individuals are strongly influenced by organizational membership and by other groups to which the individuals belong or to which they want to belong. Organization members are rewarded for conforming to group standards and values and are punished for deviating from them. Group pressures on the individual are especially strong when public commitment or expression is given by the individual. The manner in which individuals' expectations and behaviour are shaped by organizational experience has been called the 'law of adaptation' by Louis Davis (1979). People act out the roles required of them, and to a large extent, accommodate themselves to circumstances imposed on them. Once they have struck the bargain, the personal costs of adjusting to the inevitable become acceptable, and the situation becomes normal and perhaps even expected.

brium, in the number of concepts necessary to define equilibrium, and in their theories about how equilibrium is achieved.

DYNAMICS OF CONGRUENCE

The theory guiding this research on workplace democracy is based on four central concepts: the values of organization members, the formal structure of the organization, interpersonal and intergroup interactions within this structure, and the attitudes, reactions, and adjustments of organization members.[9] Within any organization at any point in time there will be an internally consistent relationship among values, structure, processes, and outcomes. This congruence is achieved through the reciprocal relations among the four concepts. The degree of congruence is never perfect, however, and there are many conditions – some internal to the organization, others external to it – which shape the level of congruence, and define its nature.

Environmental influences on the organization are rarely constant, and changes in economic conditions, political pressures, labour markets, and the public's perception of the organization exert powerful influences on the nature of the interactions among organization members. Organizations isolated from their environments are able to achieve higher levels of congruence than organizations open to shifting environmental pressures. 'Total institutions' such as company towns, prisons, ships at sea, and workplaces in remote areas are examples of organizations in which congruence will tend to be high. Interactions with others who are not members of the organization can upset the organization's equilibrium by introducing new ideas, perspectives, and expectations.

---

9 Other organizational theorists have described the phenomenon of congruence and have examined its dynamics. Gouldner (1960) proposed that an implicit agreement among parties to interact with other parties according to certain principles (which he termed 'reciprocity') had a stabilizing effect on social systems.

Fox (1974) traces the congruence among work technology, trust, and power relations at the workplace. Two types of dynamics, 'low trust' and 'high trust,' lead to internally consistent relationships among the concepts.

Schein (1965) uses the term, 'psychological contract' to describe the implicit set of expectations between the individual and the organization. The psychological contract governs the relationship between the individual and the organization.

Blau (1964) contrasts two types of 'exchange' between the individual and the organization: economic and social. The nature of the relationship between the parties, their commitment to the relationship, their satisfaction with the relationship, and the values underlying the relationship will differ in the two types of exchange.

Although relationships among values, structure, process, and outcomes will tend to be congruent in any organization, inevitable and persistent environmental changes or changes in leadership will lead to a state of temporary incongruence. The relationships among the concepts perpetually tend towards congruency, but congruence may be temporary.

The formal structure of the organization and the design and flow of work are easily changed, while changes in outcomes take longer, and changes in values take longer still. Only those organizations in placid environments or organizations which have managed to buffer themselves from external environmental pressures are able to obtain high levels of congruence. A new technology, for example, may significantly increase the discretionary element of the jobs of lower-level members, but managers may still retain values which are inconsistent with those required by the new technology. The nature of the congruence between these inconsistent pressures depends on the relative strength of the two pressures and the extent to which other forces within the organization or in the environment support one or other of the pressures. In this case the technology might be altered to limit employee discretion or the values of upper-level members might change if the new technology and the added discretion of the job worked out well.

Threats to organizational congruence can be dealt with in several ways. If possible, the environment of the organization can be regulated or influenced through advertising, public relations, or political lobbying. Some organizations seek a constant external environment by physically relocating to less turbulent or benign environments. Industries in urban areas move to rural areas; industries in countries with a truculent or demanding work-force move to countries with a compliant work-force. Further, human inputs to the organization can be regulated through careful selection, or alternatively through more intensive training, socialization, and indoctrination of new recruits.

For many organizations the socialization of new members is vital to their survival. 'Normative' organizations such as fraternities, military organizations, and cults demand the sacrifice and devotion of members. These organizations generally have long and sometimes unpleasant initiation rites to encourage total commitment to the organization's values.

Organizations in environments in which recruiters cannot always control entry to the organization face special problems. Garnier (1972) describes the socialization process in an organization in which values are supremely important, England's Royal Military Academy at Sandhurst. This organization's ideology has remained unchanged over many years, despite substantial changes in its membership. The values and attitudes of new entrants in the pre-World War II era could be taken for granted, since most recruits came from elite public schools such as Eton. Today new entrants come from a wide variety of public and private schools, and their attitudes and values are quite heterogeneous. Nevertheless, the 'culture' of Sandhurst is passed on to each new generation of incoming students. Each individual is expected to accept the values of the institution and those who assume new responsibilities in the management of the school tend to have accepted completely the values of their predecessors.

THE DEMOCRATIC AND HIERARCHICAL ORGANIZATIONS

Through the dynamics of congruence theory, an internally consistent pattern will emerge among values, structure, process, and outcomes, and the relationship among these concepts will be consistent with environmental pressures on the organization. The democratic and hierarchical organizations are 'ideal types.'[10] These ideal types are presented in table 4.

Few organizations will fit either ideal type; the two ideal types are end points on a continuum, and properties of any organization will be a product of the organization's leadership and the unique environmental pressures on the organization. In the following chapter we shall explore the properties of the two ideal types by comparing ten democratic and ten hierarchical organizations. The analysis which follows is primarily statistical in nature; detailed descriptions of the democratic organizations are found in appendix I.

In chapter 6 the characteristics of work in democratic and hierarchical organizations will be compared and the role of the workplace in shaping employee needs will be explored.

10 Other 'ideal types' based on the concept of power, authority, and participation have been proposed. They include: Bennis's (1969) 'mechanical system' and 'organic system'; Argyris's (1964) 'mechanistic' and 'organic' ideal types; Burns and Stalker's (1961) 'mechanistic system' and 'organic system'; Gouldner's (1955) 'punishment centred' and 'representative' bureaucracies; and Likert's (1967) 'System 1' through 'System 4.'

TABLE 4
The democratic and hierarchical organizations compared

The democratic organization	The hierarchical organization
Values	**Values**
a) average employee not only capable of assuming responsibility but given the opportunity will willingly undertake responsible assignments	a) average employee incapable of assuming responsibility and will avoid it if he can
b) employees most productive when given an opportunity to govern their own conduct	b) employees work best under directive and forceful supervision
c) average employee will willingly pursue organizational objectives when given a hand in creating them	c) average employee will not willingly pursue organizational objectives and cannot be trusted to work on his own without supervision
d) average employee capable of making responsible decisions on his own	d) average employee easily swayed by group pressure and incapable of making responsible choices for himself
e) average employee hard-working; can be trusted to play a creative and productive role in the management of the organization; apathetic and counter-productive behaviour the result of the frustration of positive motives, not the result of destructive motives.	e) average employee apathetic; cannot be trusted to play a creative and productive role in the management of the organization
Structure	**Structure**
a) employees at all levels given the right to participate in decision-making	a) decision-making responsibilities centralized at upper hierarchical levels
b) opportunities given to employees to exercise initiative and discretion in the conduct of their work	b) employees given few opportunities to exercise initiative and discretion at work
c) few rules, regulations, operating procedures, or detailed job descriptions	c) emphasis on codification of rules, procedures, job descriptions, and reporting relationships
d) no control or surveillance mechanisms to monitor employee performance	d) employee performance closely monitored by controls and close supervision
e) broad spans of control	e) narrow spans of control
f) de-emphasis on hierarchical referral; persons immediately involved make decisions	f) use of hierarchical referral to handle contingencies

Processes

a) frequent work-related communication from superior to subordinate, subordinate to superior, and from peer to peer
b) frequent communication among organization members on non-work-related matters
c) high confidence in the accuracy of communication
d) relations among work group members open, trusting, cohesive, friendly, and participative
e) infrequent conflict among groups
f) conflict resolution practices based on open confrontation and problem solving
g) supportive and participative supervisory practices

Outcomes

a) high member satisfaction with a broad range of organizational conditions
b) strong loyalty to the organization and commitment to its objectives
c) low alienation
d) high satisfaction with life
e) good member physical health
f) few stress symptoms
g) frequent social interaction among members outside of the workplace
h) high levels of member involvement in voluntary organizations and in social and political affairs
i) positive reactions to change
j) mutual trust among members of different hierarchical rank

Processes

a) frequent work-related communication from superior to subordinate, limited communication from subordinate to superior and peer to peer
b) infrequent communication among organization members on non-work-related matters
c) low confidence in the accuracy of communication
d) relations among work group members are guarded, less trusting, fragmented, and non-participative
e) frequent conflict among groups
f) conflict resolution practices based on hierarchical forcing, smoothing over differences and ignoring conflicts
g) non-supportive and non-participative supervisory practices

Outcomes

a) low member satisfaction with a broad range of organizational conditions
b) little loyalty to the organization or commitment to its objectives
c) high alienation
d) low satisfaction with life
e) poor member physical health
f) many stress symptoms
g) infrequent social interaction among members outside of the workplace
h) low levels of member involvement in voluntary organizations and in social and political affairs
i) negative reactions to change
j) low mutual trust among members of different hierarchical rank

5

The democratic and hierarchical
workplaces compared

Research and theory on workplace democracy have been inspired by a vision of the workplace which allows self-determination, development of skills and abilities, and personal fulfilment in the broadest sense of the term. As compelling as this vision is, there is no systematic comparison – in any country – of democratic organizations with organizations of conventional hierarchical design.

This study was undertaken to fill this void. The comparison of democratic and hierarchical organizations reported here is guided by the theory outlined in chapter 4. Each of the concepts of this theory – values, structure, processes, and outcomes – will be compared in this sample of ten democratic and ten hierarchical organizations. Following these comparisons the relationships among the concepts will be examined through canonical analysis; and the empirical profile of the two types of organization will be compared with the ideal types outlined in chapter 4.

The issues discussed in chapter 2 – power, authority, and consent – will also be examined. This analysis will focus on the nature and determinants of employee expectations regarding participation in decision-making; the gradients of power in the democratic and hierarchical organizations; and the relationship between supervisory style and the formal decision-making structure of the organization.

Before explaining the differences between the democratic and hierarchical organizations, we shall examine the sample of organizations and the respondents from whom the data have been collected. Details on the data collection methods and the research instruments are presented in appendix II.

SAMPLE OF ORGANIZATIONS

The sample consists of twenty industrial organizations, ten of which are democratically managed and ten of which are hierarchically managed. Each democratic organization is matched with a hierarchical counterpart on the following dimensions: (1) technology of the production process, (2) number of full-time employees, (3) plant type (branch plant or parent plant), (4) the union / non-union status of the work-force, (5) the size of the urban area in which the plant is located and from which it draws its work-force, and (6) the ethnic composition of the work-force.

The matching of the democratic and hierarchical organizations is outlined in table 5. The democratic organizations have on average 227 employees and the hierarchical organizations have on average 213 employees. Because of the limited sample of industrial organizations in Canada which satisfy all six criteria, some modest compromises in the matching were required.

The ten democratic organizations in this sample are among the most democratically managed industrial organizations in Canada. To qualify for the sample the democratic firms must be economically viable, that is, the organization must not be losing money and must not be financially dependent on a parent firm or on the government. In addition, the program of workplace democracy must have been in operation for at least three years, so that 'Hawthorne effects' do not bias the results in favour of the democratic organizations.

The firms were selected to represent diverse forms of workplace democracy. Included in this sample are producer co-operatives, autonomous work group organizations, a 'Scanlon plan' organization, an organization with a 'multiple management board' structure, organizations with an elected works council, and organizations with employee representation on the board of directors.

Five of the ten organizations have profit-sharing plans; three of these five have stock purchase plans, and in two other organizations employee-owners share dividend income.

Each of the ten democratic organizations has a formal structure which permits significant employee participation in decision-making. The organizations were selected on the basis of documents (such as the collective agreement or the company charter) which guarantee decision-making rights to employees. No assessment of the extent to which the organizations *actually* are participative in their day-to-day practices was made at the point of sampling.

SAMPLE OF RESPONDENTS

Within each of the twenty organizations a stratified random sample of fifty respondents was selected. The sample design has two objectives: (1) to

TABLE 5
Matched sample of democratic and hierarchical organizations

Matched pairs of organizations	Type of workplace democracy	Products	No. of employees	Location*	Plant type†	Unionized employees	Ethnic composition‡
Canadian Tire	elected works council	bulk distribution /	550	L	B	no	E
Canadian Tire match	employee ownership	warehousing	450	L	B	yes	E
Lincoln	elected works council	machining-	150	L	P	no	E
Lincoln match	employee ownership	assembly	145	L	P	no	E
Supreme	elected works council	aluminum	375	L	P	no	E
Supreme match	employee ownership	fabrication-assembly	183	L	P	yes	E, I
Tembec	workers on board	fine paper	560	S	B	yes	E, F
Tembec match	employee ownership		617	S	B	yes	E, F
Cox	elected supervision	metal / wood	47	M	P	no	E
Cox match	'town hall' meetings	machining-assembly	40	M	P	no	E
Laidlaw	autonomous work groups	wood processing	148	M	B	no	E
Laidlaw match			118	M	P	yes	E, F
Hayes-Dana	Scanlon plan	automobile parts	125	M	B	yes	E
Hayes-Dana match		machining	162	M	B	yes	E
Club House	multiple management	food processing	136	M	P	no	E
Club House match			234	M	P	no	
Harvey	producer cooperative	transport short /	110	S	P	yes	F
Harvey match		medium haul	60	S	P	yes	F
Saguenay	producer cooperative	foundry /	70	M	P	yes	F
Saguenay match		machining	125	M	P	yes	F

* L – large city > 100.000 population. M – medium-sized city < 100.000 population. S – small town < 3.000 population.
† B – branch plant; senior manager title 'plant manager.' P – parent plant; senior manager title 'president.'
‡ E – English. F – French. I – Italian.

equalize (in so far as possible) the number of respondents drawn from upper, middle, and lower hierarchical levels; and (2) to sample respondents randomly within each of the three hierarchical levels. The upper hierarchical level includes the chief executive officer and all of his immediate managerial subordinates; the middle hierarchical level includes all other managerial and supervisory personnel; and the lower hierarchical level includes all organization members who do not have subordinates. The lower hierarchical level encompasses both white- and blue-collar workers.

The application of the first rule requires that seventeen respondents be selected at each of two hierarchical levels and sixteen respondents at a randomly selected third level. However, since most organizations are pyramidal in shape, the upper hierarchical level typically will not contain sixteen or seventeen respondents, particularly in small organizations. In organizations where the number of respondents at the upper level is less than this number, all organization members at that level are selected. If, for example, the chief executive officer has nine immediate managerial subordinates, the upper hierarchical level would contain ten respondents. The remaining forty respondents are divided equally in so far as possible between the middle and lower hierarchical levels. If there were more than twenty middle managers and first-line supervisors in the organization, then twenty would be randomly selected. If there were fewer, all would be selected. If, for example, there were only fifteen middle managers and first-line supervisors, all would be selected and the remaining twenty-five respondents (50 − (10 + 15) = 25) would be selected from the lower hierarchical level.

In this study all upper-hierarchical-level organization members in all companies were selected with certainty; in most organizations, all middle managers and first-line supervisors were selected with certainty; and organization members at the lower hierarchical level were randomly sampled. In two of the companies all respondents were sampled.

Of the 1,000 individuals asked to participate in the study twenty refused and were replaced by random selection. Of the twenty employees who declined to participate in the study fifteen were employed in democratic organizations. The higher refusal rate in democratic organizations is surprising. Organization members in democratic organizations may feel freer than their counterparts in hierarchical organizations to refuse to participate in studies of this kind. Although great care was taken to point out to respondents that their participation in the study was voluntary and that individual responses would be held in the strictest confidence, these instructions may have been less than convincing. This survey (and possibly others like it)

TABLE 6
Comparison of socio-demographic characteristics of respondents in democratic and hierarchical organizations

	Upper hierarchical level		Middle hierarchical level		Lower hierarchical level	
	Democratic	Hierarchical	Democratic	Hierarchical	Democratic	Hierarchical
Age (years)	44	44	40	42	35	35
Company seniority (years)	14	14	12	14	7	7
Job security (years)	5	7	6	5	6	6
Education (years)	14	14	12	11*	11	10*
Salary	$29,414	$29,040	$19,659	$19,213	$13,474	$12,836
Male (per cent)	96	98	97	97	73	89*

* $p < 0.01$ (two-tailed).

may have involved some coercion, and respondents in democratic organizations, who are more practised at making decisions on their own, may have felt freer to decline to participate in the study.

Respondents were not matched in the democratic and hierarchical pairs of organizations. The matching of organizations on the six criteria and the random sampling of respondents within organizations provide comparable samples of respondents at each of the three hierarchical levels. The matching of respondents on socio-demographic characteristics is presented in table 6.

Respondents in the democratic and hierarchical organizations are closely matched. Of the eighteen comparisons (two-tailed), three are statistically significant. Middle-level respondents in the democratic organizations have more formal education than their counterparts in the hierarchical organizations (twelve years vs. ten years, respectively); lower-level respondents in the democratic organizations have more formal education than their counterparts in the hierarchical organizations (eleven years vs. ten years, respectively); and there is a higher percentage of females at the lower hierarchical level in the democratic oganizations than in the hierarchical organizations (28 per cent vs. 11 per cent, respectively).

The average number of respondents at upper, middle, and lower hierarchical levels is seven, twelve, and thirty-one, respectively, in the democratic organizations, and six, eleven, and thirty-three, respectively, in the hierarchical organizations.

COMPARISON OF STRUCTURE

Although the democratic and hierarchical organizations can be contrasted in terms of their values, structure, processes, and outcomes, the manner in which power is exercised forms the core of the two ideal types of organization. The structure of the hierarchical organization does not permit rank and file participation in decision-making; decisions are centralized at upper hierarchical levels. Job descriptions, formal rules, and regulations govern the activities of organization members at all hierarchical levels. Autonomy, discretion, and responsibility are allocated to persons at each hierarchical rank, so that each level has greater amounts than the level immediately below.

The democratic organization, on the other hand, allows lower-level members the right to participate in decision-making – either on issues of immediate relevance to the work itself or on issues of organization policy. Less emphasis is placed on the chain of command, and greater latitude, responsibility, and autonomy are permitted in the conduct of the work.[1]

Any organization possesses a given potential for workplace democracy. This potential depends on the following factors:

1 The work technology; the degree of specialization of tasks, capital intensity, opportunities for self-control and self-direction.
2 The size of the organization; co-operation, trust, and effective communication – factors essential to workplace democracy – are easier to attain in small than in large organizations.
3 The autonomy of the organization; ownership and control in the hands of distant and dispersed shareholders make workplace democracy difficult to implement; freedom from control of the parent firm or from government influence and local trade union autonomy from the national or international union enhance the amount of participation attainable. To be effective work-place democracy must be tailored to the unique expectations and experiences of management and labour in each organization.
4 The human resources of the organization; management and worker values, skills, and willingness to undertake employee participation set limits on the amount of participation which can be achieved.

Most organizations never achieve their full potential; none of the examples of workplace democracy in this study can be said to have fully achieved its potential.

Workplace democracy differs from the participation in the human relations tradition on one critical dimension: participation in the democratic workplace provides employees with decision-making *rights* which are *formally defined*. Participation in the human relations tradition is based on an informal relationship between superior and subordinate and confers no decision-making rights on subordinates.

It is this structural dimension of participation to which we now turn. The dimensions of workplace democracy – the degree of power exercised, the groups which exercise this power, and the issues subject to this power – will be defined. A technique for scaling the degree of democratic decision-

1 Autonomy and responsibility may be limited by the work technology. Since the work technology constrains participation in decision-making, comparisons of democratic and hierarchical organizations must control for the work technology. An especially innovative program of workplace democracy in one industry or sector may not in another setting be particularly far-reaching.

making will be presented and the scores on this measure of each of the ten democratic organizations in this sample will then be reported.

Scaling the dimensions of workplace democracy

The degree of power
The degree of power is measured on an 8-point Likert scale. The scale below is adopted from versions proposed by Walker (1974), Bernstein (1976), Kwoka (1976), and Dachler and Wilpert (1978).

1 Employees need not be informed about decisions made by management (except as necessary to conduct their work).
2 Employees have the right to be informed after decisions are made.
3 Employees must be informed ex ante and given an opportunity to voice their opinions.
4 Employees are consulted informally before a decision is made.
5 Employees must be consulted before a decision is made.
6 Employees participate informally with management in decision-making; management (through 'residual rights') and employees (through the collective agreement) retain the right of veto over some issues.
7 Management and employees jointly make decisions; in some cases employee representatives have parity with shareholder and management interests; in others shareholder and management interests dominate.
8 Employees have the final say in decision-making.

Issues subject to participation
The issues subject to participation are of two types: 'shop-floor' and 'policy.' Democratic organizations give employees the right to participate in most shop-floor issues, as well as in some policy issues. Since workplace democracy in North America has no statutory or legislative base, programs of workplace democracy vary widely on the issues subject to participation.

Shop-floor issues
 1 Determining unsafe working conditions
 2 Due process, grievance procedures
 3 Wages and benefits
 4 Seniority rights
 5 Overtime, hours of work, holidays
 6 Contracting out

7 Bidding on jobs
8 Technological change
9 Establishing piece rates, manning of machines, work standards
10 Establishing qualifications for jobs
11 Salary grades
12 Recruitment, selection, and training of new employees
13 Appointment of supervision
14 Purchase of machinery

Policy issues
15 Wage and benefit policy
16 Disposition of profits and shares to capital and labour
17 Choice of products and markets
18 Investments
19 Capitalization
20 Reorganizations, mergers, acquisitions

This scaling of issues is based on the importance or centrality of each issue to organizational survival. The importance of these issues as perceived by employees in particular organizations will vary. It is likely that employees at lower hierarchical levels in this country would consider some 'shop-floor' issues to be more important than many 'policy' issues.

The relationship between degree of power and issues subject to participation is illustrated in figure 3 (see appendix I for descriptions of companies identified in figure 3). Any organization can be represented by a point on this two-dimensional plane. This point represents the most important issue subject to rank and file participation. Democratic workplaces tend to cluster in the upper right-hand corner of the figure. Most organizations cluster along the diagonal.

Membership
The right to participate in decision-making may be given to top management, top and middle management, all managers and supervisors, or all employees. The form of member representation may be direct or indirect. The membership given the right to participate is not always clearly specified; often participation rights and responsibilities are based on implicit criteria about 'employees immediately affected.'

Each organization's score on workplace democracy is obtained by aggregating the products of the degree of power and the score of the issue subject

FIGURE 3 The relationship between issues and degree of power

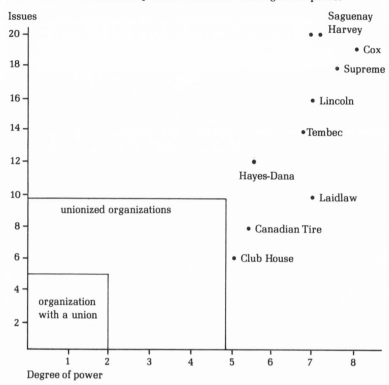

to this power. The weighting is calculated for each of the three hierarchical levels and then averaged:[2]

$$\text{score on workplace democracy} = \sum_{L=1}^{3} \left(\sum_{i=1}^{20} D_i \right),$$

where L is the hierarchical level and D_i is the degree of power exercised by employees over issue i. For each of the three hierarchical levels, the degree of power exercised over each of the twenty issues is summed. The total for each level is then aggregated over the three hierarchical levels. The lowest possible score is 60 (for each of the twenty issues, degree of power is 1; the

2 Kwoka 1976

FIGURE 4 Workplace democracy scale

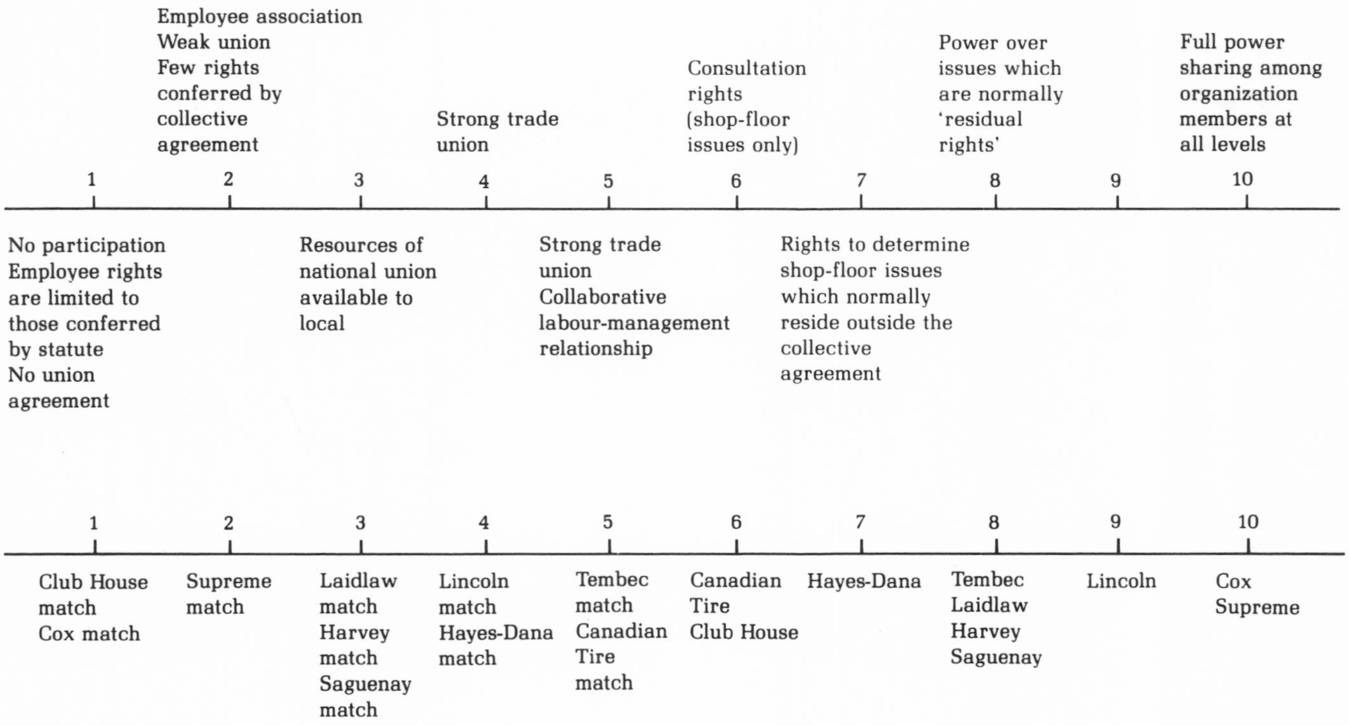

			Strong trade union		Consultation rights (shop-floor issues only)		Power over issues which are normally 'residual rights'		Full power sharing among organization members at all levels
Employee association Weak union Few rights conferred by collective agreement									
1	2	3	4	5	6	7	8	9	10

No participation Employee rights are limited to those conferred by statute No union agreement		Resources of national union available to local		Strong trade union Collaborative labour-management relationship		Rights to determine shop-floor issues which normally reside outside the collective agreement			

1	2	3	4	5	6	7	8	9	10
					Canadian Tire Club House	Hayes-Dana	Tembec Laidlaw Harvey Saguenay	Lincoln	Cox Supreme

1	2	3	4	5	6	7	8	9	10
Club House match Cox match	Supreme match	Laidlaw match Harvey match Saguenay match	Lincoln match Hayes-Dana match	Tembec match Canadian Tire match					

sum of 20 for each level is then aggregated over the three levels). The highest possible score is 480 (for each of the twenty issues, degree of power is 8; the sum of 160 for each level is then aggregated over the three levels). The lowest score would be obtained by a branch plant in which employees at all levels, from plant manager to the rank and file, have no decision-making rights on any issue. The highest score would be obtained by a fully democratic workplace in which all issues were subject to complete participation by all employees. Since the decision-making rights of upper and middle hierarchical levels are similar in most organizations, differences in the score on workplace democracy arise from differences in the decision-making rights of rank and file employees.

The scores on this measure have been converted to a 10-point scale. This scale covers the spectrum of workplace democracy currently found in North America. The scale is presented in figure 4. The weight of organizations in North America is found to the left of this scale, but the centroid is shifting to the right over time by virtue of federal, state, and provincial legislation. The weakest examples of workplace democracy fall very close to organizations with powerful trade unions.

Employee perceptions of their power are not always identical to this formal power defined by collective agreements and company documents. That is, the *formal* structure defining decision-making rights of employees is not identical to the *perceptions* of employees of their influence in decision-making.

The twenty organizations in this sample are ranked according to rank and file and manager response to the question 'Do employees participate in making important decisions relating to their work?'[3] The rank order is presented in table 7. Rank and file perceptions and manager perceptions are similar but not identical. Further, the perceptions of workers and managers are not identical to their power as formally defined by organizational documents. Not surprisingly, the democratically managed organizations with direct participation on shop-floor issues are ranked by both managers and workers as highly participative.

Congruence theory predicts that structure and process will be mutually reinforcing. That is, organizations with democratic decision-making structures will be participative in day-to-day decision-making, and hierarchically structured organizations will be non-participative in day-to-day decision-making. By splitting each distribution at the median, the twenty organizations in this sample can be placed in the four cells in table 8.

3 See question 9 in appendix III.

TABLE 7
Rank order of organizations, most to least participative as perceived by (A) the rank and file and
(B) upper- and middle-level managers compared to (C) formal structure

(A)	(B)	(C)
Laidlaw	Laidlaw	Cox
Cox	Tembec	Supreme
Harvey	Cox	Lincoln
Tembec	Supreme	Tembec
Supreme	Club House	Harvey
Lincoln	Lincoln	Saguenay
Hayes-Dana match	Canadian Tire	Laidlaw
Club House	Harvey	Hayes-Dana
Canadian Tire	Hayes-Dana	Canadian Tire
Tembec match	Lincoln match	Club House
Lincoln match	Tembec match	Tembec match
Club House match	Cox match	Canadian Tire match
Cox match	Harvey match	Lincoln match
Hayes-Dana	Canadian Tire match	Hayes-Dana match
Canadian Tire match	Supreme match	Laidlaw match
Laidlaw match	Laidlaw match	Harvey match
Saguenay	Hayes-Dana match	Saguenay match
Harvey match	Club House match	Supreme match
Supreme match	Saguenay match	Club House match
Saguenay match	Saguenay	Cox match

TABLE 8
The formal structure–informal process relationship

	Formal structure	
Informal process	Democratic	Hierarchical
Participative	8	2
Non-participative	2	8

The two democratic organizations which are perceived by the rank and
file to be less participative than average in day-to-day decision-making are a
producer co-operative and a Scanlon organization. The two hierarchical
organizations which are perceived by the rank and file to be participative are

unionized (UAW and IAM); there is a relaxed, non-adversarial relationship between employees, their unions, and management.[4]

Arnold Tannenbaum (1974a) and his colleagues found that the day-to-day relationship between superior and subordinate in Yugoslavia was less participative than the legislated requirements of the workers' council system of self-management. The day-to-day practices are determined by the culture, traditions, habits, and skills of organization members, as well as by legislation. Yugoslavs (Slovenes) are individualistic and in general have little regard for the philosophical underpinnings of self-management.

The measure of workplace democracy does not differentiate between collaborative and adversarial forms of power-sharing. However, collaborative forms of workplace democracy hold greater potential for rank and file influence in decision-making than adversarial forms, because of the greater freedom of action allowable when trust exists between parties. That is, the total power exercised by organization members over one another can be greater when relations between the parties are collaborative rather than adversarial in nature. With collaborative conditions, mutual influence is willingly granted; one party cannot ignore or block the other party's wishes without destroying the relationship. The power-sharing opportunities are greater under conditions of 'power with,' compared to 'power over.'[5] When the relationship between labour and management is adversarial, attention focuses on issues which divide, rather than on issues which unite, and the area of mutual influence shrinks accordingly.

Structure emerges from the patterns of actions and interactions of organization members. These actions and interactions are directed towards the control of other organization members. The structure of the organization is the resolution of the competing claims for control over the organization and its members. An organization's structure has emerged from the resolution of competing interests in the past, and is a determinant of how future claims will be resolved. Four dimensions of structure (in addition to the measure of workplace democracy just discussed) are compared in the democratic and hierarchical organizations. The comparisons are presented in table 9.[6]

---

4 If the informal process were measured by upper- and middle-level managers, the congruence between formal structure and informal process would be greater than the congruence reported in figure 4.

5 Mary Parker Follett in Fox and Urwick 1973

6 The following tables summarize the comparisons of values, structure processes, and outcomes in the democratic and hierarchical organizations. T-tests are calculated separately for respondents at upper, middle, and lower hierarchical levels. The T-value with one-

TABLE 9

Comparison of structure of democratic and hierarchical organizations[a]

	Respondents' hierarchical level					
	upper		middle		rank and file	
	D	H	D	H	D	H
Rule emphasis	(4.59)	(4.16*)	(4.94)	(4.60*)	(5.37)	(5.06‡)
Surveillance	2.74	2.76	3.19	3.50*	3.69	4.22‡
Opportunities for initiative	4.32	4.15	4.17	3.87*	(4.13	3.84†
Hierarchy of authority	3.55	3.60	3.96	4.04	4.30	4.65‡

a Measured on a 7-point scale. Statistically significant comparisons in a direction opposite to those predicted by the theory are in parentheses.
* $p < 0.05$.   † $p < 0.01$.   ‡ $p < 0.001$.

The three comparisons for the 'rules emphasis' measure of structure are statistically significant, but in the non-predicted direction. Democratic organizations keep more written records of employee performance and place greater emphasis on rules and procedures to cover contingencies than hierarchical organizations. Although the democratic organizations place greater emphasis on rules, the rules are not perceived as inhibiting personal initiative and discretion.

Respondents at lower levels in the hierarchical organizations experience more surveillance of activities, fewer opportunities to exercise personal initiative, and greater emphasis on the hierarchy of authority than their counterparts in the democratic organizations. However, the differences for upper and middle hierarchical levels are in general not statistically significant. Respondents at upper and middle levels in both democratic and hierarchical organizations view their organizations as less 'hierarchical' than respondents at lower levels. The effects of democratic decision-making on other dimensions of structure impact most strongly on organization members at lower hierarchical levels and on the whole do not affect upper- and middle-level members.

tailed level of significance is entered in each table. Statistically significant comparisons in the direction opposite to the prediction of the theory are in parentheses. Since the comparisons are not statistically independent, care should be taken in interpreting individual comparisons. The probability of finding a statistically significant difference, when none exists, increases with the number of comparisons.

COMPARISON OF VALUES

The decision-making structure of an organization is founded upon and justified by a value system. Values provide the organization member with a guide to an ordered relationship with others. Values encompass the moral codes by which people live and the principles upon which they act.

A broad consensus of 'understood' meanings facilitates the mutual influence of organization members, aids communication, and creates a patterning of behaviour without reference to explicit and formalized rules. The interactions among people, which define organization, both create and embody values. The organization takes on a value system from the environments in which it operates and from its influential individual members. The values of the organization are sometimes created and manipulated self-consciously, but often they emerge spontaneously from the interactions of organization members.

The organizational value system ensures institutional continuity by providing a rationale justifying the actions and policies of leaders, by defining the commitments of the organization, and by symbolizing the aspirations of organization members. The pressures on organization members to accept the dominant ideology may represent infringements on personal liberty (especially when employment alternatives are limited); they may reduce the capacity of the organization to respond to change; and they may reduce the diversity of perspective and sensitivity to diverse environments essential to survival.

The decision-making structures and processes of the organization are founded on and are consistent with the values of the most influential organization members. Each of the democratic workplaces in this sample is the product of a single individual or a group of individuals whose values are supportive of democratic decision-making.[7]

A comparison of the six measures of values in the democratic and hierarchical organizations is presented in table 10. Fifteen of the eighteen comparisons are statistically significant and all statistically significant comparisons are in the predicted direction. The value system in the democratic organizations can be characterized as more theory Y than the value system in the hierarchical organizations. Respondents at all levels in the democratic organizations have greater trust in organization members, hold more optimistic beliefs about the honesty and motivation of the average person,

7 McGregor 1960

TABLE 10
Comparison of values in democratic and hierarchical organizations[a]

	Respondents' hierarchical level					
	upper		middle		rank and file	
	D	H	D	H	D	H
Participation potential	3.23	3.01[†]	3.05	3.06	2.89	2.77*
Motivation of average person	3.53	3.29*	3.43	3.16[†]	3.45	3.31[†]
Honesty of average person	2.97	2.74[†]	2.75	2.59*	2.82	2.72*
Leadership qualities	3.44	3.25*	3.12	2.98*	3.14	3.10
Trust in people	3.24	3.17	3.26	2.93*	3.27	2.88[†]
Equality	2.91	2.66*	3.08	2.85*	3.62	3.52

a Measured on a 5-point scale
* $p < 0.05$.   † $p < 0.01$.

believe that most people if given the opportunity will participate meaning-fully in the affairs of the organization, and believe that the participative management style works best.

Middle-level respondents (in both democratic and hierarchical organizations) in comparison to respondents at other hierarchical levels, endorse the most 'hierarchical' values; upper-level respondents endorse the most 'democratic' values and respondents at lower hierarchical levels fall between upper- and middle-level respondents.

Comparison of process
The nature and quality of the interactions among individuals and groups make up the third major dimension on which the democratic and the hierarchical organizations are compared. Dimensions of process compared here include interpersonal relations, conflict and conflict resolution, communication, influence, and decision-making, and the bases of power.

Interpersonal relations
Positive interpersonal relations at the workplace are essential to personal adjustment and well-being. The need for human interaction is universal; people like to be with others and they derive much of the variety and stimulation in their lives from social interaction. As Warr and Wall (1975) have observed, when people discuss recent events at work, they are very likely to devote most attention to co-workers and less attention to supervisors or to the work they perform.

What we know and accept as real, valid, or true is determined in large part by those with whom we interact. As Festinger (1954) has demonstrated, interpersonal encounters provide the opportunity for an individual to compare beliefs, perceptions, and values with others. We adjust our beliefs and perceptions – particularly on issues without an immediate and tangible referent – to correspond to those of persons whose friendship and continuing support we value. How one reacts to the foreman's order, to a promotion, or to the shop steward is shaped to a large extent by norms and shared beliefs of the work group.[8]

The relations among work group members in this study of democratic and hierarchical organizations are assessed on four dimensions: openness, cohesiveness, friendliness, and participativeness. The comparisons are presented in table 11.

The relations among upper-level members in the two types of organizations do not differ significantly on any of the four dimensions. At the middle hierarchical level, however, all comparisons are statistically significant in the predicted direction. The relations among work group members are more

---

8 An equally important function of the work group is the social support it provides each member. The role of the work group in providing psychological support for members was dramatically demonstrated in the study of coal-getting methods made by Trist and Bamforth (1951). In the hazardous and hostile physical setting of the coal mine, the work team was a major source of support for the miners. Under the 'tub stall' and 'short wall' methods of coal-getting the members of a team (consisting of two to eight men) selected their team-mates largely on the basis of mutual compatability. New recruits began with the least pleasant duties. Lasting friendships were formed among group members, and when a team member was killed or injured, other team members looked after the miner's family. Each team was autonomous from supervision and from other groups, and team members shared, according to their specific functions, the proceeds from the day's work. Each team performed a complete cycle of work, including cutting, loading, and removal of the coal. Under these systems morale was high, and illness and absences were rare.

   However, a new coal-getting technology which promised significant advances in productivity disrupted this social system which had been so important to the well-being of the miners. Under the new 'longwall method,' teams of forty to fifty men reporting to a single supervisor were created. Each team was divided into three shifts and each team was responsible for only one part of the coal-getting cycle. Team members were now physically separated along the 200-yard coal face and could not interact with one another. Despite the high degree of interdependence of the three shifts (the oncoming shift would continue the activities of the previous shift), miners on different shifts had no opportunity to interact. Since the cycle of the previous shift needed to be completed before the next shift could complete its task successfully, conflicts often broke out between members on different shifts. The production of the longwall method was far below expectation; illness and absenteeism increased dramatically.

TABLE 11

Comparison of group and intergroup processes in democratic and hierarchical organizations[a]

	Respondents' hierarchical level					
	upper		middle		rank and file	
	D	H	D	H	D	H
Relations among work group members						
openness	4.85	4.68	5.09	4.49[†]	5.08	4.81*
cohesiveness	6.01	6.09	6.05	5.84*	5.86	5.48[†]
friendliness	5.63	5.77	5.72	5.14[†]	5.42	5.23
participativeness	5.52	5.44	5.31	5.04*	5.03	4.44[‡]
Intergroup conflict	2.60	2.97	2.76	3.20[†]	2.98	3.15
Conflict resolution practices						
problem-solving	2.89	2.84	2.80	2.58[†]	2.70	2.37[‡]
ignoring	1.82	1.95	1.79	1.95*	1.87	2.16[‡]
smoothing	2.33	2.48	(2.41)	(2.25*)	2.43	2.40
forcing	2.49	2.84[†]	2.51	2.54	2.25	2.22
Communication re: work matters						
peers	4.49	4.55	4.32	4.32	4.12	3.92[†]
superiors	3.81	4.20[†]	4.07	4.10	3.45	3.18[†]
subordinates	4.42	4.44	4.18	3.87*	–	–
Communication re: non-work matters						
peers	3.49	3.60	3.71	3.63	3.79	3.64*
superiors	3.03	3.32[†]	3.32	2.99[†]	2.85	2.57[†]
subordinates	3.49	3.30	3.39	3.19	–	–
Influence						
plant manager	4.49	4.39	4.34	4.21	4.19	4.08
managers and supervisors	3.65	3.81	3.44	3.56	3.65	3.54
workers	3.52	3.15[†]	3.28	3.17	3.15	2.74[‡]
employee representatives	3.48	3.18*	3.39	3.38	3.02	3.06
personal	3.73	3.93	3.21	3.05	2.53	2.30[†]

a Conflict resolution practices are measured on a 4-point scale; relations among work group
   members are measured on a 7-point scale; influence and communication are measured on a
   5-point scale. Statistically significant comparisons in a direction opposite to those predicted
   by the theory are in parentheses.
* $p < 0.05$.   † $p < 0.01$.   ‡ $p < 0.001$.

open, more friendly, more participative, and more cohesive in the democratic than in the hierarchical organizations. At the lower hierarchical level,
all comparisons except 'friendliness of co-workers' are statistically significant in the predicted direction.

On the measure of social relations with fellow workers away from the workplace,[9] there are no differences between respondents in democratic and hierarchical organizations at the upper hierarchical level, but there is significantly more social interaction for respondents at the middle and lower hierarchical levels in the democratic than in the hierarchical organizations.

Conflict and conflict resolution
Conflict is inevitable in work organizations. The purposes, goals, and activities of any diverse group of individuals will never be identical. However, democratic forms of decision-making can create a widening agenda of common interests. If these common interests include the survival and profitability of the organization, disagreements can be settled within the wider agenda of common interests. Several of the hierarchical organizations in this sample suffered from conflicts over values, such as management endeavouring to break the union or the workers through the union carrying on a class war against management. Without acceptance of the right of the other to exist or to pursue its self-interest the parties are caught in a process of mutually heightening hostility through the reaction of each party to the other.[10] Under these conditions effective problem-solving is impossible, and 'conflict traps' (patterned ways into which all new conflicts tend to fall) emerge.

Comparisons of the amount of conflict between groups and four methods of resolving these conflicts are presented in table 11. All three groups of respondents report less intergroup conflict in democratic than in hierarchical organizations, but the comparison is statistically significant only for middle-level members.

In democratic organizations problem-solving is the most frequently used mode of conflict resolution, followed by forcing, smoothing, and ignoring. In hierarchical organizations problem-solving and smoothing are used about equally and are followed by forcing and ignoring.

For organization members at middle and lower hierarchical levels, problem-solving modes of conflict are used significantly more often in democratic than in hierarchical organizations, and ignoring is employed significantly less often. Surprisingly, the smoothing mode of conflict resolution is employed significantly more often by middle-level managers in the democratic than in the hierarchical organizations. Perhaps the emphasis on friendly relations among employees in the democratic workplaces puts pressure on superiors to smooth over differences of opinion.[11]

9 See interview question 7 in appendix III.
10 This dynamic is called a 'Richardson process.'
11 This finding, however, contradicts the greater openness found among middle-level managers in democratic organizations.

Communication

The democratic organizations are hypothesized to have more communication, between superior and subordinate and between peers, as well as more accurate and open communication than their hierarchical counterparts. The comparisons are presented in table 11.

There is more frequent communication on both work and non-work matters in the democratic organizations as predicted, although the differences are neither consistent nor dramatic. The similarity of the amount and accuracy of communication in the democratic and hierarchical organizations is surprising. Although members of the democratic organizations share a value system which is consistent with open communication, and although the formal decision-making structure requires frequent consultation and interaction among members, the communication patterns in the democratic workplaces are similar to those in the hierarchical workplaces.

Influence over decision-making

The day-to-day influence processes should, in theory, mirror the formal decision-making structure of the organization; that is, the process should follow the structure. However, as pointed out earlier, the day-to-day practices do not always follow the formal structure of the organization.

The question, 'Do employees participate in making important decisions relating to their work?'[12] was answered affirmatively significantly more often by respondents at all levels in the democratic organizations than in the hierarchical organizations.

However, not all groups within the democratic organizations exercise more influence than comparable groups in the hierarchical organizations. The comparisons are presented in table 11. Neither the plant manager and his executive group, nor all other managers and supervisors are believed to exercise more influence over day-to-day decisions by respondents at any level in the democratic than in the hierarchical organizations. Apparently the democratic practices do not give managers more influence.[13] Significantly, however, the democratic programs have not *reduced* the influence of upper- and middle-level managers.

Workers as a group are believed (by upper- and lower-level respondents) to exercise significantly more influence in the democratic than in the hierarchical organizations. The democratic decision-making structure impacts

12 See question 9 in appendix III.
13 This finding contradicts Arnold Tannenbaum's (1968) theory that democratic decision-making increases the power of organization members at all hierarchical levels.

more on the rank and file worker than on any other group in the organization. Employee representatives are perceived to be more influential in democratic than in hierarchical organizations only by upper-level managers. The personal influence of the respondent[14] is significantly greater in the democratic than in the hierarchical organizations only at the rank and file level.

The control graphs for democratic and hierarchical organizations obtained from managers and the rank and file are found in figure 5. The control graph for both managers and the rank and file confirms that employees at the rank and file level in democratic organizations exert significantly more influence over decision-making than their counterparts in hierarchical organizations. The influence exerted by upper- and middle-level employees in democratic organizations does not differ significantly from the influence exerted by the counterparts in hierarchical organizations.

As Tannenbaum (1974b) and his colleagues have theorized, the total amount of influence is greater in the democratic than in the hierarchical organizations. Only for the middle hierarchical level (in part A of figure 5) does the influence in democratic organizations fall below that for hierarchical organizations. The often-voiced fear that democratic decision-making will infringe on the traditional prerogatives of supervisors and middle managers finds some support in this study. The challenge posed by this redistribution of power is discussed in chapter 9.

Bases of power
The way power is exercised in the workplace has changed dramatically in recent years. The power of contemporary managers and supervisors is increasingly subject to both formal and informal limits. Power is frequently bound by company policy, limited by labour contracts, and dependent on subordinate consent and goodwill. Even in areas in which the manager has complete discretion he can rarely make any decision he likes.

Young people today are less awed by hierarchical authority than were their counterparts in the past. The role of supervision is changing from directing, controlling, rewarding, punishing, and evaluating to facilitating, educating, and creating the conditions that will enable subordinates to fulfill their responsibilities.

Of the six bases of power the most frequently mentioned in both democratic and hierarchical organizations are expert, 'law of the situation,' and legitimate bases. However, the pattern of the most frequently employed bases of power differs significantly in the democratic and hierarchical

14 See question 7(e) in appendix III.

FIGURE 5 Control graphs for democratic and hierarchical organizations
obtained from (A) managers and (B) the rank and file

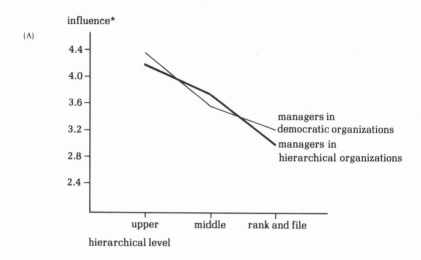

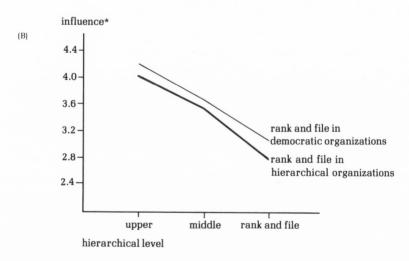

*Measured on a 7-point scale. Question 7 in appendix III

organizations.[15] The expert and 'law of the situation' bases of power are used more frequently and the coercive and legitimate bases of power are used less frequently in the democratic than in the hierarchical organizations. This pattern holds at all hierarchical levels but is statistically significant at the rank and file level only. The emphasis on the consent of subordinates and the emphasis on the common good of all organization members in the democratic organization are consistent with expectation.

COMPARISON OF OUTCOMES

The complex of outcomes, including job-related satisfactions, alienation, and mental and physical health, represents an important (yet neglected) dimension of organizational performance. The effects of work and organizational life on individual outcomes is a matter of vital interest to everyone.

Mental health
Central to the complex of psychological outcomes of organizational life is mental health. This concept has eluded careful and precise definition and is heavily value laden. Definitions of mental health depend as much on the values and orientation of the individual defining the concept as on the condition of the individual being judged. To illustrate: is the mental health of an employee who rebels against an unchallenging and fragmented job greater or less than the mental health of the employee who willingly accepts these conditions?

The enhancement of employee mental health should be a legitimate goal of the work organization in the same way that economic performance is a legitimate goal. Technological and competitive market forces will limit the capability of many organizations to meet this objective; but few firms have systematically examined these constraints to determine whether they are doing as much as they can do to improve employee well-being.[16]

---

15 $\chi^2 = 21.80$, $df = 6$, $p < 0.001$
16 The complexity of the concept 'mental health' is demonstrated by Jahoda's (1958) review
    of definitions of the concept: (1) positive attitudes toward self; self-respect; self-esteem,
    and an accurate perception of self; (2) growth, development and self-actualization; a
    drive to maximize potential, and to develop skills; (3) personality integration; a balanced
    personality; an absence of mental conflicts; (4) autonomy; self-direction, independence,
    self-mastery; (5) accurate perception of reality; an ability to perceive other persons and
    events accurately without undue influence of personal attitudes and biases; (6) environ-
    mental mastery; the healthy person is able to deal successfully with those areas of life
    important to the person.

TABLE 12

Comparison of member outcomes in democratic and hierarchical organizations[a]

| | Respondents' hierarchical level | | | | | |
| | upper | | middle | | rank and file | |
	D	H	D	H	D	H
Mental health	6.04	5.93	5.91	5.86	5.87	5.60[†]
Alienation	2.63	2.54	2.82	2.98	3.32	3.71[‡]
Behavioural outcomes						
job upgrading[b]	51%	34%	50%	52%	20%	15%[*]
voting in political elections[b]	97%	97%	91%	85%	79%	78%
voting in union elections[b]	–	–	–	–	68%	70%
Satisfaction						
pay	6.15	5.78[*]	5.41	5.07[*]	5.28	4.76[†]
fringe benefits	6.11	5.95	5.50	5.37	5.31	4.75[‡]
job security	6.19	6.07	5.87	5.33[†]	5.59	5.01[†]
participation	6.27	6.22	5.84	5.40[†]	5.00	4.33[‡]
freedom on the job	6.47	6.42	6.22	5.91[*]	5.29	5.42[†]
opportunities						
promotion	5.90	5.49[*]	5.23	5.09	4.78	4.30[†]
learn new things	6.12	5.98	5.81	5.64	5.30	4.78[‡]
develop skills	6.26	5.85[†]	5.82	5.65	5.23	4.77[‡]
accomplishment	6.38	6.24	5.85	5.68	5.55	4.95[‡]
respect from co-workers	6.24	6.15	5.97	5.75[*]	5.69	5.34[†]
social relations	6.27	6.37	6.06	5.86[*]	5.98	5.58[†]
Attitudes towards management	6.47	6.19[*]	5.98	5.66[*]	5.44	4.63[‡]
Commitment to organization	6.41	6.45	6.28	6.01[*]	6.02	5.67[‡]
Negative reactions to change	2.64	2.81	3.02	3.50[†]	3.86	4.52[‡]

a Measured on 7-point scales

b Questions on job upgrading and voting in union and political elections are answered 'yes' or 'no.'

* $p < 0.05$.   † $p < 0.01$.   ‡ $p < 0.001$.

The importance to mental health of experiences at work cannot be over-estimated. In voluntary leisure activities like tennis or poker an individual can decide how much self-esteem or self-worth he wishes to risk or invest and how visible this investment will be. At work, however, this option is rarely available and the outcome is central to each person's well-being.

The measure of mental health[17] is compared in the democratic and hierarchical organizations in table 12. The differences are modest; respondents

17 See appendix III.

at all hierarchical levels in both democratic and hierarchical organizations report high levels of mental health. Only at the rank and file level is there a statistically significant difference between democratic and hierarchical organizations.

Physical health
In a longitudinal study of the determinants of longevity, Palmore (1969a; 1969b) considered life-style habits such as smoking and drinking, income, socio-economic status, retirement security, incidence of previous ailments, and religious attitudes. The most significant predictor of longevity was job satisfaction. People who enjoyed their work were more likely to live to an old age than people who did not enjoy their work.[18] Physical health is an outcome of obvious importance to everyone. The link between the workplace and physical health is largely unrecognized.

Two measures of physical health – an overall appraisal of health[19] and a physical symptom checklist[20] – are compared in the democratic and hierarchical organizations. There are no differences at any hierarchical level in the two types of organization on the overall measure of physical health. On the physical symptom checklist there are few consistent and significant differences at the upper and middle hierarchical levels.

At the lower hierarchical level, however, three comparisons are statistically significant. Respondents at the lower hierarchical level in democratic organizations compared to their counterparts in hierarchical organizations report fewer colds,[21] fewer instances of loss of appetite,[22] and fewer cases of heart condition.[23]

Two other comparisons approach significance; respondents at lower hierarchical levels in democratic organizations report more instances of rapid heartbeat than their counterparts in hierarchical organizations[24]; and managerial respondents in democratic organizations report greater nervousness than their counterparts in hierarchical organizations.[25]

---

18 Lawrence Kelly (1975) reports that the loss of man-days due to absenteeism exceeds the loss attributable to strikes and lock-outs by a factor of ten.
19 See question 20 in appendix III.
20 See question 21 in appendix III.
21 Mean scores are 4.25 and 4.08 respectively; $t = 2.13$.
22 Mean scores are 4.54 and 4.36 respectively; $t = 2.43$.
23 Mean scores are 4.92 and 4.84 respectively; $t = 2.05$.
24 Mean scores are 4.39 and 3.77 respectively; $t = 1.80$.
25 Mean scores are 3.95 and 3.77 respectively; $t = 1.80$.

Alienation

Perhaps more than any other outcome alienation is identified with the modern work organization. Alienation, as a condition of modern man, has been closely identified since the time of Marx with the absence of employee control over the workplace. The Marxian perspective on alienation focuses on the worker and the industrial workplace and has built upon the meaning first given the concept by western social philosophers such as Hegel, Simmel, and Durkheim.

Although the Marxian perspective dominates current thinking about the concept, no definition of alienation could reflect the diverse intellectual traditions and perspectives which have used the term as a central concept. Within the contemporary sociological tradition,[26] the construct alienation has been defined to include a wide variety of psychosocial disorders, such as anomie, despair, powerlessness, rootlessness, apathy, loss of self-esteem, and isolation from others. As Johnson (1973) notes, the term alienation is rich in meaning but it conveys this meaning in an inexplicit and often perplexing manner.[27]

---

26 Reviewed by Geyer (1972) and Bonjean, Hill, and McLemore (1967).
27 The diversity of meaning of the concept alienation as used in comtemporary empirical research can be summarized in five dimensions: (i) dimensionality: unidimensional / multidimensional; (2) meaning: subjective / objective; (3) referent: workplace / broader social focus; (4) level of analysis: individual / group / society; (5) causes: contemporaneous / historical. The dimensionality of the concept alienation is an issue which has not been resolved. Evidence for the multi-dimensional view of alienation comes from Dean (1961), Streuning and Richardson (1965), and Seeman (1967). Countervailing evidence and support for the unidimensional view of alienation comes from Nettler (1957), Rhodes (1961), Middleton (1963), Couch (1966), Tannenbaum et al., (1974b), Sheppard and Herrick (1972), and Gordon (1978).

There are several variants of the multi-dimensional viewpoint. Browning, Farmer, Kirk, and Mitchell (1961), for example, argue that Seeman's (1959) five concepts are not part of a unitary construct but rather should be viewed as sequential stages, beginning with experienced powerlessness leading to feelings of meaninglessness and resulting in normlessness. Kirsch and Lengermann (1972) also argue that the dimensions of alienation are independent and should be viewed sequentially. In their view self-estrangement follows from powerlessness, meaninglessness, and isolation.

The temporal and conceptual primacy of the five subdimensions has not been worked out, nor have the relations among the subdimensions been well explained by those who hold the multidimensional view. Neal and Rettig (1967) conclude that a researcher's orientation and data should determine whether alienation is considered to be uni- or multidimensional.

Alienation has also been variously used to refer to objective alienating conditions and to subjective (feeling) states. For Blauner (1964) the division of labour and the mechanization of the work process are objective alienating conditions, and individuals working

Alienation is considered here as a unidimensional concept referring to an alterable (but not momentarily transient) and subjective state of the individual which reflects the individual's sense of powerlessness in the larger

under these conditions are assumed to be alienated. Hopp (1976) examines alienated behaviours which result from objective conditions of work such as supervisory practices and the work technology. Hulin and Blood (1968) examine population and demographic characteristics to identify those who are assumed to be alienated from middle-class values. Others, notably Seeman (1967) and Dean (1961), view alienation as a subjective psychological state of the individual.

For those who hold the subjective view of alienation, there remains the problem of differentiating the concept of alienation from other constructs such a work satisfaction and locus of control. Aiken and Hage (1966), for example, measure alienation from work and alienation from expressive relations by asking questions of the sort ('How satisfied are you with ...?'), and Seeman's measures of alienation are very similar to Rotter's (1966) measures of internal-external locus of control.

Thirdly, should alienation be considered as a general philosophical view of life which reflects one's attitude towards the larger social and political order, or should alienation refer specifically to the workplace? Examples of the latter viewpoint include Pearlin (1962), Kirsch and Lengermann (1972), and Aiken and Hage (1966). Examples of the large referent include Dean (1961), Neal and Rettig (1963), Srole (1956), Sheppard and Herrick (1972), and Tannenbaum, et al., (1974b).

The concept 'generalization theme' (Seeman 1971) has been used to broaden the concept of alienation to an all-encompassing, pervasive phenomenon in contemporary industrialized society. That is, alienation from work is associated with alienation from the political system, social relations, and the family. Although Seeman (1967; 1971) finds little support for the 'generalization theme,' Whitehorn (1979) finds that 'work alienation' is correlated with 'societal alienation.'

When alienation if defined in terms of specific workplace referents, it is difficult to distinguish alienation operationally and conceptually from concepts such as job satisfaction. When alienation is defined as a subjective state, a broad referent is desirable – especially in studies linking objective conditions of work and alienation. When alienation is given a broader meaning, the researcher is able to address the question, 'to what extent do conditions in the workplace influence one's views and perspectives on issues beyond the organization's boundaries?'

Alienation has also been used to refer to a subjective state of individuals as well as to the state of groups (such as social classes) or to societies at large. Research in the Blauner and Seeman tradition has generally accepted alienation as an individual rather than a group characteristic.

Finally, the concept of alienation has been used implicitly to refer to a subjective state caused by historical factors such as socialization practices, social class influences, and other historical experiences, as well as to a subjective state caused by contemporaneous environmental factors (Seeman 1959). In the latter view alienation is situation-specific and is not an enduring and unalterable state of the individual.

Since alienation can, and has been used in a manner which reflects varying combinations of the above five dimensions, the concept has taken a great diversity of meaning in the contemporary literature.

society; isolation from affairs in the society; belief that rules or norms no longer govern events in the society; and perception of the meaninglessness of events in the larger social and political order. This subjective state has behavioural correlates, such as non-participation in social events outside of the workplace, and decreased propensity to vote in political and union elections or to upgrade skills through training and participation in voluntary organizations; but the term alienation refers to the experienced (feeling) state of the individual.

The comparison of the index of alienation[28] in the democratic and hierarchical organizations is presented in table 12.

Upper-level respondents in both democratic and hierarchical organizations are less alienated than middle-level respondents; and middle-level respondents are less alienated than lower-level respondents. Only at the lower level is the alienation of members greater in the hierarchical than in the democratic organizations. Again, the effects of democratic decision-making are greatest at the rank and file level.

Behavioural outcomes
The measures of behaviour – taking courses or training to upgrade skills, voting in federal and provincial elections, and voting in union (or employee association) elections – are compared in democratic and hierarchical organizations. Only one comparison is statistically significant: a greater percentage of the rank and file in democratic than hierarchical organizations have upgraded their jobs in the recent past.

There are no differences at any level in the two types of organization in voting patterns. The failure to find differences between democratic and hierarchical organizations in members' voting behaviour contradicts Pateman's (1970) hypothesis that employees who are given the opportunity of participating in decision-making will be more effective contributors to the democratic process in the larger society. Organizational participation and participation in the political process are not mutually reinforcing as Pateman suggests.

Job-related satisfactions
The satisfaction of respondents with eleven dimensions of the workplace is reported in table 12.[29] The levels of satisfaction reported by members of democratic organizations are significantly more positive than the levels

28 See question 13 in appendix III.
29 See question 3 in appendix III.

reported by members of hierarchical organizations. The differences are most pronounced for members at lower hierarchical levels (where all comparisons are statistically significant). Six of the eleven comparisons are statistically significant for middle-level members and three comparisons are significant for upper-level organization members.

The effects of democratic decision-making on outcomes are greater at lower than at upper hierarchical levels. Workplace democracy may have a powerful effect on rank and file employees, because few employees at that level in North American workplaces enjoy the privilege. Participation in decision-making is a gratifying and rewarding experience, but some of the satisfaction derived from participating in decision-making comes from engaging in an activity which goes beyond the norm. Rights and privileges which are commonplace do not satisfy. The due process rights enjoyed by most North American workers were far beyond the imagination of employees sixty or seventy years ago, yet these rights are rarely a source of employee satisfaction. Democratic decision-making practices are not a source of satisfaction to faculty members, because faculty members at most universities accept these practices as the norm. The absence of rights or privileges accepted as the norm brings great dissatisfaction, but their presence does not create satisfaction.

With existing evidence it is difficult to assess how much of the positive effect of workplace democracy is attributable to intrinsic qualities of participation and how much is attributable to comparisons with practices in referent organizations in the same region or sector. In any event, there will always be opportunities for organizations to go beyond the norm and to derive benefits in so doing. As the norm moves towards more democratic practices the innovative organization will have to seek new frontiers of employee participation.

Why is satisfaction with pay, benefits, and conditions of work greater in the democratic than in the hierarchical organizations, when there are no differences between the two types of organization in these characteristics? This study is not the first to identify this anomaly. Tannenbaum (1974b) and his colleagues find positive relationships in four countries between self-reports of influence and a variety of outcome measures which are unrelated to the exercise of influence.

Apparently, satisfaction with one dimension of organizational life (such as the qualities of the job or the amount of participation in decision-making) generalizes to other dimensions of organizational life. Conversely, dissatisfaction with some condition can generalize to other conditions. Employees who are dissatisfied with their jobs will tend to be dissatisfied with pay,

TABLE 13
Summary of analysis of variance

	Alienation		Reactions towards change		Commitment		Attitude towards management	
	F	Sig.	F	Sig.	F	Sig.	F	Sig.
Main effects								
structure	9.08	$p < 0.001$	5.14	$p < 0.001$	2.64	$p < 0.005$	9.57	$p < 0.001$
style	10.01	$p < 0.001$	30.00	$p < 0.001$	25.52	$p < 0.001$	32.54	$p < 0.001$
Interaction								
structure × style	1.58	$p < 0.008$	1.13	N.S.	1.78	$p < 0.001$	1.03	N.S.

co-workers, supervision, and the amount of influence they exercise over decision-making.

Other outcomes
Three other outcomes – attitudes towards management, commitment to the organization, and negative reactions to change – are compared in the democratic and hierarchical organizations. The three outcomes are significantly more positive at the rank and file and middle levels in democratic than in hierarchical organizations. These three comparisons support the data reported earlier: employee reactions to the workplace are significantly more positive in democratic than in hierarchical organizations.

STRUCTURE AND STYLE

The supervisor plays a major role in shaping the outcomes of subordinates. Research in the human relations tradition[30] has demonstrated that open, trusting, participative, and supportive supervision creates committed, loyal, and productive subordinates. How does the effect of workplace democracy on subordinate outcomes compare to the effect of supportive supervision? Is there an interaction between democratic structure and supportive / participative supervisory style?

To test the effects of style and structure and their interaction on employee outcomes a measure of supervisory style[31] and the measure of the workplace democracy[32] are examined by an analysis of variance. Four outcome measures are selected to represent diverse elements from the domain of outcomes.[33]

A summary of the analysis of variance with style and structure main effects and style-structure interaction is presented in table 13. Both organization structure and supervisory style have significant effects on the four outcomes. Style has a more significant effect than structure. The style-structure interaction is significant for the alienation and commitment measures, but not for the measures of attitudes towards change or attitudes towards management.

30 Likert 1961; 1967
31 See appendix III.
32 Ibid.
33 The correlation between supervisory style and democratic structure is 0.21 ($p < 0.001$) for the total sample; 0.09 (not significant) for upper-level respondents; 0.16 ($p < 0.01$) for middle-level respondents; and 0.24 ($p < 0.001$) for lower-level respondents.

TABLE 14
Mean scores of outcome measures for each structure-style combination*

Structure	Style	Alienation	Negative reactions to change	Commitment	Attitude towards management
Democratic	Participative	2.99 (1)	3.25 (1)	6.28 (1)	5.93 (1)
Democratic	Non-participative	3.31 (3)	3.88 (3)	5.71 (3)	5.28 (3)
Hierarchical	Participative	3.18 (2)	3.53 (2)	6.08 (2)	5.53 (2)
Hierarchical	Non-participative	3.62 (4)	4.57 (4)	5.37 (4)	4.55 (4)

* Rank order in parentheses, most to least positive

The mean scores of the four outcomes for each of the four combinations of style and structure are presented in table 14. Outcomes are most positive for the democratic structure / participative style combination; second most positive for the hierarchical structure / participative style combination; third most positive for the democratic structure / non-participative style combination; and least positive for the hierarchical structure / non-participative style combination.

T-tests on two orthogonal contrasts for each outcome measure (row (1) vs. row (3) and row (2) vs. row (4)) reveal statistically significant contrasts for all four outcome measures. That is, all four outcomes are more positive under the democratic structure / participative style combination than under the hierarchical structure / participative style combination; and outcomes are most positive under non-participative style when the structure is democratic rather than hierarchical.

A participative supervisory style tends to be found in democratic organizations. Fifty-eight per cent of the 1,000 cases in this study are found in congruent pairings of style and structure (2 × 2 table, splitting style and structure at the mean); 58 per cent of incongruent pairings are found in the hierarchical structure / participative style combination. In other words, participative styles are found more frequently in hierarchical organizations than non-participative styles are found in democratic organizations.

The congruence of supervisory style and organization structure is not surprising. The value system underlying participative management and the self-reinforcing nature of style and structure contribute to congruence between the concepts.

Organization member outcomes are found to be more positive in democratic organizations than in hierarchical organizations. That is, structure has significant effects on member outcomes and these effects are independent of the effects of supervisory style. However, the effects of supervisory style on subordinate outcomes are stronger, probably because supervisory style is more salient to organization members than is organizational structure.

Senior executives and union officials in several of the democratic organizations in this study revealed during interviews that a major problem in their organizations is authoritarian supervision, that is, supervisory styles which are inconsistent with the formal decision-making rights of subordinates. These data suggest, however, that in general, organizational structure and supervisory style tend towards congruence. The greatest discrepancies between style and structure occur in organizations where the shift from hierarchical decision-making to democratic decision-making structures is recent and where supervisory staff were retained after the shift. These data suggest that one way to change supervisory style is to change the larger organizational context, although the expected congruence between style and structure may take some time to evolve.

WORKPLACE DEMOCRACY AND
THE ROLE OF THE FIRST-LINE SUPERVISOR

The role of the first-line supervisor has long been considered one of the least desirable in the organization. This job is one of the most powerless in the organization. First-line supervisors cannot control events; they must react to them. They are asked to explain and justify policies they rarely had a hand in formulating. The role is often a dead-end job lacking the security of rank and file jobs covered by collective agreements.

Occasionally, the turnover among first-line supervisors is so high that when relations with subordinates are poor, the subordinates are prepared to out-wait the superior. Stress-induced ulcers are also frequent among the ranks of first-line supervisors. Under these circumstances increased rank and file participation can be threatening to the first-line supervisor. It is more comforting to give orders from a position when you are not called upon to justify your decisions or from a position in which you are not accountable to those below you in the chain of command.

The influence that first-line supervisors exert over their subordinates and the influence directed towards first-line supervisors by others are compared in the democratic and hierarchical organizations. Surprisingly, there are no significant differences in the two types of organization in supervisors' freedom to make decisions on their own, the extent to which their decisions are subject to review by others, and the amount of influence they exert over the day-to-day operation of the office or shop floor.

On measures of outcome, however, there are many differences between supervisors in the democratic and hierarchical organizations. Overall job satisfaction, commitment to the organization, attitudes towards change and satisfaction with intrinsic aspects of work are greater in the democratic than in the hierarchical organizations.

GRADIENTS OF SATISFACTION

A gradient defines differences in outcomes for respondents at different hierarchical levels. Upper-level organization members in general are more satisfied than middle-level members who, in turn, are more satisfied than lower-level members. However, lower-level members in democratic organizations express degrees of satisfaction which approach those expressed by middle-level managers in hierarchical organizations. Even in the formally participative organizations such as Israeli kibbutzim and organizations with the workers' council system of self-management in Yugoslavia, lower-level respondents do not approach levels of satisfaction of middle-level respondents in the non-participative organizations in the United States, Austria, and Italy.[34] The levels of satisfaction of lower-level members in this sample of democratic organizations are as high as those reported in kibbutzim and Yugoslav organizations.[35]

EMPLOYEE EXPECTATIONS

Employee aspirations for a greater voice in decision-making will shape the work organizations of the future. In chapter 1 the case was made that much of the pressure to extend democratic practices to the workplace will come from young employees. Greater employee expectations are indeed found among younger employees at every level.[36]

More importantly, however, employee expectations are found to differ in the democratic and hierarchical organizations. The expected level of participation[37] for respondents in democratic and hierarchical organizations is presented in table 15. The expectations of middle- and lower-level members are

34 Tannenbaum et al. 1974b.
35 Ibid.
36 The correlation between age and expectations is -0.07; $p < 0.01$.
37 See question 10 in appendix III.

TABLE 15
Expected participation in
democratic and hierarchical organizations

Hierarchical level	Democratic organizations	Hierarchical organizations
Upper	3.01	2.92
Middle	3.14	2.81
Lower	3.17	3.05

significantly greater in democratic than in hierarchical organizations.[38] Having experienced democratic decision-making, employees at middle and lower levels feel that their new responsibilities are legitimate and proper – and they desire more.

Expectations are greater at lower than at upper hierarchical levels in both democratic and hierarchical organizations. The differences between expected participation of upper- and lower-level respondents is as large in the democratic as in the hierarchical organizations. That is, the ideal participation of the rank and file in democratic organizations exceeds the ideal participation of managers in democratic organizations by the same amount as their counterparts in hierarchical organizations. This discrepancy between the expectations of employees at different hierarchical levels is a source of conflict and a source of continuing pressure on those who manage work organizations.[39,40]

Another type of discrepancy – the difference between the participation actually practised and employee expectations – is also a source of conflict.[41]

38 $p < 0.05$.
39 Expected participation in decision-making is a function of many factors. Hespe and Wall (1976) report that employees who are most satisfied with their jobs desire less participation in decision-making. In other words, employees look to participation as a means of resolving some of their dissatisfactions at work. In this study no support is found for this notion. Job satisfaction does not correlate significantly with expected participation for respondents on any hierarchical level.
40 An analysis of variance testing the main effects of democratic/hierarchical structure, level and their interaction indicates that both structure and level are statistically significant factors in predicting expected participation; democratic/hierarchical structure: $F = 16.33$, $df = 1$, $p < 0.001$; level: $F = 4.52$, $df = 2$, $p < 0.01$; interaction: $F = 2.07$, $df = 2$, $p < 0.13$.
41 This concept is operationalized as the absolute difference between question 9 and question 10 in appendix III.

TABLE 16
Discrepancy between actual and expected participation
in democratic and hierarchical organizations

Hierarchical level	Democratic organizations	Hierarchical organizations
Upper	0.28	0.42
Middle	0.55	0.63
Lower	0.69	1.00

TABLE 17
First canonical correlations for
each pair of concepts

Values-structure	0.48
Values-process	0.37
Values-outcomes	0.46
Structure-process	0.50
Structure-outcomes	0.50
Process-outcomes	0.74

The discrepancy between actual and expected participation in democratic and hierarchical organizations is presented in table 16.

The discrepancy between actual and expected participation is smaller for lower-level respondents in democratic than in hierarchical organizations (there are no differences at middle and upper hierarchical levels). Predictably, the discrepancy increases from upper to middle to lower levels in both democratic and hierarchical organizations.[42]

RELATIONS AMONG THE CONCEPTS

A canonical analysis of the measures of the six pairs of the four concepts is performed to determine the relationships among groups of measures. Canonical correlation finds linear combinations of two sets of measures which

42 An analysis of variance testing the main effects of democratic/hierarchical structure, level, and their interaction shows that structure and level but not their interaction are significant determinants of the discrepancy between actual and ideal participation; structure; $F = 27.39$, $df = 1$, $p < 0.001$; level; $F = 44.50$, $df = 2$, $p < 0.001$; interaction: $F = 2.12$, $df = 2$, $p = 0.12$.

maximize the correlation when the linear combinations themselves are correlated in the two-variable sense.

The first canonical correlations for each pair of concepts are presented in table 17. All six of the first canonical correlations are statistically significant.[43] The outcomes measures are most strongly related and the values measures most weakly related to measures of the other concepts.

The canonical function coefficients for the measures of each pair of concepts are presented in table 18. The canonical function coefficients provide the weighting of each measure in the linear combination and show the direction of the relationship.

The pattern of canonical function coefficients offers strong support for congruence theory. All of the canonical function coefficients for the measures of values are internally consistent and are in the direction predicted by the theory.

The canonical function coefficients for the measures of structure are also consistent with the theory, except for the 'rules' measure in the structure-process and structure-outcomes relationships. In these relationships, emphasis on rules is associated with positive relations with group members, high personal influence over day-to-day work activities, low levels of intergroup conflict, low alienation, positive reactions to change in the organization, and high job satisfaction.

Two of the three canonical function coefficients for the 'supportiveness of supervision' measure of process are in the non-predicted direction, suggesting that high supportiveness is associated with hierarchical values and hierarchical structure. Participativeness of supervision, however, is related to the other measures as predicted by the theory.

Of the twenty-one canonical function coefficients for outcomes, all but two are in the direction predicted by the theory.

To determine the extent to which the ten democratic and the ten hierarchical organizations conform to the two ideal types of organization defined in chapter 4 a discriminant analysis is performed on a subset of the measures employed in the canonical analysis. Discriminant function coefficients identify measures which contribute to the differentiation between the two types of organization. Each coefficient represents the relative contribution of the variable to the function, and the sign of the coefficient denotes the effect (positive or negative) of the variable.

Three measures of each concept are selected from the original twenty-eight measures. The measures are selected in order to represent diverse

43 $p < 0.001$.

TABLE 18
Canonical function coefficients

	Values-structure	Values-process	Values-outcomes	Structure-process	Structure-outcomes	Process-outcomes
Values						
participation potential	0.33	0.14	0.17			
motivation	0.20	0.60	0.46			
honesty	0.08	0.21	0.33			
leadership qualities	0.67	-0.02	0.13			
trust	0.06	0.28	0.40			
equality	0.07	0.33	-0.02			
Structure						
rules	-0.24			0.44	0.38	
surveillance	-0.49			-0.45	-0.74	
opportunities for initiative	0.29			0.56	0.18	
emphasis on hierarchy	-0.28			-0.42	-0.35	
democratic decision-making	0.36			0.08	0.20	
Process						
group relations		0.52		0.30		0.33
problem-solving		0.21		0.11		0.15
intergroup conflict		-0.32		-0.32		-0.35
supportiveness of supervision		-0.21		-0.14		0.24
participativeness of supervision		0.28		-0.01		0.06
personal influence		0.17		0.59		0.41
communication re: work		0.03		-0.07		0.03
communication re: non-work		0.07		0.36		-0.07
Outcomes						
alienation			-0.64		-0.23	-0.09
mental health			0.05		-0.27	0.28
commitment			-0.15		0.15	0.07
stress			0.21		0.32	0.00
job satisfaction			0.25		0.21	0.38
negative reactions to change			-0.47		-0.72	-0.37
attitudes towards management			0.00		0.03	0.29

TABLE 19
Standardized discriminant function coefficients

Values	
motivation	0.26
honesty	0.10
trust	0.29
Structure	
surveillance	−0.11
opportunities for initiative	0.11
emphasis on hierarchy	−0.05
Process	
intergroup conflict	−0.01
group relations	0.05
supportiveness of supervision	0.31
Outcomes	
attitudes towards management	0.37
commitment	0.03
negative reactions to change	−0.10

domains from each concept (i.e., intercorrelations with the measures of the same concept are significant, but not among the highest of the set) and such that the correlations of the measure with other measures of different concepts are high. The following measures are selected: 'motivation,' 'honesty,' and 'trust' measures of values; 'rules emphasis,' 'hierarchy of authority,' and 'opportunities for initiative' measures of structure; 'intergroup conflict,' 'group relations' and 'supportiveness of supervision' measures of process; and 'attitudes towards management,' 'commitment to the organization' and 'negative reactions to change' measures of outcome.

The standardized discriminant function coefficients are presented in table 19. On the basis of the twelve measures in table 19, 66 per cent of the 1,000 cases are correctly classified.[44] Eleven of the twelve discriminant function coefficients are in the predicted direction (the intergroup conflict measure of process is hypothesized to have a positive discriminant function coefficient, but its value is −0.01). The 'hierarchy of authority,' 'intergroup conflict,' 'group relations,' and 'commitment' measures do not play a significant role in discriminating the democratic and the hierarchical organizations. The 'motivation' and 'trust' measures of values, the 'supportiveness of supervision' measure of process, and the 'attitudes toward management' measures

44 $\chi^2 = 102.96$, $df = 1$, $p < 0.001$.

of outcomes are the major variables in discriminating the democratic and the hierarchical organizations.

SUMMARY

The comparison of democratic and hierarchical organizations on the dimensions of values, structure, process, and outcomes suggests that there are predictable and statistically significant correlates of democratic decision-making. The ten democratic workplaces in this sample possess the properties of the 'democratic' model of organization, and their matched counterparts are significantly closer to the 'hierarchical' model.

The differences between democratic and hierarchical organizations are greatest for organization members' values, followed by interpersonal and intergroup processes, and outcomes (great differences for measures of job-related satisfactions but not statistically significant for stress, physical health, and mental health), and weakest for the job codification, hierarchy of authority, and formalization measures of structure (although some of the differences are significant for lower-level organization members).

The absence of significant differences in stress symptoms, mental health, physical health, and voting in political and union elections in democratic and hierarchical organizations is surprising. The effects of workplace democracy are less general than hypothesized and most strongly affect member outcomes directly concerning the workplace.

The differences between democratic and hierarchical organizations are strongest for organization members at lower hierarchical levels, weakest for organization members at the upper hierarchical level, and intermediate for organization members at middle hierarchical levels.

The canonical analysis demonstrates that measures of the four concepts of the theory are related almost exactly as predicted by congruence theory.

The democratic organizations are found to have more participative supervisory styles than their hierarchical counterparts, as congruence theory predicts. Both structure and style are found to have independent and significant effects on outcomes; however, style has a more significant effect on outcomes than structure.

The increased influence over decision-making of the rank and file in democratic organizations is not purchased at the price of reduced managerial influence. That is, the total amount of power is greater in the democratic than in the hierarchical organizations.

This analysis leaves a major question unanswered: is the nature of work different in the democratic and hierarchical organizations? If work were more enjoyable, fulfilling, or rewarding in the democratic organizations, then the differences in outcomes in the democratic and hierarchical organizations might be explained (at least in part) on this basis.

We now turn our attention to work. The effects of work on employee well-being will be examined briefly, followed by a comparison of characteristics of work in the democratic and hierarchical organizations.

6

The nature of work in
democratic and hierarchical workplaces

The importance of work in our lives is difficult to overestimate. More than any other activity, work provides an opportunity for fulfilling human needs for competence, mastery, and achievement. Whether rewarding or not, work remains a central preoccupation of most people. Studies of the unemployed[1] demonstrate the profound importance of work to our sense of well-being and to our mental health. Those without jobs (the young, the retired, the unemployed) often feel like outsiders and find it difficult to participate in the life of our society.

In response to the now classic question posed by Nancy Morse and Robert Weiss (1955), 'If by chance you inherited enough money to live comfortably without working, do you think you would work anyway?' 80 per cent of working people answered 'yes' (86 percent of the middle class and 76 per cent of the working class). 'Interest' and 'accomplishment' were cited as the most important reasons for continuing to work by the middle class; 'to keep occupied' was cited as the most important reason by the working class. Most of the working-class respondents indicated that they would quit their present jobs and look for other work.

A similar study reported by Michael Kirby (1980) demonstrates that work is an important activity for most Canadians. When asked to rank in order the importance of church, family, work, friends, and union, work is ranked only second to the family. Ninety-seven per cent of Canadians say that they would prefer to work, even if they were able to collect UIC benefits. Undoubtedly, many respondents would prefer to work because UIC payments are less than regular earnings, but 70 per cent of Canadian workers say that they work because they *like to* more than because they *have to*.

1 Slote 1969

Our sense of personal worth and importance is defined in large measure by the work we do. Activities in our society which are not defined as 'work' (such as the activities of a homemaker) are not considered important. Homemakers seek 'fulfilling' work outside of the home (which by any objective standard is less intrinsically rewarding than housework), because 'work' is recognized as important to the society and confers an identity on those who perform it.

Our jobs are measures of our importance to the organization and of our worth in the larger society. Jobs bind us to the organization and represent the most visible and tangible aspect of our organizational lives. The rhythms of work mark the passage of time and provide continuity to our lives. Cycles of work and leisure provide 'time anchors' which give some measure of regularity and closure to our daily lives.

Work also provides many people with the only continuing and significant human interaction outside of the immediate family. This interaction is important not only because it satisfies an important human need but also because it is an essential means of testing and affirming many of our personal beliefs and values.

No other human activity provides as many continuing and important opportunities for meeting basic human needs. Recent research has reshaped and refined beliefs about the relationship between people and their jobs. In total, this research amounts to a condemnation of work in the modern work organization.

Attitudes towards work, like attitudes towards authority, have changed over this century. At the turn of the century, the design of work was dominated by a single-minded preoccupation with economic efficiency. Today, demands are heard for work which enhances employee well-being. The idea that work should be a means of satisfying the personal needs of the job-holder is of recent origin; and although not yet widely accepted, this idea increasingly governs the design of work systems in this country. For example, virtually all major projects in the resource sector in Canada incorporate, from the beginning design stages, work that meets human needs for variety, challenge, and freedom.

The failure to create intrinsically satisfying work has produced a generation of workers with a purely instrumental attitude toward work. Today's workers have been persuaded that intrinsically interesting work is out of the question, the only reward being relief from work in the form of shorter hours and longer vacations. Work which cannot satisfy deeper human needs and aspirations becomes nothing more than a means of supporting a valued way of life away from the workplace. The often-quoted remark of William

Winpisinger (1973), 'if you want to enrich the job, enrich the pay cheque,' reflects this instrumental view of work.

The proposition that work should be changed to make it more intrinsically rewarding rests on the assumption that work *should* be a central life interest and *should* reflect the dignity and worth of the individual. It might be argued that fulfilment is more easily attained through leisure activities than through work itself. According to this perspective leisure pursuits provide the best opportunity for individuals to meet their needs for self-enhancement; work should be tolerated merely as a means to achieve this end.

The relationship between work and leisure remains a subject of controversy. Research on this issue is guided by one of three competing theories. The 'compensatory' theory hypothesizes that when gratifications are absent at the workplace, workers obtain compensatory gratifications from activities outside workplace.

The second or 'segmentation' theory argues that life is divided into separate segments, each representing different activities and interests, and each is experienced independently of the others.

The third or 'spill-over' theory proposes that the work experience generalizes to other non-work activities. This theory is not necessarily supported by research evidence showing a correlation between work and leisure activities. Since work is a major part of most people's lives, attitudes towards work would correlate substantially with attitudes towards other areas of life even if no spill-over occurred. Furthermore, leisure experiences and attitudes could spill over into work; that is, causality might flow in the other direction. The 'spill-over' of work to non-work is not purely psychological in nature. Non-work (leisure) activities are often constrained by time, money, and energy, all of which may be limited because of the job.

Most research supports the spill-over theory.[2] Meissner (1971) finds that workers in highly specialized jobs are less active in leisure activities than workers in less specialized jobs. That is, there appears to be a 'carry-over' from work to leisure. If so, then work should have some intrinsic quality, even if it is used simply for instrumental purposes.

Parker (1971) points out that leisure cannot be substituted for work which is not personally absorbing or worthwhile. Leisure has become a respite from the regimentation, subordination and meaninglessness of the work-

2 Kasl's (1973) review of the literature finds little support for either the 'compensatory' or the 'segmentation' theories.

place. Without meaningful work leisure often becomes nothing more than a passive state of exhaustion, 'fantasy' and vicarious experience.

VALUES AND WORK

The nature of work in the modern workplace is shaped not only by technological and economic forces, but also by the assumptions and values of those who design the work technology. When systems engineers and production specialists believe the technical system to be reliable and the social system to be unreliable, the socio-technical design will endeavour to optimize solely on technological deminsions; people will be employed as addenda only when necessary. The technology will be primary, and the employee, his activities, and his responsibilities will be shaped by this technology. However, if those who design work systems believe that the social system is reliable – that is, that the work force is composed of committed and responsible people – then the technological system will be designed to utilize these human resources effectively.

The unwillingness of people to accept work which deprives them of opportunities for making decisions and exercising discretion has led to a reassessment of the principles of work system design. It is increasingly recognized that a person becomes himself by making decisions and by accepting responsibility for these decisions. This process of identification of self comes from the conduct of work. Opportunities for self-identification and self-determination are absent in workplaces in which what to do and how to do it are determined not by the individual but by supervision or by the work technology. The absence of opportunities at work for self-directed activity leads to predictable outcomes: alienation, conformity, and underdeveloped aptitudes and abilities. In an earlier generation these outcomes were accepted as necessary in the pursuit of economic efficiency.

The criteria employed by manufacturing designers and information systems designers in planning jobs have been assessed by Taylor (1979a). Taylor asked a sample of designers to rank the importance of several criteria for subdividing the work flow into tasks. The rankings of seven criteria for manufacturing designers and information systems designers are presented in table 20.

According to these data work systems designers prefer to minimize the immediate costs of production, rather than to consider long-term costs (which include undeveloped and unused abilities, worker alienation, and dissatisfaction). Taylor observes that these designers know and understand

TABLE 20
Importance of criteria for breaking workflow into tasks

	Engineers	Systems analysts
Maximizing throughput per unit of time	1	1
Efficient use of machine resources	2	2
Making jobs as simple to perform as possible	3	4
Reducing manpower	4	5
Providing management with better information	5	3
Providing more job satisfaction	6	6
Minimizing floor-space requirements	7	7

the debilitating effects of routine work on employees, but few feel obliged to design systems which minimize these effects. However, increasing pressures on management will lead to new initiatives to design the work technology to meet human needs.[3]

PERSPECTIVES ON WORK

Contemporary perspectives on work have been shaped by the changing values and perspectives of the past eighty years. Three perspectives appear to have been especially important. The first is the factory system at the turn of the century with its technological determinism and the supporting justifications of Frederick Taylor's 'scientific management.' The second is the human relations perpective based on the Roethlisberger and Dickson study of Western Electric's Hawthorne Works. The third is the socio-technical system perspective of Eric Trist.

Each of these three perspectives has its contemporary interpretations: scientific management has culminated in Allen Mogenson's (1963) 'work simplification'; the Hawthorne studies have led to the orthodox job enrichment of Frederick Herzberg (1966); and the Trist studies continue with the work of Louis Davis, Albert Cherns, and James Taylor of UCLA.[4]

The deterministic character of the early industrial technology demanded strict division of labour and standardization of jobs. In this era the manner in which the work was to be performed, who was to perform it, and when it was to be performed could be precisely determined. A technological deter-

3 See the description of the Laidlaw Lumber Division of McMillan Bloedel in appendix I.
4 Davis and Cherns 1975; Davis and Taylor 1979

minism dominated the thinking of those who designed work systems. The work technology was to be designed according to strict engineering criteria, and it was not to be compromised by human or social considerations.

The values of the early industrial era supported this technological determinism.[5] Working people with few alternatives and no clear concept of a better method accepted the imperatives of this technology and concentrated on obtaining improved wages, benefits, and conditions of work.

Frederick Taylor in his two major works, *Shop Management* (1903) and *The Principles of Scientific Management* (1911), provided an underlying rationale for this system. Scientific management appealed to rational and empirical grounds for the settlement of disputes over work. This new approach marked an improvement over the subjective and arbitrary judgments of superiors which passed for managerial practice in that era.

However, even in that era many found Taylor's single-minded pursuit of economic efficiency to be dangerous and demeaning. Scientific management provided a rather incomplete perspective on job design. Under scientific management choices in job design were made without considering hidden costs such as inflexibility, loss of employee commitment, and under-utilized human resources. Scientific management was based on a strategy of minimizing short-term costs, rather than minimizing total cost. An assessment of total cost must include the costs of labour turnover, absenteeism, lack of flexibility in work skills, substandard products, and overhead costs attributed to supervision and other forms of control.

Since great gains were to be achieved in this era from the rigorous application of scientific management, the less obvious externalities could be ignored. It is increasingly apparent however that the marginal gains to be made through the effective use of human resources are more substantial today than they have been at any time in the past.

The second tradition, following from Roethlisberger and Dickson (1939), is important not so much for its perspective on work itself, but rather for the strong moral and normative tone of the 'human relations' movement. Although the nature of work was not manipulated as an independent variable in the Hawthorne studies, important changes to the work were made in both the bank wiring room and the relay assembly area. Employees were given greater autonomy in the conduct of their work, their needs and wishes were more closely attended to, and they were told that the experiment was part of a larger endeavour which might significantly alter the workplace in the future.

5 See chapter 3.

The work of Frederick Herzberg (1966) on job enrichment follows in the human relations tradition. Although seriously flawed by methodological difficulties,[6] Herzberg's work stands as one of the seminal contributions to the theory and practice of job design. Herzberg stressed that enriched work would release untapped skills, motivations, and abilities and would thereby enhance the performance of the organization. Herzberg's work more than any other stimulated job redesign innovations in the workplace.

The third major perspective on job design began with the work of Trist and his colleagues at the Tavistock Institute in London. Trist's work marks a shift in concern from the design of specific jobs to a concern with the work system. The 'socio-technical system' perspective considers the output of a work system to be the function of two independent but correlated systems – a social system made up of individuals and groups and a technical system made up of the work technology. Trist argues that productivity cannot be maximized by considering only one system. Both dimensions must be jointly optimized to achieve the greatest overall effectiveness.

Socio-technical design is an area of active current interest. However, the application of principles of socio-technical design requires substantially greater management commitment than does the redesign of individual jobs under classic job enrichment. Management, however willing to redesign individual tasks on the shop floor, may reject changes in the work system because such modifications touch their work lives directly and require major changes in control procedures and superior-subordinate relationships.

THE JOB SATISFACTION PARADOX

Research on the question 'Are employees satisfied with their jobs?' reveals a puzzling inconsistency. Surveys of work attitudes report that very high percentages of working people are satisfied with their jobs;[7] however, there is substantial and growing evidence from other sources that employees are dissatisfied with their work.

Regardless of the type of questionnaire measure employed, over 80 per cent of Canadians and Americans surveyed in recent years report satisfaction with their jobs. Surveys of the Institute for Social Research at the University of Michigan over the past twenty years report that 79 per cent to 95 per cent of employees are satisfied to some degree with their work. The Centre for Research on the Utilization of Scientific Knowledge at the Uni-

6 House and Wigdor 1967; Graen 1968
7 Thurman 1977

versity of Michigan reports that in surveys of over 20,000 working people between 1960 and 1970, over 85 per cent report no dissatisfaction with their jobs.

A recent Canadian survey by Burnstein et al. (1975) for the Economic Council of Canada reports that 40 per cent of respondents are 'very satisfied' with their jobs and fully 89 per cent of Canadians are at least 'somewhat satisfied' with their jobs. These reports of high job satisfaction are found in most industrialized western countries.[8]

Despite the reported high levels of job satisfaction, other evidence of dissatisfaction at the workplace (including strikes, grievances sent to arbitration, careless and indifferent work performance, decreased willingness to accept supervision without question, and continuing high rates of employee absenteeism) suggest that all is not well at the workplace.

Can this paradox between reported levels of job satisfaction and conflicting evidence from other sources be reconciled? If the job satisfaction figures are correct, there appears to be little incentive to change conditions of work. Some argue[9] that levels of employee satisfaction are indeed high, and that recent changes in absenteeism and turnover can be explained by changes in the demographic composition of the work-force (young and female employees just entering the work-force with skills inappropriate for their jobs).

The job satisfaction figures obtained from questionnaire and interview surveys of working people should be interpreted with caution. There are several reasons for suspecting that the reported levels of satisfaction are inflated.

First, when asked about levels of satisfaction with their jobs, working people may give perfunctory answers. That is, the question 'All in all, are you satisfied with you job?' may lead to the socially desirable response 'yes' in the same manner that 'How is it going today?' leads to an affirmative answer. An honest response to the question may require a long-standing and trusting relationship between the respondent and the interviewer – a relationship which is rarely obtained in large sample surveys of working people.

The interviewer can never be certain that social desirability bias does not contaminate the data. To test for social desirability in this study the following question was asked of each respondent: 'Did you vote in the last provincial of federal election?' Seventy-nine per cent of rank and file respondents and 92 per cent of managers said 'yes.' The actual figures for citizens of the

8 Bolweg, 1979.
9 Flanagan, et al. 1974

same socio-economic status are 74 per cent and 83 per cent respectively. It is clear that in this survey there is some socially desirable responding.[10]

Secondly, reported levels of job satisfaction are a function of an individual's ability to come to terms with the work situation. A job may contribute little to an individual's sense of purpose or well-being, but the individual may express satisfaction because there is no escape and no alternative. In this case most individuals adjust their needs, their hopes, and their aspirations to a job which holds little prospect of improvement. Acting otherwise ensures continuing frustration and dissatisfaction, with debilitating effects on one's personal health and social and family life.

Thirdly, the question 'All in all, are you satisfied with your job?' does not make the frame of reference of the respondent clear. We do not know the expectations of the respondent nor the norms which the respondent employs when responding to the question. What we want and what we accept as desirable is a function of what we have seen and what we know exists. Employees with limited horizons may know nothing other than what they are doing, and they cannot, therefore, be dissatisfied. An employee could well be satisfied with a job which would be defined as intolerable if the employee could compare it with other jobs.

A worker who carried ladles of molten aluminum from a furnace to moulds expressed a very high level of satisfaction with the job during an interview in this study. By any objective standard, the job was unpleasant; the heat was searing, the work was dangerous and heavy, and the air was filled with smoke. When asked why he enjoyed his work, the worker reported that the job was one of the few in his organization which permitted a three-day, thirty-seven-and-one-half-hour work week. The schedule enabled the worker to hold a second job and thereby to enjoy a life-style otherwise beyond his means.

Fourthly, responses to job satisfaction questions are confounded with the 'ego involvement' of the respondent. In western societies, notions of self-importance and self-worth are inextricably intertwined with one's job. If we despise our jobs, we despise ourselves. Few individuals are likely to disparage their jobs without feeling some loss of personal worth.

The selection of a job is one of the most important decisions a person will make in his lifetime. A question about attitudes towards the job may well elicit a defensive reaction which biases results in favour of high job satisfaction. Furthermore, dissonance tends to bias reported job satisfaction in the

10 The comparisons of democratic and hierarchical organizations are not affected by social desirability bias, since the bias operates in both samples.

favourable direction. Dissatisfaction with a job may be seen as one's own fault because of having chosen the wrong job or having failed to get another job.

Finally, rather than reconcile themselves to the demands of their jobs, people can also 'adjust their jobs' to their liking. Taylor (1979b) describes an example of a 'hiker' in an automobile assembly plant (a hiker drives cars from the storage lot to railway cars) who reports high levels of satisfaction with the job simply because he can take breaks from the work by losing ignition keys, discharging batteries, or flooding carburetors in a manner which escapes detection. While the hiker apparently is 'satisfied' with his job, other measures of satisfaction (absenteeism, sabotage of the work) might suggest that he is dissatisfied with the job.

For these reasons the reported levels of job satisfaction must be interpreted with caution. Employee surveys are able to identify categories of workers who are less satisfied with their jobs than others, and to identify organizations in which attitudes are more positive than in others, but the overall level of reported satisfaction is probably inflated.

DIMENSIONS OF WORK

In this study ten dimensions of work were measured by means of observations and interviews. These ten dimensions assess the major psychological qualities and physical conditions of work. The ten dimensions will be described and then comparisons reported of the tasks performed by senior managers, middle managers, and workers in the democratic and hierarchical organizations. The measures of the ten dimensions are found in appendix III.

Variety
Variety defines the extent to which a particular job involves a variety of activities, differences in the pace of work and changes in the location of work. In some jobs the individual responds to the exigencies and unvarying rhythms of the machine. The work is conducted in a single location, its pace and the nature of its activities are invariant. Other types of production floor work permit the individual to vary the pace of work according to the individual's needs (as long as production targets are met) and the job may be 'enlarged' to include a variety of support activities (such as quality control and machine repair). The three dimensions of variety – activities, pace of work, and location of work – may vary independently, although in general the three dimensions are positively correlated.

Task completion

Task completion measures the extent to which a job involves the performance of a complete cycle of activities or a 'whole' unit of work from
beginning to end. The greater the degree of task completion, the greater the
individual's sense of personal responsibility for the work, and the less likely
he is to assign blame for inadequate performance to someone else. Individuals on the shop floor who perform a complete cycle of activities may be
permitted to attach their names to the product. For example, in the Aston-
Martin automobile factory in Great Britain tradesmen who complete an
entire engine are permitted to affix their names to the motor.

Autonomy

Autonomy measures the extent of personal discretion allowed by the job.
Autonomous work allows the individual to initiate activity and to exercise
discretion over the pacing of work rather than to respond simply to the
demands of the work technology. Frederick Taylor argued that autonomy
from supervision should be limited on the shop floor: 'the management must
think out and plan the work in the most careful and detailed way, demanding the worker not to seek to increase production by his own initiative, but
to perform the orders given down to the slightest detail.'[11]

For managerial and supervisory personnel controls over work may be
administrative in nature, or limits on autonomous action may come from
external agencies (e.g., safety legislation, professional norms). Professional
norms represent a significant limit on the individual's autonomy. That is, the
controls come not from without but from within; Perrow (1979) points out
that organizations which must deploy members to places where they cannot
be under close surveillance by supervision have the choice of creating rules
and reporting procedures to keep control of 'professionalizing' personnel so
that they can be trusted to act in the organization's interests. Most professionals feel that detailed and impersonal rules are inappropriate and that
constraints on free activity should be self-imposed, and self-enforced.

Autonomy at work is more popularly labelled 'freedom.' A recent study of
people's experience of 'freedom' as they went about their daily activities[12]
employed a technique called 'experiential sampling.' At randomly selected
times throughout the day, electronic pagers on 107 volunteers were activated by means of a radio signal. Each volunteer was asked to fill out a
questionnaire which he carried with him, indicating where he was, what he

11 Friedman 1961, 34, quoting Taylor
12 Czikszentmihalyi and Graef 1979

was thinking about, how he felt, and to what degree he would prefer to be doing something else. A total of 4,700 reports were obtained from assembly-line, clerical engineering, and managerial workers.

The results indicate that of all their daily activities people feel least free at work. Only 15 per cent of subjects who were at work said that they wanted to do whatever they were doing when the pager was activated. White-collar workers feel freer than blue-collar workers. An employee's sense of freedom is linked to the amount of variety and responsibility on the job. When someone believes that an activity was freely chosen, regardless of external circumstances, the person is more cheerful, happy, and involved with the task.[13]

Skills
This dimension includes requirements of the work for sophisticated or complex skills, abilities, and knowledge. It also includes the amount of initial training demanded by the job and the frequency with which the individual is expected to upgrade his skills. This dimension is often difficult to measure, because individuals performing seemingly unskilled work have nevertheless accumulated a breadth of knowledge and insight over the years which enables them to perform their jobs in a manner that new recruits could not. Employees who perform work of this nature may accumulate considerable insight into the work flow itself, machinery, clients, customers, and suppliers. These important dimensions are often overlooked in research, because it is difficult to assess the length of time it would take an individual to learn the job as thoroughly as the present incumbent.

Novelty
This dimension measures the extent to which tasks are incompletely defined and the extent to which the individual must be prepared to handle surprising or unpredictable situations. In some types of work the frequency of novel events is virtually non-existent while in other types of work the individual has almost no sense at the beginning of a work day of what he will be doing during the day. Few individuals, it seems, prefer completely unstructured work, although some degree of novelty is desired by most employees.

13 The authors also report a surprising finding; blue-collar workers spend significantly more time than white-collar workers actually working while they are on the job. Blue-collar workers work 70 per cent of the time and white-collar workers work 61 per cent of the time. Socializing, relaxing, and day-dreaming consume a significant portion of the workday.

In work with little novelty employees may create their own through horse-play or social interaction.

Intellectual demands
This dimension assesses the extent to which the quality of the work is determined by the employee, not by the machine technology or factors beyond the employee's control. The degree of attention, concentration, and mental effort demanded by the job are important facets of this dimension. Managerial work typically places greater intellectual demand on the individual than shop-floor work.

Required interaction
This dimension measures the extent to which direct interaction with others is required by the job. Some work demands constant and intensive interaction with others (whether clients or other organization members) while other jobs isolate the individual from any social interaction. This dimension does not assess the extent to which the individual actually interacts with others, but rather measures the *required* interactions with others on the job. Individuals who converse with one another while at work, but who nevertheless perform separate and unrelated tasks, are performing work with low required interaction.

This dimension has remained largely unexplored. The size of the 'role set' of the individual, the frequency of required interaction of others in this role set, and the intensity of this required interaction are all dimensions of the concept.

Conflicting demands
This concept measures the extent to which members of the role set place conflicting pressures on the individual. The demands may take the form of 'inter-sender conflict' whereby two individuals expect the job incumbent to perform in a manner such that both cannot be satisfied; or the conflict may take the form of 'role overload' whereby the individual cannot simultaneously meet all the demands of members of the role set.

Physical conditions of work
This dimension measures the quality of the physical working environment, including cleanliness of the work area, the ambient temperature of the workplace and its variation by season, the amount of physical effort involved in the conduct of the work, and the extent to which the work is dangerous and unhealthy.

Feedback

Feedback defines the extent to which the individual performing the job is provided with information about the performance of the work. Machine-paced work often provides immediate and direct feedback on the individual's performance. Work with a high discretionary component is generally characterized by less immediate and frequent feedback.

The nature and quality of feedback on the job is dependent upon the existence of external and independent standards by which performance may be judged. Many aspects of managerial and supervisory work cannot be objectively evaluated, and hence feedback tends to be irregular and unreliable. Under such circumstances subjective criteria (such as loyalty to the organization) tend to predominate, and feedback on task performance tends to emphasize these qualities.

Jaques (1964) has examined the concept 'time-span of discretion.' This concept refers to the period of time in which an individual could exercise inadequate discretion or could perform below standard before that fact would come to the attention of the individual's immediate superior. Jaques argues that this concept is the only job dimension required to explain most of the variance in individuals' reactions to the job. The longer the time span of discretion, the greater the job satisfaction, the greater the loyalty and commitment to the enterprise, and the greater the individual's sense of self-esteem.

COMPARISON OF TASKS

The ten dimensions of tasks are compared in the democratic and hierarchical organizations in table 21. Six of the thirty comparisons are statistically significant (three at the rank and file level, one at the middle level, and two at the upper level). At the lower hierarchical level there is greater autonomy from supervision, more required interaction with co-workers, and fewer conflicting demands in democratic than in hierarchical organizations.

At the middle level there is less variety to work in democratic than in hierarchical organizations. This result is surprising; it is commonly believed that managing an autonomous and self-directing work-force offers challenges and variety missing from hierarchically managed organizations.

At the upper hierarchical level managers in democratic organizations perform work which involves significantly less completion of a cycle of activities, and they work under less pleasant physical conditions. The day-to-day activities of upper-level managers in democratic organizations have less closure than the activities of their counterparts in hierarchical organizations,

TABLE 21
Comparison of work in democratic and hierarchical organizations[a]

| | Respondents' hierarchical level | | | | | |
| | upper | | middle | | rank and file | |
	D	H	D	H	D	H
Variety	5.00	4.73	4.30	4.55*	3.30	3.29
Task completion	3.29	4.11[†]	3.10	3.10	2.47	2.45
Autonomy	4.39	4.36	3.92	3.82	2.72	2.44[†]
Skills	4.20	4.14	3.60	3.58	2.74	2.77
Novelty	4.80	4.61	3.97	4.12	2.72	2.63
Intellectual demands	5.01	5.07	4.45	4.34	3.66	3.54
Required interaction	5.22	5.08	4.85	4.72	2.92	2.45[†]
Conflict demands	2.81	3.00	3.40	3.15	4.32	4.56[†]
Physical conditions	4.96	5.22*	4.27	4.20	3.41	3.38
Feedback	3.69	3.63	3.62	3.52	3.60	3.56

a Measured on a 7-point scale, except physical conditions, which is measured on a 6-point scale
* $p < 0.05$.   † $p < 0.01$ (two-tailed).

because there is more sharing of responsibility and more frequent joint activities in the democratic organizations. Upper-level managers in democratic organizations also spend more time on the shop-floor than their counterparts in hierarchical organizations; their physical working conditions are consequently less attractive than those of upper-level managers in hierarchical organizations.

The overall similarity of tasks in the two types of organization indicates that workplace democracy does not substantially affect task attributes. The absence of major differences in task between democratic and hierarchical organizations suggests that differences in outcomes cannot be attributed entirely to differences in task attributes.

The task characteristics were compared separately in each of the ten pairs of democratic and hierarchical organizations. In only two democratic organizations are the tasks significantly more enriched and challenging than the tasks in their hierarchical counterparts; these organizations are Laidlaw Lumber and The Group at Cox. In Laidlaw Lumber employee participation is linked directly to the work itself, and predictably, the work is more autonomous, challenging, and varied than the work in its hierarchical counterpart. In The Group at Cox employees have chosen to enrich their work as a means of maintaining high quality standards and as a means of promoting employee interest in the job.

TABLE 22
Work enrichment, democratic decision-making,
and their interaction as determinants of outcomes

	Job satisfaction	Intrinsic job satisfaction	Commitment	Mental health
Work enrichment	0.30*	0.48*	0.42*	0.20*
Democratic decision-making	0.28*	0.29*	0.40*	0.19
(Work enrichment) × (democratic decision-making)	−0.22	−0.21	−0.35	−0.17

* $p < 0.01$.

THE JOINT EFFECTS OF WORK AND
WORKPLACE DEMOCRACY ON OUTCOMES

In chapter 5 evidence was presented which showed the significant effect of democratic decision-making on a variety of employee outcomes. Employees in organizations which permit significant participation in decision-making are significantly less alienated, more committed to the organization, and more satisfied with a wide range of organizational conditions than their counterparts in organizations which do not permit significant participation in decision-making.

There remains, however, an important question which has never been answered: what are the relative effects of work and workplace democracy on employee outcomes? The intrinsic qualities of work (variety, autonomy, responsibility, uncertainty) have been found in previous research to lead to positive outcomes.[14] These qualities are labelled 'work enrichment.'[15] The standardized regression coefficients for work enrichment, democratic decision-making, and their interaction as predictors of four outcome measures are presented in table 22.

Work enrichment is a significant predictor of all four outcomes; democratic decision-making of three outcomes; and their interaction of one outcome. The effect of work enrichment is significantly greater than the effect of democratic decision-making for one outcome measure: intrinsic job satisfaction. The effects of democratic decision-making are nearly as great as the effects of work enrichment, except for the outcome with a specific job referent. This finding suggests that workplace democracy may be a means of

14 Herzberg 1966; Wanous 1974
15 See appendix III for measures.

improving employee morale and satisfaction when technological constraints limit the opportunity to enrich the work.

INDIVIDUAL DIFFERENCES AND JOB DESIGN

The debate about what people seek from their work inevitably touches on the issue of individual differences. While some employees react negatively to routine and closely supervised work, others do not.

The effect of individual differences on the relationship between the job and the attitudes and reactions of the individual performing the job has been a major preoccupation of behavioural scientists for over a decade. It is clear that all workers do not respond in the same way to enriched work. Most studies[16] indicate that individuals react positively to enriched jobs but some react more favourably than others.

Research on individual difference moderators of the task-outcomes relationship has examined the following moderators: Alienation from middle-class norms[17]; 'cultural predisposition' (urban / rural upbringing)[18]; education, need for achievement, and need for autonomy[19]; protestant work ethic[20]; need for achievement[21]; growth need strength.[22] Of these moderator variables growth need strength (GNS) has been most consistently related to the task attributes-outcomes relationship.[23] Growth need strength refers to a mixture of higher-order needs such as achievement, recognition, challenge, and variety.[24]

The strength of growth needs varies from individual to individual. For example, in this study the strength of senior managers' growth needs is significantly greater than the strength of middle managers' growth needs; and middle managers' growth needs in turn are significantly greater than the growth needs of rank and file employees.[25]

Although work is central to the lives of most Canadians, individuals vary in their desire for challenge and growth opportunities at work. Yankelovich

16 Except Hulin and Blood 1968; Turner and Lawrence 1965
17 Hulin and Blood 1968
18 Turner and Lawrence 1965
19 Seybold 1976; Stone, Mowday, and Porter 1977
20 Stone 1976
21 Steers and Spencer 1977
22 Hackman and Lawler 1971; Wanous 1974
23 Wanous 1974
24 See measures in appendix III.
25 Mean GNS of upper-level respondents is 4.15; middle-level respondents, 3.74; and lower-level respondents, 3.10.

(1974) points out that the demand for self-fulfilment through meaningful work is found primarily among young workers (under thirty-five years of age); by and large, workers over thirty-five years of age are willing to settle for economic rewards.

There are two possible interpretations of this relationship between age and the desire for challenging work. The 'psychology of entitlement' may not guide the expectations of older workers because of their experiences in a less affluent era. The demand for challenging work and a voice in how it is performed, according to this interpretation, will gradually spread as the new generation of workers and those who follow after them become a greater percentage of the work-force.

A second interpretation rests on the effects of a job on employee growth needs. One way of coping with a routine and uninspiring job which holds little prospect of improvement is to lower expectations so that work becomes instrumental to the fulfilment of needs which cannot be met away from work.

What is not clear from any research evidence is the proportion of individuals whose growth needs would be strong (and who would find intrinsic work satisfying) if their past experiences and current opportunities at the workplace were to encourage the development of these needs. Unfortunately, anyone's guess about this proportion is as much an expression of his philosophy as it is a statement of empirical fact.

For whatever reason, individuals differ in the extent to which they desire challenge, variety, and autonomy at work. Workplaces which permit significant employee participation in decision-making and which treat individuals as autonomous and responsible contributors to the organization should encourage the development of growth needs. Surprisingly, however, the data from this study indicate that no differences in GNS are found for employees at any level in the democratic and hierarchical organizations. These data suggest that the larger organizational context does not significantly shape member needs.[26]

However, on closer examination, it is clear that the organizational context does shape individual needs. The correlation between strength of growth needs and organizational context is significantly higher for organization

26 Mean Growth Need Strength for (1) upper hierarchical levels in democratic and hierarchical organizations are 4.08 and 4.06 respectively (not significant); (2) middle hierarchical levels in democratic and hierarchical organizations are 3.65 and 3.64 respectively (not significant); and (3) lower hierarchical levels in democratic and hierarchical organizations are 3.04 and 3.06 respectively (not significant).

members with low organizational tenure.[27] Socialization experiences and exposure to organizational norms and practices consequently do have an effect on individual needs.

At the two lower hierarchical levels tasks which allow greater variety, autonomy, responsibility, and challenge tend to be performed by persons who desire jobs of this character.[28] This association between task enrichment and growth needs supports the proposition that employees select jobs which match their growth needs.

Again, the role of leisure activities in fulfilling growth needs can be raised. An individual with high growth needs performing impoverished or uninspiring work may find opportunities outside of work to fulfil these needs. However, as indicated earlier, there is evidence of a 'spill-over' effect from the work experience to leisure. To the extent that our educational system fosters independent thought and to the extent that it creates individuals who expect growth opportunities at work, changes in the methods of work will continue to evolve in the direction of greater autonomy, variety, and challenge.

An individual's reaction to a job is not simply a function of the interaction between the characteristics of the job and personal needs; it is also a function of the interaction between the job and the availability of alternatives to the job. This sample of respondents was divided into two groups: (1) employees who are above the average age of the sample, with higher than average seniority, with lower than average education, and performing jobs with lower than average skill requirements; and (2) employees who are below the average age, with below average seniority, with higher than average education, and performing jobs with higher than average skill requirements.

The levels of satisfaction of these two groups were compared on a variety of job related factors. Overall there are few statistically significant comparisons on variables such as satisfaction with pay, promotion opportunities,

---

27 Correlations between growth need strength and democratic hierarchical structure for employees of high and low tenure are as follows.

level	high tenure	low tenure
upper	0.18	−0.09
middle	0.09	−0.09
lower	0.08	−0.06

28 The correlation between growth needs and the index of task enrichment is 0.01 (not significant) for upper level members; 17 ($p < 0.001$) for middle level members; and 0.22 ($p < 0.001$) for lower level members.

attitudes toward management, commitment to the organization, and mental health. However, on the overall measure of job satisfaction,[29] members of the first group are significantly more satisfied with their jobs than members of the second group.[30] That is, persons performing low-skill jobs can be quite satisfied with the work when by virtue of their age, skills, and seniority there are few other alternatives.

It could be argued that individuals should not have 'jobs' defined as specific sets of tasks or responsibilities. People are not inert automatons; they are developing, complex, emotional, and unique beings with a changing set of skills, abilities, attitudes, and interests. These needs and abilities should be primary; jobs should be created or altered to match them. Ideally, the individual should have a voice in the assignment of jobs and should be free to take on temporary and different assignments for the purpose of training, broadening horizons, or simply alleviating boredom.

Most systems designers and managers would not agree that the individual is primary, and that tasks should be designed to be psychologically rewarding for the worker, rather than simply efficient in the economic sense. It should be noted, however, that notions of self-actualization and personal growth are fundamental tenets of contemporary liberal democracy. Western liberalism, above all else, values the individual, and the institutions of society (including work organizations) are intended to regulate the free competition among individuals in maximizing their potentialities. The design of most Canadian workplaces can be justified neither by appeals to classic liberalism nor by appeals to humanist socialism.

29 See question 4 in appendix III.
30 Mean of group 1 is 5.21; mean of group 2 is 4.94; $t = 1.96$; $p < 0.05$.

7

Workplace democracy
and trade unionism

The varieties of workplace democracy described in this study have been greeted with suspicion and outright hostility by most Canadian trade unionists. This response contrasts with the strong support given by most western European trade unionists to the co-determination and works councils forms of employee participation.

The source of Canadian trade union opposition to workplace democracy is easily identified but less easily rectified. In Europe employee participation is generally viewed as strengthening collective bargaining, while in Canada participation is believed by many trade unionists to weaken collective bargaining. European collective bargaining is typically conducted at the national or industry level, and programs of employee participation are designed to strengthen plant-level bargaining by extending consultation to include issues normally covered by collective bargaining in this country.

In Canada, by contrast, collective bargaining is conducted largely at the plant level, and forms of workplace democracy are seen as directly competitive with (and consequently a challenge to) the trade union. Ironically, the Canadian worker who does not seek participation as an end in itself has more control over shop-floor issues than his European counterpart, who is more ideologically committed to the principle of workers' control.

In Canada trade union opposition to workplace democracy arises because the established rights of shop stewards are often threatened by such arrangements. Many trade unionists feel that the introduction of workplace democracy without direct union involvement may weaken benefits (such as job jurisdictions and seniority clauses) which unions have won on behalf of their members. Programs of workplace democracy (such as self-governing work groups) often blur the boundaries between work jurisdictions, combine worker and supervisory functions, and upset work rules established through collective bargaining. Further, they feel that attempts to involve the worker in decision-making will weaken worker attachment to unions by making workers more satisfied and by dealing with workers and their concerns through mechanisms other than shop stewards and the trade union.

Trade union scepticism about workplace democracy is understandable. This is not to say, however, that trade union opposition is desirable or even that this opposition is in the long-term interests of the trade union movement. Union leaders perceive little demand for increased participation from the rank and file, and they are not willing to compromise concrete gains (such as wage increases or job security) for the uncertain benefits of greater participation in decision-making. They cannot fit the collaborative forms of workplace democracy into the adversarial relationship which has characterized labour-management relations in this country over this century.

Throughout the careers of most Canadian trade union leaders the role of the trade union as a legitimate institution in our society has been hotly contested, and many trade unionists feel that employee participation programs threaten the very existence of the trade union movement. They cannot accept changes in the workplace which do not involve the trade union as a significant partner. The desire to contain, restrict, and regulate unilateral managerial authority has been the driving force behind the trade union movement since its beginning. New ventures in workplace democracy are viewed with suspicion not only because the results are unpredictable, but also because collaborative power-sharing must necessarily diminish the historical mission of the trade union movement.

Trade unionism itself is a form of workplace democracy. Through the collective agreement and the grievance process workers have direct control over some conditions of work. The history of trade unionism has been a struggle to broaden the issues subject to collective bargaining into the domain of 'management rights.' These rights were once absolute, but increasingly, issues of vital interest to employees fall under the collective agreement and hence are bilaterally determined. The UAW, for example, brought the issue of pensions to the bargaining table in 1949. Previously, pensions had been the exclusive domain of management. Later, health insurance, protection against lay-offs, due process in hiring and promotion, the introduction of technology, and the speed of the production line were subject to collective bargaining.

However, there is a major difference between trade unionism and the forms of workplace democracy studied here. This difference centres on the collaborative / adversarial nature of the relationship between the parties. It is a fundamental tenet of this book that conflict between labour and management is inevitable. In fact, conflict is inevitable in any social grouping and in any socio-political system – slave-holding, feudal, capitalist, socialist, or communist. The distinction between collaborative and adversial relations is not the distinction between the absence or presence of conflict. In a collaborative relationship the perception of common interests governs the relationship between parties, and differences are settled within this framework of common interests. In an adversarial relationship, the interests which divide the parties outweigh those which unite the parties. Trade unionism is *not* fundamentally incompatible with collaborative forms of workplace democracy.

It is becoming increasingly apparent that the process of periodic collective bargaining has become excessively burdened by plant-level problems which have remained unresolved over the life of the contract. This trend is manifested by the lengthening negotiation periods beyond the expiry of the collective agreement. The increasing frequency of open conflict, legal and illegal strikes, and walk-outs also reflects the failure of collective bargaining to resolve issues which accumulate during the life of the contract. Unsettled grievances are generally negotiated away by both sides during contract negotiations, and this process generally follows the logic of power, not the logic of fairness or the correctness of the decision. Collaborative forms of workplace democracy might well unburden the collective bargaining process by encouraging continuous negotiation-consultation-participation during the life of the agreement. Workplace democracy, however, would go well beyond forms of 'continuous bargaining' now popular in some jurisdictions in Canada.

THE CANADIAN INDUSTRIAL RELATIONS SYSTEM IN TRANSITION

A number of significant changes are under way which will significantly alter the nature of the relationship between labour and management in Canada and will eventually alter the way in which decisions are made in work organizations.

Perhaps the most basic changes are the emerging values and attitudes of managers and workers. Employee participation in decision-making is now more acceptable to managers than it has ever been in the past. Part of this value change may be nothing more than a simple recognition that the older, authoritarian styles no longer work; but nevertheless the ethic of participative management is now a part of management thinking in this country.

Furthermore, members of the blue-collar labour force are better educated than their parents and are less amenable to traditional management practices of command-and-obey. The growth of white-collar unions, particularly in the skilled and professional occupations, has led to a greater willingness to consider participation as a viable means of increasing the quality of work-life of union members. The Public Service Alliance of Canada, for example, is the first Canadian union to express openly a willingness to participate in quality of worklife programs with management.

The official position of the Public Service Alliance of Canada is illustrated in the following statement:

The Alliance needs to play a major role in Quality of Working Life projects initiated in the Public Service. Political pressure against public servants and economic and legislative restrictions on collective bargaining impose severe restrictions on the means by which Public Service employees can improve their working conditions and benefits. QWL is a means through which it is possible to improve the working environment in the Public Service, something that is not possible to achieve through the traditional means. QWL is designed to improve the work life of public servants on the job by increasing participation in decision making, improved communications, broadening of responsibilities, greater self-determination, and more open and cooperative human relations. The results will be improved productivity, improved labour-management relations, increased purpose and involvement of employees, and greater personal and job satisfaction.[1]

If forecasts of limited economic growth and stiffening taxpayer resistance to real dollar increases in public service salaries are accurate, then democratic decision-making may well be one of the few avenues open to public service unions to improve the conditions of their members.

Non-union companies are beginning to exert considerable pressure on unionized companies to alter inefficient work practices. In cases where self-governing work group forms of workplace democracy are both more efficient (and consequently more attractive to management) and more satisfying to workers, trade unions will be pressured to allow such practices.

Favourable media reports about varieties of workplace democracy also exert pressure on managers and trade union officials. In response to the concerns of the alienated worker the parties may increasingly look to collaborative and participative programs.

The decision-making rights of employees in both the unionized and non-unionized sectors are being extended by federal and provincial legislation. This process has been under way in Canada for some time. Perhaps the most

1 Policy Paper #18, 1979

dramatic change in recent years concerns the right to direct the work. According to principles established by collective agreements, judgments of labour arbitrators, and court opinions, employees must perform tasks assigned by management. If the employee believes the work assignment to be illegal, unsafe, or otherwise ill-advised, he must still perform the work, pending review of his complaint. This principle, however, which management believes to be essential to the preservation of the orderly conduct of the work, is under continuous review, and in some jurisdictions the right of management to direct the work is severely limited. Health and safety legislation in several Canadian provinces, for example, gives workers the right to refuse to perform work until a review of the complaint is heard.

It is increasingly clear that labour-management co-operation cannot be legislated. The arbitration process, for example, is time-consuming and expensive. In many firms grievances are allowed to accumulate and generate unrest. The eventual resolution of these grievances – when used by one side to pressure the other – may not be based on the merits of the cases. Grievance arbitration was intended as a substitute for labour law. It has become increasingly legalized as a result of the intricacies of modern collective agreements and the complex of laws which pertain to collective bargaining. The overregulation of our industrial relations system and the reliance on legal means for the resolution of industrial disputes are symptoms of a failing system.

We shall now examine labour-management negotiation as a means of resolving organizational conflicts and then proceed to two models of collective bargaining which could guide labour-management relations in the future.

NEGOTIATION AND WORKPLACE DEMOCRACY

The right of labour and management to negotiate the terms of their relationship is a cornerstone of our industrial relations system. However, negotiation has not always been a part of the collective bargaining process. Before negotiation was introduced into collective bargaining, disputes between labour and management were handled without exchange of viewpoints. An employer would establish a scale of wages without consultation with workers. Journeymen would establish their own scale of wages, sometimes inserting the scale in a Bible on which all swore that they would not work for less. The scale was then presented to the employer, and if it was not accepted, the workers stayed away from work until one side conceded to the other. There were no discussions, negotiations, or counter-proposals.

About 1850 Horace Greeley, an American who was both an employer and a union sympathiser, proposed that workers come forward and negotiate with the employer on the basis of reasoned arguments and statistics. This suggestion led eventually to what we now call 'collective bargaining.'

The invention of negotiation represented a significant advance in human relations. Max Ways observes, 'Despite its limitations, abuses, and hazards, negotiation has become an indispensable process in free societies. More effectively than any alternative anybody has thought of so far, it enables us to realize common interests while we compromise conflicting interests. Since these are among the objectives of rational people, negotiation has to be counted among the greatest of human inventions.'[2]

However, negotiation as a process governing the relationship between labour and management is subject to a number of drawbacks. First, the process of negotiation is surrounded by certain ethical ambiguities. Negotiation as best practised is seldom open and candid and is often simply dishonest. Hiding one's true intentions, misinforming the other party, and exploiting the other party's weakness while appearing sincere are all part of the process.

The process of negotiation is not an appropriate way to settle all industrial disputes. Wage negotiations, for example, become a balancing act for the union. Union representatives must expand their constituents' welfare without placing the efficiency of the enterprise in jeopardy. Unfortunately, however, the union has limited information from management about the true competitive position of the firm. Often the two parties become so concerned with victory in a dispute that they forget their mutual obligations and common interests. Ultimately, the interests of both managers and workers may be harmed. The strike or lock-out – the ultimate weapons in the arsenals of labour and management – are tests of will and staying power, not rational means of settling a dispute.

Negotiation is a process that generally results in either domination or compromise – rarely in integration.[3] With domination one side gets what it wants; with compromise neither side gets what it wants. When there is no integration, each party retains the original motives that led to the conflict, and the 'conflict trap' will inevitably lead to new conflicts. As soon as it can the subordinate party will alter the balance of power in its favour.

The process of negotiation itself is flawed because it shapes the perspectives of parties in a manner which makes integration of divergent interests

---

2 Ways 1979, 90
3 Fox and Urwick 1973

difficult. Negotiations often do little more than temporarily paper over divergent interests among parties. When disagreements are not mediated by reference to common goals, there is no incentive for either party to do more than carry out the minimum terms of their agreement, because to do so would be interpreted as weakness by the other party. Divergent interests become more salient and more issues become subject to negotiation. Inevitably accusations of dishonesty, bad faith, and negligence follow.

Negotiation, however, need not take this form. Walton and McKersie (1965) describe 'integrative bargaining' in which goals of the parties are not perceived to be in fundamental conflict; the preferences of the parties can be integrated to the benefit of both or at least to the benefit of one without disadvantage to the other. Integrative bargaining focuses on problem-solving, gathering of information, searching for alternatives, and mutual persuasion – all on the basis of mutuality of interests.

MODELS OF COLLECTIVE BARGAINING

The trade union as 'loyal opposition'
The trade union as 'loyal opposition' has been advanced by Hugh Clegg (1951; 1960) and by Sidney and Beatrice Webb (1894). According to Clegg, opposition is the sine qua non of political democracy. This principle, he contends, is as applicable to the economic enterprise as it is to the larger political system. Just as opposition is a necessary condition for political democracy, so is opposition a necessary condition for industrial democracy. Workers must have countervailing power against management, and the trade union fulfils this role of opposition.

According to this perspective unions cannot join with management in co-managing the enterprise, because the union's role as loyal opposition would thereby be undermined. Clegg observes, 'the trade union cannot ... become the organ of industrial management; there would be no one to oppose the management, and no hope of democracy. Nor can the union enter into an unholy alliance for the joint management of industry, for its opposition functions would then become subordinate and finally stifled.'[4]

Clegg feels that unions run the danger of being co-opted in collaborative arrangements with management and they run the risk of being destroyed in the process. Unions must never become concerned with issues of profits, productivity, or economic survival. The union does not have the technical or

4 Clegg 1951, 131, as quoted by Blumberg 1968, 142

administrative experience to co-manage the business, and hence cannot contribute meaningfully to decision-making in these areas. Clegg insists that the trade union must be autonomous: 'trade unions may negotiate with managers and sign agreements with them, hold discussions with them and try to foster good relations with them, but they must not take this beyond the point where they can choose to act independently if they wish to, for at this point they have ceased to be able to limit and control management; they have become a part of management.'[5]

The fundamental question raised by Clegg is whether or not an opposition is a necessary condition for workplace democracy, as it is for political democracy. Is the trade union to management what the official opposition is to the government in power? Paul Blumberg (1968) argues that it is not. He observes that the essence of democracy is the accountability of leadership to the electorate which has the power to remove that leadership. An opposition may facilitate the selection of alternate leaders, but it is not the essence of democracy. All organizations need criticism from within for the purpose of renewal and the adjustment of goals and priorities among stakeholders. Participation is the process which brings forth new ideas, fresh perspectives, and new leadership. When the trade union becomes the 'loyal opposition,' it becomes an opposition which can never assume power; any opposition party which can only check, protest, or veto the party in power is not a genuine opposition.

The adversarial relationship between the union and management is eloquently supported by Eric Hoffer. Like Clegg, Hoffer feels that it is dangerous for the union to meld its interests with management:

The important point is that this taking the worker for granted occurs not only when management has unlimited power to coerce but also when the division between management and labor ceases to be self-evident. Any doctrine which preaches the oneness of management and labor – whether it stresses their unity in a party, class, race, nation, or even religion – can be used to turn the worker into a compliant instrument in the hands of management. Both Communism and Fascism postulate the oneness of management and labor, and both are devices for the extraction of maximum performance from an underpaid labor force. The preachment of racial unity facilitated the exploitation of labor in our South, in French Canada and in South Africa ... Our sole protection lies in keeping the division between management and labor obvious and matter-of-fact. We want management to manage the best it can, and the workers to protect their interests the best they can. No social

5 Clegg 1960, 28

system will seem to us free if it makes it difficult for the worker to maintain a considerable degree of independence from management ...

The question is whether an independent labor force is compatible with efficient production. For if the attitude of the workers tends to interfere with the full unfolding of the productive process, then the workingman's independence becomes meaningless.

It has been my observation for years on the docks of San Francisco that, while a wholly independent labor force does not contribute to management's peace of mind, it can yet goad management to perfect its organization to keep ever on the lookout for more efficient ways of doing things. Management on the San Francisco waterfront is busy twenty-four hours a day figuring out ways of loading and discharging ships with as few men as possible ...

It is true, of course, that the cleavage between management and labor is a source of strain and strife. But it is questionable whether tranquillity is the boon it is made out to be. The late William Randolph Hearst shrewdly observed that 'whatever begins to be tranquil is gobbled up by something that is not tranquil'. The constant effort to improve and advance is neither automatic nor the result of a leisurely choice between alternatives. In human affairs, the best stimulus for running ahead is to have something we must run from. The chances are that the millennial society, where the wolf and the lamb shall dwell together, will be a stagnant society.[6]

Some unions continue to take the position that increasing productivity is solely management's responsibility, and that unions serve their members best by pursuing improvements in wages, benefits, job security, and working conditions. This adversarial dynamic generally creates a large agenda of unresolved conflicts. The adversarial relationship is a convenient – but nevertheless increasingly inappropriate – way of dealing with issues over which management and the union disagree. This dynamic locks parties into a 'win-lose conflict' which often requires adjudication by impartial third parties.

Ed Finn, the public relations director of the Canadian Brotherhood of Railway Transport and General Workers, observes that the win-lose dynamic is often destructive. 'No doubt, many of our business and union leaders are sophisticated and flexible enough to play this Jekyll-and-Hyde role to be able to distinguish between situations where the adversary approach is appropriate, and where it isn't. But the same cannot be said for most rank and file union members. They can't turn their aversion to the boss on and off, to look upon him as an enemy during contract talks, and as an ally at other times.'[7]

6   Hoffer 1952, 79–82
7   Finn, *Toronto Star*, 7 May 1979, B10

Although the role of trade unions as irretrievably and unequivocably opposed to management is common in the United Kingdom it is usually less so in Canada. However, one example is the relationship between International Nickel Company and the United Steelworkers of America in Sudbury, Ontario. The union endured in a bitter eight-month strike for the sole purpose of bringing the company to its knees. Stephen Lewis, who followed the conflict closely observed, 'I failed to understand the depth of feeling – a feeling so suffused with rage and frustration that whether or not to have a strike was beyond the pale of rational determination. It was irresistible. Unavoidable. So long as Inco behaved like a four-letter word, the union would respond in kind ... This is a fight to the finish.'[8]

The role of union as loyal opposition has become the 'mind set' of this generation of trade union leaders, and this role is carried out even when it is obviously inappropriate. The York University Faculty Association in Toronto, for example, has assumed an adversarial relationship in its dealings with the university administration. The union has insisted that management raise salaries, reduce student / teacher ratios, and avoid faculty lay-offs when these conditions are imposed on the university community by the provincial government. The Faculty Union appears to harbour the belief that the administration ('management') is responsible for the dire financial straits of the university (which it is not) and that management must find a way out of the difficulties (which it cannot do without union support and assistance).

The collaborative model
A second model of collective bargaining is the collaborative model. It is clear from the Swedish experience that collective bargaining can be collaborative and can fit with other forms of workplace democracy. The Tembec experience,[9] the Pioneer Chainsaw experience,[10] and the producer co-operative examples in this study[11] illustrate that workplace democracy is not inconsistent with trade unionism. However, there must be a collaborative relationship between parties. A crisis may be necessary to show that both 'sides' can be reasonable and that both sides have common interests. When common interests are emphasized rather than ignored, there is a far greater potential for a broadening of the collective bargaining agenda to matters of vital concern to management as well as to the rank and file.

8 Lewis, *Sunday Star*, 15 April 1979, A20
9 See appendix I.
10 Clarke 1979
11 See appendix I.

The movement towards collaborative as opposed to adversarial relations is possible for most Canadian unions. There are some unions, however, which are unlikely to enter into collaborative relations with management. Two examples are the Confederation of National Trade Unions (CSN) in Quebec which is engaged in 'war against capitalism,' and the Canadian Union of Postal Workers (CUPW). The constitution of the CUPW explicitly forbids any union collaboration with the management of the Post Office.

The rebuilding of relationships between labour and management is possible if local trade union leaders and local plant managers have the will. Trade unions in Canada have a long-standing tradition of local autonomy, with minimum interference from the national or international union. To the extent that the national office of the union bargains with national objectives in mind and to the extent that the national office pursues ideologically motivated objectives, the less emphasis there will be on building a collaborative relationship with management at the local level.

The increasing complexity of the collective bargaining process also works against collaborative relations. Both management and unions now require the services of technical and professional staff; this development has contributed to the increasing centralization of power and the increasing bureaucratization of both unions and corporations.

A survey of union activists by Kochan, Lipsky, and Dyer (1974) in New York state assesses the issues that are perceived as amenable to joint union-management solution. The results are presented in table 23. It is apparent from this table that a majority of these union activists do not believe that both the company and the union can achieve their objectives at the same time in most areas. However, there does appear to be some union support for joint union-management programs.[12]

Participative mechanisms can arise in unionized organizations. For example, the 'Council of York University Libraries' emerged from the collective bargaining process, and provision for the library council is included in the collective agreement.[13] Among the council's responsibilities is the determination of the merit component of salary increases by peer review. Subjecting isues of this sort to participation can be divisive (as many university faculties will attest) and there must be agreement on basic principles before such a process will work. When the definition of merit is subject to widely varying judgments, and when these differences are not easily reconcilable,

12 Other data reported in the article indicate that collective bargaining was not felt by these activists to be effective in dealing with these issues.
13 See Brown 1979.

TABLE 23
Attitudes of union officers towards selected issues

	Per cent rating issue 'very important'	Per cent rating issue integrative*	Per cent rating issue appropriate for joint program†
Earnings	92	26	6
Fringe benefits	79	48	4
Safety	75	68	41
Job security	68	44	12
Control of work	47	34	54
Adequate resources	46	46	61
Interesting work	41	39	68
Productivity	30	30	51
Work-load	22	29	44

* Per cent reporting that with regard to given issue 'my company and union want to accomplish completely the same thing' or 'my company and union want to accomplish somewhat the same thing.'
† Per cent feeling that the 'best way' to deal with the issue is to 'set up a joint program with management outside collective bargaining.'

participation may not be appropriate. If the divisions within the organization are great, and if the organization is crippled by political factions and antagonisms, then more modest forms of workplace democracy may be appropriate than the forms studied here. With a legacy of acrimonious labor-management conflict, considerable groundwork may be necessary to build up a base of goodwill and common purpose.

The collective agreement negotiated by the Energy and Chemical Workers Union and management at the Shell Chemical Plant in Sarnia, Ontario provides a model of the collaborative relationship. The foreword to the agreement is as follows.

The purpose of the agreement which follows is to establish an enabling framework within which an organizational system can be developed and sustained that will ensure an efficient and competitive world-scale chemical plant operation and provide meaningful work and job satisfaction for employees. Recognizing that there are risks involved and that there are many factors which can place restraints on the extent to which changes can occur, both management and union support and encourage policies and practices that will reflect their commitment to the following principles and values:

Employees are responsible and trustworthy, capable of working together effectively and making proper decisions related to their spheres of responsibilities and work arrangements – if given the necessary authorities, information and training.

Employees should be permitted to contribute and grow to their fullest capability and potential without constraints of artificial barriers, with compensation based on their demonstrated knowledge and skills rather than on tasks being performed at any specific time.

To achieve the most effective overall results, it is deemed necessary that a climate exists which will encourage initiative, experimentation, and generation of new ideas, supported by an open and meaningful two-way communication system.

The remainder of the agreement briefly covers the following ten issues.[14]

1 Recognition: recognizes the union as the sole bargaining agency
2 Plant committee: states the union's right to have a plant committee for negotiation or otherwise and to have a shop steward on every team
3 Grievances: states only that 'there shall be developed and maintained a system to ensure the prompt and equitable resolution of problems at the Plant'
4 Hours of work and rates of pay: states that the basic work week is thirty-seven and one-third hours, that workers are paid on salary, gives the salary levels, and describes schedules, shifts and how they may be altered, overtime pay, and shift bonus
5 Deduction of union dues: company deducts monthly dues for the union
6 Seniority: states that seniority applies only to lay-off and defines seniority and conditions of recall
7 Vacations: the vacation entitlements by years of service are given
8 Statutory holidays: the ten holidays are described as are statutory holiday pay conditions
9 Safety and Health: 'the union, in consultation with team representatives, may appoint two representatives on the Safety Committee ... meetings of this committee which have been called for purposes of Safety or to investigate accidents involved in injury to employees.'
10 Termination of agreement: gives dates of the term of the agreement and time required for notice of termination or revision

This collective agreement has created a good deal of controversy in management and trade union circles. None the less, contracts of this kind will

14 Taken from Davis and Sullivan 1980

become more common as managers and trade union leaders discover that their individual and common interests are best furthered through agreements based on mutual trust and confidence, not on distrust and hostility.

EXPANDING TRADE UNION INVOLVEMENT
IN THE DEMOCRATIC WORKPLACE

Employers in this country bitterly resisted trade union efforts to limit their residual rights outside the boundaries of traditional personnel concerns. However, management decisions in areas which do not directly concern employment (such as changes in production methods and new technology) may nevertheless seriously affect such conditions. Participation in these broader concerns is of obvious advantage to the union. However, participation in these matters in the adversarial mode is to the obvious disadvantage of the employer. In Italy, for example, where the relationship between unions and employers is particularly acrimonious, the trade unions in some sectors have negotiated the right to bargain investment policy and company contributions to local charities.

In the future collective agreements will undoubtedly move towards greater comprehensiveness, more explicit detail, and greater formality. This trend is unfortunate (although it improves due process for union members), because it is excessively rigid. The collective agreement specifies what cannot be done rather than what can be done. The win-lose mentality, and the 'low trust dynamic' generated by the adversarial relationship will inevitably colour all aspects of the relationship between labour and management.

Trade union involvement in collaborative forms of participation will accelerate when management and trade unionists realize that their respective interests can be furthered by co-operation and consultation. Management must perceive that the union will be helpful in obtaining stability in promoting rank and file support of negotiated agreements and in promoting effective communication with the rank and file. Similarly, union officials must feel that management will not attempt to destroy the union, that management will not take arbitrary or unilateral action without union involvement, and that management will support the concept of free collective bargaining.

The movement towards collaborative union-management relations will not come easily or quickly. In cases where trust between the parties has been destroyed (at Inco, for example) collaborative, problem-solving relations may never be achieved. However, the cases studied here (Tembec and Hayes-Dana) demonstrate a possibility and provide an ideal towards which labour and management in other firms might move.

Our discussion of trade unions and workplace democracy will continue in chapters 8 and 9. Before examining how labour and management might move towards collaborative workplace democracy in Canada, we shall examine profit-sharing and employee ownership – two issues which can assist in the movement.

8

Profit-sharing and employee ownership: the economic dimension of workplace democracy

Profit-sharing and employee ownership, like workplace democracy, have remained largely outside the mainstream of management practice in this country. The reason has less to do with objective evidence concerning the effectiveness of these programs than with prevailing management and trade union ideologies.

Stock purchase, incentive, and bonus plans based on profits have long been considered effective means of motivating executives. However, these plans are not generally considered appropriate for production and clerical employees. There is a widespread belief among Canadian and American managers that employee motivation and commitment to the enterprise are purchased by the prevailing wage rate; furthermore, it is widely believed that profit-sharing – by increasing labour's share of profits – reduces the return to shareholders.

Trade union officials fear that profit-sharing does little more than include the worker as a partner with management in assuming the risks of the business, without offering commensurate control over decisions which affect profits. They also fear that the role of the union under profit-sharing will be weakened by dividing worker loyalty between the union and management.

Profit-sharing and employee ownership are rarely discussed in books on workplace democracy, despite the mutually reinforcing relationships among the three concepts. The economic dimension of workplace democracy has been virtually ignored by the organizational theorist. In this chapter profit-sharing and ownership will be defined; the relationship between these concepts and democratic decision-making explored; the empirical evidence concerning the effects of profit-sharing and ownership evaluated; and the potential of profit-sharing and employee ownership to improve the quality of work life of working people will be examined.

PROFIT-SHARING

Profit-sharing may be defined as any arrangement whereby an employer shares with all (or a designated group of) employees the profits derived from the employer's business. The International Congress on Profit Sharing held in Paris, France in 1899 defined profit-sharing as 'An agreement freely entered into, by which the employees receive a share, fixed in advance, of the profits.'[1] The Council of Profit Sharing Industries in Chicago defines profit-sharing as 'Any procedure under which an employer pays or makes available to regular employees subject to reasonable eligibility rules, in addition to prevailing rates of pay, special current and deferred sums based on the profits of the business.'[2]

There are three basic types of profit-sharing plans:[3,4] (1) current distribution plans, (2) deferred pay-out plans,[5] and (3) combination plans. Any of the three major types of plans may be either 'top-hat' or 'broad-based.' A top-hat plan, as the name implies, is restricted to senior managers, while a broad-based plan includes all regular employees, subject to reasonable eligibility rules. In most profit-sharing plans, a formula specified in advance determines how profits will be shared among employees and shareholders. Typically, this formula is stated as a percentage of pre-tax earnings. The formula may also be expressed as a percentage of profits remaining after accounting for shareholder equity.

Current distribution plans
A current distribution plan allocates a share of the firm's profits directly to employees in cash or in company shares. This distribution is typically made annually but may be made at more frequent intervals.

---

1 Metzger and Colletti 1971, 5
2 Ibid.
3 There is a fourth plan – the Profit Sharing Pension Plan – in which payments to the employee pension trust are related to profits. Since the Profit Sharing Pension Plan is a form of pension plan and is designed for the sole purpose of providing retirement security, it is not related to employee participation. The Profit Sharing Pension Plan is described in section 248 of the Income Tax Act.
4 Canadian profit-sharing plans are defined in *Information Circular* 77-1 of the department of national revenue and sections 144 and 147 of the Income Tax Act.
5 The term 'deferred,' when it stands alone, differs in the American and Canadian literatures. In the American literature 'deferred' refers to 'deferred income,' while in the Canadian literature the term refers to 'deferred tax.'

Deferred pay-out plans
Under deferred pay-out plans an employee's share of company profits is placed in a trust fund and distributed at a later date, usually upon the member's retirement, termination of employment, disability, death, or, when permitted, for the purpose of meeting special needs. Also credited to each employee's profit-sharing account are investment earnings, capital gains (or losses), appreciation (or depreciation), and forfeited balances arising from the non-vested termination of other employee accounts.

Combination plans
Combination plans can be based on any combination of current distribution and deferred pay-out plans. One of the great advantages of profit-sharing is its flexibility. A profit-sharing plan can be tailored to reflect the expectations and purposes of any particular company. Plans can be designed according to the philosophy of the employer, the financial condition of the firm, the nature of the work-force, and the nature of the firm's business. By combining current distribution and deferred pay-out plans an employer has available a means of addressing the special needs of some employees or of providing immediate rewards for increased productivity while providing the employee with long-term investment income. One plan can be created for all employees and another for some class of employees (e.g., sales, executive, or blue-collar employees).

Some companies provide 'cafeteria' plans which allow the employee to select a plan with benefits tailored to his or her individual needs. For example, some firms allow the employee to decide the proportion of the profit-sharing allocation to be taken in cash and the proportion to be placed in a deferred trust. Employees with pressing cash requirements can elect to take their profit-sharing allocation in cash, while employees nearing retirement can elect to place their profit-sharing allocation in a trust to provide retirement security.

An evaluation of profit-sharing
Although profit-sharing has attracted relatively little attention in Canada, there is substantial and growing interest in profit-sharing in the United States. In 1954 there were 8,242 registered deferred pay-out profit-sharing plans in the United States; in 1974 this number had grown to 186,244. Currently there are over 250,000 registered deferred payout profit-sharing plans and an estimated 80,000 cash profit-sharing plans in the United States. Today, 26 per cent of all manufacturing companies in the United States with over fifty employees share their profits; one out of three retailers shares its

TABLE 24
Comparison of profit-sharing and non-profit-sharing companies

	Profit-sharing companies	Non-profit-sharing companies
Ratios (1969)		
net income to net worth (%)	12.78	8.00
net income to sales (%)	3.62	2.70
Indices (1969; 1952 = 100)		
sales	358.4	266.0
net worth	376.1	256.7
earnings per common share	410.5	218.8
dividends per common share	293.7	175.3
market price per common share	782.1	397.6
Other measures		
approximate company earnings per employee (1969)	$1,165.00	$647.00
growth of the invested dollar (1952–69)	$9.89	$5.61

profits with its employees; and 44 per cent of banks and trust companies share their profits.

The effects of profit-sharing on company performance have been examined in two major studies by Bert Metzger of the Profit Sharing Research Foundation.[6] The first study compares eight large department store chains with six non-profit-sharing counterparts. A financial comparison of the profit-sharing firms with the non-profit-sharing firms for the period 1952 to 1969 is outlined in table 24.

On all financial measures the profit-sharing companies outperform the non-profit-sharing companies by a substantial margin. Metzger further notes that the superiority of the profit-sharing firms is increasing. The differences in performance in 1958 and 1969 are reported in table 25.

Metzger and Colletti conclude:

On all measures of significance to stockholders, the profit sharing group of companies outperformed the non-profit sharing by *substantial* and *widening* percentages.

Employees in the profit sharing companies helped generate almost twice the level of company earnings per employee as were generated in non-profit sharing com-

6 Metzger and Colletti 1971; Metzger 1975a

TABLE 25
'Superiority gap' of profit-sharing companies
over non-profit-sharing companies

	1958	1969
Ratios		
net income to net worth (per cent)	+54.3	+59.8
net income to sales (per cent)	+36.8	+34.1
Indices		
sales	+7.0	+34.7
net worth	+10.9	+46.5
earnings per common share	+29.5	+87.6
dividends per common share	+18.7	+67.5
market price per common share	+26.9	+96.7
Other measures		
approximate company earnings per employee	+50.3	+80.1
growth of the invested dollar (per cent)	+18.0	+76.3

panies. The profit sharing group also demonstrated more vigorous growth in sales, net worth, average market price, earnings, and dividends per common share.

Department store chains with profit sharing surpassed the non-profit sharers on both profitability ratios (net income to net worth, and net income to sales).[7]

In the second study Metzger (1975a) compares the economic performance (using 1974 data) of thirty-three large, profit-sharing companies with the average economic performance of comparable, but non-profit-sharing firms. Examples of profit-sharing firms in this sample include Xerox Corporation, Procter and Gamble Co., and Sears, Roebuck. The performance comparisons are presented in table 26.

The return on sales for the twenty-three profit-sharing industrials is 28.3 per cent higher than the return on sales for the Fortune 500 industrials; and the return on equity is 5.3 per cent greater. The return on sales for the ten profit-sharing retailers is 96.9 per cent higher than the return on sales for the forty-one Fortune retailers; and the return on equity is 5.2 per cent greater.

In a survey of eighty-three member firms of the Profit Sharing Council of Canada Nightingale (1980) reports that profit-sharing is strongly endorsed by management as an effective means of improving employee morale as well as of enhancing the profitability of the firm. Employee attitudes towards profit-sharing are reported to be positive in 89 per cent of com-

7 Metzger and Colletti 1971, 25

TABLE 26
Performance comparison of profit-sharing and non-profit-sharing companies

Classification	Return on sales (per cent)	Return on shareholder's equity (per cent)
Industrials		
median of Fortune 500 industrials	4.3	13.6
median of twenty-three profit-sharing industrials	6.1	14.6
Retailers		
median of Fortune 41 retailers (excluding nine profit-sharing firms)	1.00	9.1
median of ten profit-sharing retailers	1.85	11.0

panies in this sample. In none of the firms is the attitude judged to be negative. In 84 per cent of the firms, profit-sharing is reported to be an effective means of attracting and holding desirable employees; and 72 per cent of firms report that profit-sharing is effective in improving employee team-work and co-operation.

Survey results indicate that profit-sharing has been installed in these firms for three basic reasons: improving team-work and co-operation; providing economic security for employees; and giving employees a better understanding of the factors entering into business success.

The macro effects of profit-sharing
Beyond the level of the individual firm profit-sharing has the potential for addressing many social and economic ills. Profit-sharing, if widely adopted throughout North American industry, could significantly improve labour-management relations. The abysmal strike and lock-out record of Canadian and American firms over the past decade has drawn frequent comment. Labour and management all too frequently view the other party as an adversary, locked into an inevitable 'win-lose' relationship. Labour, with no interest in the firm and no sense of responsibility for the firm's future, uses its power to wring as many concessions as possible from management. Management views the union as an obstacle to the efficient operation of the enterprise and deals with it accordingly.

By giving employees a tangible financial stake in the enterprise and the opportunity of seeing how company profits are generated and distributed, the spirit of adversarial relations might well be significantly reduced.

A profit-sharing payment is also a non-inflationary wage because the wage is tied to the creation of wealth. By encouraging saving, profit-sharing may also have a counter-inflationary impact. Further, when profits are calculated according to an established and explicit formula, profits provide an 'objective' standard by which employee wages can be determined.

Profit-sharing also provides a means of broadening capital ownership. Increasingly, capital is concentrated in fewer and fewer hands, and consequently, fewer and fewer people have any stake in our economic system other than a wage or pension which most take for granted.

Peter Drucker (1976) has argued that in the United States capital ownership is widely distributed through employee claims on pension trusts. Pension trusts currently own 25 per cent of the equity capital of major American companies, and Drucker predicts that this figure will rise to 50 per cent by 1985. This phenomenon has been called 'pension fund socialism.'

Drucker's analysis, however, is flawed in several respects. First, socialism in practice has generally led to centralized state control of the means of production. Employee ownership of the means of production is capitalism, not socialism.[8]

Secondly, Drucker overestimates the control which pension funds exercise over companies. Drucker argues that if 'control' of a corporation is defined as control of one-third of the corporation's common stock, then most large American corporations are indeed controlled by pension funds. Control of one-third of a corporation's shares might well be sufficient to give an individual control (assuming other holdings are scattered), but most pension trusts hold no more than 5 per cent of the shares of any individual company. The pension fund consists simply of a class of small investors, and this class in no way exercises control over the corporation.

Thirdly, Drucker misunderstands the meaning of 'ownership' and the role of pension funds. A pension fund, like a bank, trust company, or insurance company, is a form of financial intermediary. The balance sheet of a financial intermediary shows large assets offset by nearly as large liabilities and the relatively small equity of the residual owners. The earnings of the intermediary are derived from the difference between the yield of the assets and the amount paid on the liabilities. The highly levered equity owners consequently have an incentive to invest the assets of the intermediary in high-yield uses.

In a pension fund the employer assumes the role of residual owner and the employee the role of the owner of the fund's liabilities. The employee is

---

8 Not all socialists are centralists; however, the dominant form of socialism has been centralized state control.

typically offered a pension the value of which remains fixed, regardless of the performance of the fund. The employer wants to fulfil his obligations to pensioners as cheaply as possible. Unexpectedly good performance reduces employer contributions and poor performance increases contributions. Consequently, aggregate profits do not ultimately accrue to workers as 'owners' of pension funds in the same way that they accrue to private holders of company shares.

Successful profit-sharing

Profit-sharing is not a panacea. Profit-sharing, like any management tool, can be used in an effective or ineffective manner. Some firms, such as Procter and Gamble or S.C. Johnson and Son, have shared profits with employees for more than sixty years, while other firms have discontinued their plans because few benefits either to employees or to the company were evident.

Research and experience indicate that effective profit-sharing plans are based on five principles. First, the coverage of the successful plan is as broad as possible. All employees in the firm who contribute to the generation of profits should be eligible to participate in the profit-sharing plan; eligibility rules are generous; that is, all non-probationary employees are eligible to participate in the plan, and there are few restrictions (such as rank, seniority, or income) to membership.

Secondly, the successful profit-sharing plan.is combined with some form of employee participation in decision-making. The profit-sharing plan unites labour and management in the pursuit of a common objective and ensures that decisions made by employees at all levels will be consistent with this common objective.

Thirdly, the successful plan is almost always associated with an effective means of communicating with employees. That is, profit-sharing cannot be treated simply as another benefit to be installed and forgotten. Bernard A. Diekman, former president of the Profit Sharing Council of Canada, once commented, 'The amount of profit shared – as important as this is – comes second to the manner in which profit-sharing is communicated to employees.'[9]

Fourthly, labour and management must have confidence in and respect for each other. Management must feel that workers will put forth extra effort if given the opportunity to share in the success of the enterprise; and labour must have confidence in management's honesty, good intentions, and ability to earn profits.

9 Bernard Diekman, personal communication

Finally, firms with successful profit-sharing plans provide wages and benefits comparable to those of their industry. Profit-sharing will not work if it is a substitute for prevailing wages and benefits.

Profit-sharing and trade unionism
Trade union opposition to profit-sharing is based on several considerations. First, profit-sharing is a contingent income, and is associated with an element of risk. This unpredictability conflicts with a major trade union goal: the promotion of income and employment security. Most trade unionists would prefer to bargain for a fixed wage and a guaranteed pension annuity.

Secondly, profit-sharing is a form of co-operation, and is perceived by many trade unionists as a means of persuading workers to be satisfied with gains which are less than the gains which could be guaranteed through collective bargaining.

Thirdly, many trade unionists are opposed to profit-sharing because workers do not participate in many of the decisions which affect the profitability of the enterprise. They argue that profitability is largely a function of policy decisions in which workers rarely take part and is not a function of decisions made on the shop-floor by the worker.

Fourthly, employees or their union representatives are rarely allowed any real voice in the administration of profit-sharing plans.

Despite these objections, profit-sharing is not incompatible with trade unionism. In fact, the wages negotiated through collective bargaining are a form of profit-sharing. Under collective bargaining a formula is determined for the division of the firm's surplus. This decision is made in advance of the creation of profits, and the formula is determined on the basis of the relative power of management and the union. This process is, as Douglas Fraser once described it, an attempt to 'divide up the pie before you put it in the oven.'

The difficulties with traditional collective bargaining and the advantages of profit sharing over conventional wage negotiations were seen by Walter Reuther. He once observed,

The breakdown in collective bargaining in recent years is due to the difficulty of labor and management trying to equate the relative equity of the worker and the stockholder and the consumer in advance of the facts ...

If the workers get too much, then the argument is that that triggers inflationary pressures, and the counter argument is that if they don't get their equity, then we have a recession because of inadequate purchasing power. We believe this approach [profit-sharing] is a rational approach because you cooperate in creating the abundance that makes the progress possible, and then you share that progress after the fact, and not before the fact.

Profit sharing would resolve the conflict between management apprehensions and worker expectations on the basis of solid economic facts as they materialize rather than on the basis of speculation as to what the future might hold ... If the workers had defined assurance of equitable shares in the profits of the corporations that employ them, they would see less need to seek an equitable balance between their gains and soaring profits through augmented increases in basic wage rates. This would be a desirable result from the standpoint of stabilization policy because profit sharing does not increase costs. Since profits are a residual, after all costs have been met, and since their size is not determinable until after customers have paid the prices charged for the firm's products, profit sharing as such cannot be said to have any inflationary impact upon costs and prices ... Profit sharing in the form of stock distributions to workers would help to democratize the ownership of America's vast corporate wealth.[10]

A rational, non-adversarial method of wage determination is badly needed in this country. The combination of a wage survey and profit-sharing is one such method. An annual wage survey, conducted jointly by management and union representatives, would determine the wage levels in the firm's industrial sector and in the firm's locality. For each class of employee and for each trade the ranges of wages would be determined. Any firm would have a negotiated policy about employee wages (a firm, for example, might have a policy of paying its workers at the fiftieth percentile for all classifications of employee, or at the seventy-fifth percentile of the relevant comparison group of companies). In addition to this wage employees would share in company profits.

Through this procedure employees would be guaranteed a viable wage as well as an opportunity to supplement it through profit-sharing. This process, more than our current methods, accounts for the financial condition of the firm and the role that employees at all levels play in the creation of profits.

Inevitably there will be issues at the workplace on which both parties cannot agree. These differences can be handled through the usual grievance or arbitration procedures. Profit-sharing, however, would broaden the domain of mutual interests and would provide an opportunity for more communication between the parties.

Profit-sharing need not undermine trade unionism and weaken worker loyalty to unions. Profit-sharing would undermine the union only in situa-

10 Reuther 1977, 1–2

tions where the union's sole purpose or justification is opposition to management. Profit-sharing can work only when the relationship between labour and management is based on a modicum of trust and co-operation.[11]

EMPLOYEE OWNERSHIP

Employee ownership can take one of three forms: (1) the producer co-operative, (2) ownership acquired through conventional purchase of shares, and (3) employee stock ownership plans (ESOPs). Producer co-operatives are relatively rare in Canada and the United States. Membership in a producer co-operative is typically acquired through the purchase of a 'share' of the enterprise. Every member of the co-operative must purchase a share and the share entitles the holder to a portion of the income (surplus) of the firm (usually a portion equal to that of other members) and to participate in the decision-making of the co-operative on a 'one person, one vote' basis.[12]

Alternatively, employee ownership can be acquired through conventional means. That is, employees may purchase company shares on the open market.[13,14] Stock purchase plans are based on a philosophy which holds that

11 There currently exists no objective comparison of the frequency of strikes and lock-outs in profit-sharing and non-profit-sharing firms. Among the 150 members of the Profit Sharing Council of Canada with broad-based plans, there has been only one strike among member firms in the last twenty years. This strike, at Lake Ontario Steel at Whitby, Ontario occurred in 1979 and was called by the United Steelworkers of America over the issue of vacations and vacation bonus pay. The company plan calls for the distribution of 15 per cent of company profits for the previous financial year to all employees in April of the following year. It is interesting to note that some union members collected their $1,200 profit-sharing allotment during the strike, and this payment assisted them in holding out for improved benefits.

A division of this firm, Sheerness Steel Company in England, was the only steel plant to continue operation during the 1980 steel strike. Employees, who share in company profits, voted to continue operation when union members of all other firms in England voted to strike.

12 See appendix I for a detailed analysis of the producer co-operative.

13 Stock option plans are governed by sections 7 and 53 of the Income Tax Act. Under the Act the stock option benefit is defined as the difference between the market value of the shares and the purchase price. This benefit is taxed as ordinary income in the year received except when the shares are of 'Canadian-controlled private corporations.' When the stock option plan provides shares of Canadian-controlled private corporations, the employee will be taxed on a capital gains basis in the year the shares are sold. The employee must hold the shares for two years to qualify for this special tax treatment. Since employees are not permitted to deduct any expenses incurred by the stock option plan, there is no immediate financial benefit to the employer.

14 See appendix I.

all employees should have the right to own a share of the firm which employs them.

Conventional share ownership can also be obtained through joint trusts operated by unions on behalf of employees. Tembec Forest Products Limited[15] operates on this principle.

The third form of employee ownership, the employee stock ownership plan (ESOP), has been heralded by its proponents as a means of strengthening the free enterprise system. The ESOP is a form of employee ownership that takes advantage of U.S. tax laws to encourage firms to issue stock to their employees. Although ESOPs are not currently encouraged under Canadian tax laws, there is growing interest in the concept in this country.[16]

The ESOP was first proposed by Louis Kelso in three books: The Capitalist Manifesto (1956) with Mortimer Adler; The New Capitalists (1961) also with Adler; and Two-Factory Theory: The Economics of Reality (1967) with Patricia Hetter.[17] Although there are several forms of ESOP, the most popular is the 'leveraged' ESOP.[18] A company creating a leveraged ESOP will sell, for example, $1 million worth of newly issued stock to its employee trust. The trust pays for the stock by borrowing $1 million from a bank, with the company guaranteeing the loan. The company then annually pays the trust amounts of cash equal to the loan payments and interest required by the trust. The money is then passed by the trust to the bank. As the loan is repaid, the shares (or the dollar value of the shares) are allocated to employee accounts according to a predetermined formula. Contributions to employee accounts are limited to 15 per cent of the employee's annual income and taxes are paid when the shares are withdrawn from the trust by the employee.

The money paid to the trust by the company is tax deductible. Consequently, the company obtains deductions on both principal and interest. With the principal amounting in this example to $1 million, the tax savings, assuming a 50 per cent tax rate, would be $500,000.

---

15 Ibid.
16 A recent DNR ruling in the case of Supreme Aluminum Industries has effectively created an ESOP for Canadian companies with a deferred profit-sharing plan which invests in shares of the employer.
17 The ESOP concept was translated into practice by the following bills: the Regional Rail Reorganization Act of 1973, the Employee Retirement Income Security Act of 1974, the Trade Act of 1974, the Tax Reduction Act of 1975, the Accelerated Capital Formation Act of 1975, the Jobs Creation Act of 1975, and the Tax Reform Act of 1976.
18 A non-leveraged ESOP could be created through the conversion of an existing profit-sharing plan into an ESOP.

Dividends follow the shares; that is, they become part of the holdings of individual accounts or they are added to the value of the shares held by the trust if they are not immediately allocated to individuals. Voting rights for the shares – a matter of obvious importance to employees – may be held by the trustees of the plan or may be passed on to employees as they are vested.

When employees retire or leave the firm, they may either take possession of their shares, or if permitted by the plan, 'put' the shares to the company (closely held companies should allow such 'puts,' since if they do not, employees who leave may find themselves holding unmarketable shares). The company would not ordinarily give itself a 'call' right, although it may have the right of first refusal on shares former employees wish to sell.

An ESOP differs from profit sharing in the following ways: (1) an ESOP *must* invest primarily in employer securities; (2) an ESOP *must* make distribution in employer shares; and (3) an ESOP *requires* some annual contribution to the trust, regardless of whether a profit has been made.

The ESOP in perspective
U.S. legislation requires that an ESOP must be 'for the exclusive benefit of the participants,' although financial incentives are offered to the firm to encourage the introduction of an ESOP. The principal advantage of an ESOP to the employee is the opportunity it provides to become an owner of the enterprise. An ESOP trust, unlike a profit-sharing trust, is able to utilize company credit for the purchase of shares to be given to employees. In effect, the ESOP trust incurs the same risk which the company normally assumes when it borrows money. That is, the investment from the borrowed money should earn a rate of return at least equal to the interest cost of the loan plus earnings per share equal to those before the loan.

The employee ownership achieved through an ESOP should improve morale and productivity. In the short term increased productivity results in greater dividend income; in the long term increased productivity results in increases in the value of employee shares. However, the employee has no assurance that he will ultimately receive benefits from share ownership, even if he meets or exceeds his performance targets. Even if a benefit is received, there is no guarantee that the benefit will be commensurate with his effort. When the company operates in an economic environment which provides an immediate and direct link between employee motivation and the value of the firm's shares, an ESOP can be an effective means of ensuring company survival. However, to the extent that the firm's fortunes are dependent upon general economic conditions or factors beyond the firm's control, the link between employee effort and the value of the employee's shares may be rather tenuous. In such circumstances ESOPs may do little to enhance employee motivation.

The ESOP could be used as a means of promoting 'industrial democracy,' although not all ESOPs will broaden employee participation in decision-making. Shares allocated to an ESOP need not carry voting rights. Even if shares with voting rights are allocated to the ESOP, the voting rights may be retained by the trustees. Banks loaning capital to ESOPs have insisted that the trustees control the portion of the stock which represents unpaid collateral, and in new corporations trustees have generally retained voting rights until the loan has been completely repaid.

At the very least, however, employees as shareholders will demand more information about management decisions. Management in firms with an ESOP must be psychologically prepared to accept employees as partners and to disclose financial matters and management policy to employees.

The effects of employee ownership
Most studies of the effects of employee ownership are case studies and are largely anecdotal in nature. There are four studies, however, which are based on large sample comparisons of employee-owned and conventionally managed companies. All four studies present evidence supporting the superiority of employee ownership over conventional practice.

A comparison of thirty ESOP firms with thirty conventional counterparts reported by Conte and Tannenbaum (1977) demonstrates that the ESOP firms have slightly higher profit levels than the conventional firms. Conte and Tannenbaum found that the largest single predictor of profitability was unrelated to employee participation, worker representation on the board of directors, the nature of employee-shareholder voting rights, and whether ownership was direct or based on an ESOP trust.

Friedland (1971) studied a sample of companies drawn from the Toronto Stock Exchange with and without executive stock option plans. A valuation model was used to determine the relative stock price performance of stock option and non-stock-option companies and to identify the financial variables which account for the differences. Friedland found that differences could not be accounted for by financial variables. However, an analysis of residuals (those differences not accounted for by financial variables) revealed that in three of the four industry groups studied (extraction, services, and transport, but not manufacturing) companies with stock option plans tended to outperform companies without stock option plans.

Bernstein (1974) reports a study of eighteen plywood manufacturing firms in Oregon and Washington which are owned and operated by employees.

Collectively, these firms account for one-eighth of American plywood production. The firms range in size from eighty to 450 employees. Bernstein presents evidence showing that the employee-owned firms are more productive than their conventionally managed counterparts. He observes that when several of these firms were challenged by the Internal Revenue Service to justify the higher-than-average wages paid to employees (wages are tax-deductible), the companies were able to justify this practice to the satisfaction of IRS auditors. According to the IRS ruling the higher wages were warranted by productivity levels 25 per cent to 60 per cent greater than the national average of conventional firms.

Russell, Hochner, and Perry (1977) present evidence from a dozen employee-owned refuse collection companies in the San Francisco area. They report higher wages and higher productivity in the employee-owned enterprises than in their conventionally managed counterparts.

O'Toole (1979) in a recent appraisal of employee ownership concludes that the effects of employee ownership on morale, motivation and productivity appear most positive when: (1) ownership is conventional (that is, through direct ownership of shares, rather than through an ESOP trust); (2) ownership is broad-based (that is, employees at all levels are eligible to participate); and (3) ownership represents a significant proportion of equity.

Although the evidence is not overwhelming, the few careful studies undertaken of employee ownership demonstrate that it has worked in some circumstances, and that in the short run it can be more effective than conventional owner-operated businesses.

THE EUROPEAN PERSPECTIVE ON
PROFIT-SHARING AND EMPLOYEE OWNERSHIP

Interest in profit-sharing and employee share ownership is not limited to North America. There have been calls for broadened capital ownership in most western European countries. These plans have diverse labels: in Britain, 'National Capital Saving'; in Sweden, 'The Meidner Plan'; in Denmark, 'Economic Democracy'; in the Netherlands, 'Capital Growth Sharing'; and in Germany, 'National Profit Sharing.'

Most of these European programs, however, are based on a political ideology which differs substantially from the ideology underlying profit-sharing and employee ownership in Canada. Most of the western European programs are part of a larger social program of redistributing wealth throughout all sectors of the society. If enacted, proposals in Sweden, the Netherlands, and West Germany would concentrate power in a few hands, rather than diffuse power to the rank and file employee. In addition, under some European plans employee income and benefits would not necessarily be related to employee motivation, productivity, or even company profits.

These European programs are not likely to find favour in North America; their adoption would undoubtedly intensify the battle between labour and capital. Even in Europe employer opposition has been fierce. Nevertheless, these plans are of interest, because they demonstrate that legislative initiatives in the areas of employee ownership and profit-sharing are not limited to Canada or the United States.

In *Sweden* the share ownership plan is commonly referred to as the 'Meidner Plan.' Under this plan, a 'wage earner's' fund would be established and would be administered by trade union officials. Swedish companies employing more than fifty workers would contribute 20 per cent of their annual pre-tax profits to this fund. Investment income of the fund would not be distributed to individuals but rather would be used to promote trade union endeavours in the areas of education, training, and research. A major objective of the Meidner Plan is to increase worker influence over industry. According to most estimates within thirty years control of Swedish industry would pass to unions. This plan encountered stiff management opposition, and with the defeat of the Social Democratic Party in 1976 the plan was tabled for further study.

In *Denmark* there has also been interest in union-controlled funds, although after twelve years of intensive lobbying by unions and the Social Democrats, the provisions have yet to be passed into law. The Danish plan is one of the most radical of all western European programs. The proposed legislation requires companies to contribute 0.5 per cent of their total wage bill, gradually rising to 5 per cent over a period of years, to a central fund to be administered by union officials. Employees could withdraw their allocations after seven years. This plan has encountered strong management opposition.

In 1975 the government in the *Netherlands* proposed a profit-sharing program which would allocate 20 per cent of the gross annual profits of firms making more than $90,000 per year (in 1977 dollars). The fund would be administered by government appointees and union representatives. The fund would be used to purchase shares for employees of firms which contributed to the fund as well as to increase the pensions of employees in firms not contributing to the fund.

In *West Germany* since 1959 an 'investment wage,' in addition to the regular wage negotiated by collective bargaining, has been allocated to employee accounts for a five-year period. Matching government allocations are made to employee accounts for the purpose of encouraging savings and capital accumulation. At the end of a five-year period employees can withdraw their funds. A further proposal in 1974 would have required firms with annual profits greater than $200,000 to contribute up to 10 per cent of their profits to a fund administered by the company and the union. The contributions would be frozen for up to twelve years in the fund. This fund would invest in areas of the economy where capital was required. The proposal was never enacted.

In *France* a law enacted in 1967 requires firms employing more than 100 persons and obtaining at least 5 per cent return on capital to set aside a 'special participation reserve' for employees. This fund is to be invested in shares for the benefit of employees and the government provides tax incentives to encourage employee share purchasing.

It is unlikely that any of the western European union-managed plans will be enacted into law within the foreseeable future.

THE FULLY DEMOCRATIC WORKPLACE

Profit-sharing and employee ownership, when combined with democratic decision-making structures, create the 'fully democratic' workplace. Four of the ten democratic organizations studied here (Supreme Aluminum Industries, Tembec Forest Products, Lincoln Electric, and Canadian Tire) combine all three dimensions.

The values identified in chapter 4 support all three practices: participation in profits, ownership, and decision-making. These practices are mutually reinforcing; an organization with a successful program in any one will gravitate towards introducing the others, although market or technological constraints may preclude the introduction of one or other of the practices.

The relative effects of the three programs on employee well-being cannot be assessed empirically with available evidence. Although controlled comparisons of firms with different combinations of programs have never been reported, and although such comparisons on this sample of companies would leave uncontrolled sector, technology, size, and location of the company, some predictions can be made. The most powerful of the three programs is participation in decision-making, followed by profit-sharing and ownership. Significant gains in employee outcomes beyond those of the conventional hierarchical organization can be achieved by any single program; combinations of the programs will provide further gains, although the marginal gain will be less than the marginal gain attained by adopting the first program.

Profit-sharing and employee ownership hold enormous (and as yet untapped) potential for reinforcing democratic decision-making practices in the workplace. Profit-sharing and employee ownership, because they are more compatible with prevailing ideology and practice in the workplace, may be an effective means of creating a unity of purpose and a positive labour-management climate which will facilitate the introduction of democratic decision-making.

9

Workplace democracy in perspective

Democratic workplaces have been shown to differ significantly from their hierarchically managed counterparts on the dimensions of values, structure, processes, and outcomes. The ten democratic organizations are found to fit the 'democratic' model of organization, and the ten hierarchical organizations are found to fit more closely the 'hierarchical' model of organization. The nature of work has been compared in democratic and hierarchical organizations and few differences have been found; the effects of work on employee well-being have been explored, and these effects – like the effects of workplace democracy – have been found to be significant and far-reaching. The relationship between profit-sharing / ownership and workplace democracy has been explored, and the concepts are found to be mutually reinforcing. The role of trade unionism and collective bargaining in workplace democracy was explored, and although Canadian and American trade unionists remain opposed to collaborative forms of workplace democracy, trade unionism is found to be compatible with the concept of workplace democracy.

In this final chapter the issues examined in the book will be placed in perspective. Matters of organizational and public policy will be raised and new directions proposed. This discussion will be guided by the following questions:

– What is the proper role of the work organization in promoting the values and ideals of democratic society?
– In light of the historical evolution of employee rights and managerial authority in the workplace, what forms of workplace democracy are likely to evolve in the future?
– What forms of workplace democracy – board level representation, works councils, Scanlon plans, producer co-operatives, self-directing work

groups – hold the greatest potential for reducing employee alienation, while preserving or enhancing the economic performance of the enterprise?
- What role can profit-sharing and employee ownership play in reinforcing workplace democracy?
- Do trade unions have a role to play in collaborative forms of workplace democracy?

WORK ORGANIZATIONS IN DEMOCRATIC SOCIETY

The democratic process is as applicable to the work organization as it is to the political sphere. Authoritarian practices at the workplace remain one of the more conspicuous anomalies of our democratic society. As Irving Bluestone points out, 'the workplace is probably the most authoritarian environment in which the adult finds himself. Its rigidity and denial of freedom leads people to live a double life; at home they enjoy substantially the autonomy and self-fulfilment of free citizens; at work they are subject to constant regimentation, supervision and control of others.'[1]

Democracy at the societal level as well as at the organizational level cannot function without a structure of rules to ensure fairness and equality of rights. To the question, 'are formal structures necessary for participative processes?', proponents of the human relations school answer 'no.'

The proponents of workplace democracy, however, answer 'yes.' Formal structure is a necessary (but not sufficient) condition for workplace democracy. The rules defining the decision-making rights and responsibilities of organization members are a reflection of the commitment of the two major stakeholders to workplace democracy. Rules guarantee that all parties will be bound by defined procedures, and that participation will not be a privilege to be granted and withdrawn at will but will be an ongoing right of all organization members.

Management cannot 'play' with formal decision-making rights and responsibilities. Democratic decision-making is not a management technique – such as MBO, transactional analysis, sensitivity training – to be experimented with on an ad hoc basis and then discarded when expected results are not forthcoming. By placing increased power, discretion, and information in the hands of employees (who may choose not to exercise this power or discretion in a manner acceptable to management), expectations about employee

1 Bluestone, quoted in Rosow 1974, 108

rights are greatly increased. Programs of workplace democracy cannot be withdrawn without incurring substantial rank and file dissatisfaction.

The agenda for reform
The role of the work organization must be redefined if it is to fulfil its obligations to promote and uphold our liberal democratic ideals. To begin with, the term 'efficiency' should be broadened to include the hidden costs of the workplace which are not currently reckoned in the conventional definition of 'efficiency.' The employer has a responsibility to employees as well as to shareholders. This is not to say that an employer has a responsibility to create the conditions necessary for employee self-fulfilment without considering the effects of such a policy on the economic performance of the firm, but it does mean that the employer has a responsibility to create conditions at the workplace which minimize alienation, stress, ill health, and dissatisfaction, to the extent permitted by technological and economic constraints. Unfortunately, in most workplaces technological and bureaucratic imperatives dominate considerations of human values and personal well-being.

Most individuals have little opportunity to experience the democratic process at the workplace. Our democratic political institutions will inevitably be weakened by the failure of the work organization to uphold and strengthen democratic ideals. The mission of the work organization should include, among other things, the enhancement and promotion of political and social ideals.

The mix of abilities, motivations, and creativity of the work-force should be defined as a resource to the firm just like technological and capital resources. Despite manifest evidence that those who do the work (and hence those who are most familiar with it) can play an important role in improving the economic performance of the firm, few organizations effectively utilize these resources. Management continues to oppose changes in the existing authority structure of the workplace because of the widespread perception that the worker is hired to perform a specific task and cannot be counted on to contribute his creativity and enthusiasm to the organization.

The growing recognition that there are legitimate stakeholders in addition to shareholders and management is another manifestation of the changing organizational creed. Stakeholders who are entitled to participate in the affairs of the organization are limited to those persons or groups who have demonstrated a commitment to the organization, either through financial investment or through years of service. Stakeholders entitled to participate in decision-making include owners, debtors, employees, and members of the community who require the support and income generated by the company (especially in single-industry towns). Former employees (now on pension) might also be considered legitimate stakeholders. Union efforts to improve pensions for retired employees reflect this perception of the retired employee as a legitimate stakeholder in the enterprise.

Organization theory has neglected this political dimension of the work organization. There are some obvious surface similarities between organizations and governments: organizations pay salaries, provide medical plans, and retirement income; they offer social and recreational facilities; they assist their members with personal plans, housing, and education; they have 'laws' and codes of conduct; they have a judiciary – that is, ways of resolving conflicts among competing interests; and they have 'classes,' coalitions, and interest groups.[2]

The spectre of political stalemate, internecine political intrigue, and organizational paralysis is often raised by proponents of the status quo if groups with differing interests and goals were allowed to participate in organizational decision-making. What happens if some stakeholders continue to disagree with some or all of the goals of the organization as defined by other stakeholders? Would workers, if given an opportunity to participate in decision-making, consent to economically motivated plans to reduce the size of the work-force?

The principle proposed here is that employees have the *right* to participate in decisions which affect them as legitimate stakeholders in the enterprise. They also must bear responsibility for these decisions.

In those cases where improved quality of working life adversely affects productivity, employees along with other stakeholders should have the right to participate in deciding what, if any, trade-off is to be made. The pursuit of 'efficiency' often creates costs (boredom, alienation, loss of livelihood) which must be borne by employees, and employees should have the right of determining the trade-offs between keeping their fellow-workers employed, and their incomes and long-term job security.

To be more specific, employees should have the right to decide with management on the introduction of new equipment that might displace some of them. Should they decide against the introduction of the equipment, they will all bear the costs which accrue to the organization's loss of com-

---

2 Lakoff and Rich (1973) use the term 'private government' to mean 'organization.' The view of organization as a political-economic system has been proposed by Kanter (1977), Perrow (1979), and Lindblom (1977).

petitive position. The essential point is that they have the *right* to make (and take responsibility for) this decision.

Mary Parker Follett argued that interest, responsibility and power formed an 'indissoluble partnership.' She illustrates this principle with the following example.

You should never give authority faster than you can develop methods for the workers taking responsibility for that authority. We find also that we should not give workers authority without some corresponding stake in the business. In a certain store which has a form of profit-sharing, the employees voted one December not to open the store on the day after Christmas, after taking into account the number of people likely to come out on that day against the expenses of the operation. But in the case of another holiday when the same question came up, thinking that this time there would be no appreciable effect on the numbers of people shopping, they voted to open. They had the 'power' in both cases, and if that 'power' had been divorced from a stake in the business, they would probably have voted in both cases to close the store. Interest, responsibility, power – perhaps here is an indissoluble partnership.'[3]

Employees who own the enterprise can determine any goal they wish for the organization, such as income or employment maximization, or social benefit to the community. From the evidence of this study there is no reason to believe that employees, when given the opportunity, would pursue goals which differ in any important respects from the goals pursued by professional managers. Those who believe that a more humane and socially conscious organization would emerge from significant employee participation in decision-making will be disappointed. An exception to this statement might be community relations. Since workers live in the community, not at some distance away like many influential stakeholders, they would tend to be more socially responsible regarding the impact of the organization on the community – if no loss of employment were entailed.

An organization is a resource to be used for the pursuit of certain interests. In the past the interests of the founders and owners have been predominant; in the future the interests of employees will receive greater attention. The interests of employees in the democratic workplaces in this sample are in large measure compatible with the interests of the employer. Furthermore, their positions on major organizational decisions have been similar to those of managers and owners.

3 Mary Parker Follett in Fox and Urwick 1973, 81

Many, however, would disagree with this proposition. Vanek (1971), for example, argues that those who succeed in business are motivated by materialism and individualism, and their practices are often ruthless and self-interested. Workers in control of their work organizations would, he believes, act more responsibly and selflessly.

Dominant coalitions of stakeholders may well emerge and limit the diversity of opinion within the work organization. Selznick (1949) uses the term 'co-optation' to describe the process whereby new elements are absorbed into the leadership or policy-determining structure of an organization as a means of averting threat to the stability or existence of the organization. Examples abound of trade union leaders, government regulators, and critics of organizations being absorbed by dominant stakeholder interests.[4]

Workplace democracy and the redistribution of wealth
Most of the discussion of workplace democracy in Canada has focused on institutional arrangements and representation mechanisms; to date, it has not confronted the fundamental issues of the effect of workplace democracy on the private ownership-market-economy.

Workplace democracy may be founded on the ideals of equality, but 'equality of end result' (à la Rawls 1971) is not a necessary result. Although the gradients of outcomes and power are less in the democratic than in the hierarchical organizations, the gradients of income are identical in the two types of organization. Even in co-operative organizations the gradients of income are no different from those in their hierarchically managed counterparts. Market constraints limit the ability of any organization to underpay its senior managers and overpay its rank and file workers.

THE EVOLUTION OF WORKPLACE DEMOCRACY

Employee rights, power, and freedom will continue on the trajectory established over the past century. In the future there will be more employee participation in decision-making, greater employee protection against arbitrary and subjective treatment at the workplace, and greater emphasis on the employee as a positive and valued contributor to the organization. These changes will come about partly through statutory means and partly through a change in the values of organizational leaders. Democratic values must eventually penetrate the workplace and, as they do, organizational practices will evolve in the democratic direction. These changes will require a rethinking of managerial responsibilities.

4 Dowling 1978

Leadership: new challenges
The emergence of workplace democracy in the industrialized west will present new challenges for the leaders of work organizations. Ironically, leadership is more important in the democratic workplace than in the hierarchically managed workplace. Today's business and trade union leaders, who are preoccupied with their day-to-day responsibilities, must become what Selznick (1949) calls 'institutional leaders.' They cannot allow themselves to become preoccupied with technical matters; they must shape the 'character' of their organizations by promoting and protecting the values of the organization and by guiding the multiple interests of stakeholders towards common goals.

The critical task of reconceptualizing the mission of the modern work organization and creating new values supportive of this re-defined mission has been left by default to other institutions in our society. What is needed from business and trade union leaders is a compelling statement of the principles by which they lead and a vigorous program to implement these principles in their organizations. Inspired, selfless, and moral leadership – responsible to the governed – must be developed, despite the many obstacles.

Workplace democracy limits unilateral control of superiors over subordinates and provides an institutional check on abuses of power; ironically, democratic decision-making is implemented by those who are least likely to abuse their power. Work organizations most in need of guaranteed employee rights in decision-making are those which are least likely to implement democratic decision-making. The acceptance of the inevitability of conflict between different stakeholders and the reliance on open problem-solving rather than confrontation and coercion to manage this conflict are rarely found among today's business leaders.

Supervision: new pressures
Although there is little evidence that first-line supervision and middle managers in democratic workplaces are adversely affected by the rights and prerogatives of their subordinates, supervisors rarely embrace the concept of democratic decision making with enthusiasm.[5,6] Many supervisors follow the 'command-and-obey' principles of an earlier era and cannot adopt the participative styles demanded in the democratic work organization.

5 This phenomenon has been noted by Tannenbaum et al. (1974) and by Herzberg (1966) and his colleagues: 'job enrichment for subordinates means job impoverishment for supervisors.'
6 See control graph in table 10. Supervisors in democratic organizations are less powerful than their counterparts in hierarchical organizations.

Opposition to shop-floor democracy by first-line supervisors represents one of the most serious obtacles to its introduction in North American workplaces. The successful implementation of democratic decision-making normally requires many years. Time is needed to overcome the reticence of many supervisors to experiment with new and untried methods; and time is needed to document the relative performances of those who follow the participative style compared to those who manage in the traditional way. Absenteeism, turnover, and indices of production can provide compelling evidence for the relative merits of one style of management over another.

Supervisors and middle managers fear that participative programs will give subordinates direct communication channels with senior management. Many supervisors fear also that they will lose the formal imprimateur of the organization if participation of subordinates in decision-making is permitted. The discomfort of supervisors who must now manage from a position in which their decisions are open to review and comment by subordinates is understandable. However, the most perceptive supervisors recognize that they have little more than formalized, pro forma respect of subordinates and that bases of power built on expertise and skill are far more valuable than the reward and coercive bases of power.

In most organizations employees have no say in the selection of their supervisor. The data from this study suggest that the quality of supervision has a great deal to do with subordinates' satisfaction, sense of well-being, and personal worth, yet subordinates have no control over the appointment of supervision. The absence of subordinate rights to participate in the selection of supervision is a significant (yet easily remedied) failure of the modern work organization. Many upwardly mobile supervisors view their position as a temporary assignment and endeavour to enhance the short-term performance of the work group with little concern for the quality of work life or their subordinates. Hourly employees, on the other hand, typically remain in their departments for many years and rightfully expect to build a lasting and satisfying work environment.

The appointment of supervision with the participation of subordinates will not jeopardize the effectiveness of supervision, as many fear. The role of the supervisor under such a system would undoubtedly be more difficult than it currently is. The first-line supervisor has always been 'the person in the middle' and if employees participated in the appointment decision, supervision would be caught between two powerful groups. However, the process of democratically appointing supervision is simply a recognition of reality. The best supervisors are those whose work groups are productive and those whose subordinates feel that they are fair, approachable, and attentive to their needs. Supervisors who are 'productive' in the narrow sense of the term but who leave a wake of resentment and anger behind them as they move through the ranks should not be regarded as having fulfilled their responsibilities to the organization.

The United Steelworkers of America has suggested that the union have a voice in the appointment of supervision. This suggestion is sensible, as long as the process does not become embroiled in the adversarial relationship. Subordinates might also have a say in the promotion decisions concerning their supervisors. If they did, supervisors would treat their subordinates in a more ethical and supportive manner. The voice of subordinates in the appointment and promotion process would be a key guarantor of the accountability of leadership to subordinates.

WORKPLACE DEMOCRACY: WHICH DIRECTION?

Each of the five generic forms of workplace democracy studied here – employee board-level representation, Scanlon plans, works councils, producer co-operatives, and self-directing work groups – has unique advantages and is best suited to particular circumstances. The prospects of each form of workplace democracy, however, are not equally promising. Among the dimensions which define the promise of each form of workplace democracy are the following.

- How soon do the effects of workplace democracy become evident?
- How much relearning (re-education) is required of organization members?
- Is the program reversible, that is, can changes be made in the program without disrupting organizational activities?
- Is the program acceptable to other stakeholders (unions, shareholders)?
- What are the costs of introducing the form of workplace democracy?

Of all forms of workplace democracy, self-directing work groups are the most promising. More than any other type of workplace democracy, self-directing work groups are consistent with prevailing practices. The right of management to manage is not questioned, although substantial changes are required in the values and styles of first-line supervision. Furthermore, work is the most salient aspect of work life for most employees. Enriched work which is autonomous from supervision and which involves whole task responsibility significantly improves employee reactions to the workplace.

The Scanlon plan is also an effective way to introduce democratic forms of decision-making into the workplace. Since participation in decision-making is linked to a program of productivity improvement, managers tend to be more receptive to Scanlon plans than to most other forms of workplace democracy. Trade unionists, however, remain sceptical. Forms of workplace democracy which involve sharing of productivity gains or profits are more likely to be perceived as 'genuine' by workers than forms of workplace democracy in which participation in decision-making only is permitted. The rather limited conditions for effective Scanlon plans, however, restrict the applicability of the concept.[7]

Works councils are an effective means of enhancing employee participation in decision-making. Each of the forms of works council studied here has been effective in improving employee outcomes and in maintaining a collaborative labour-management climate. Works councils have been used as an alternative to trade unions and will continue to be opposed by the trade union movement.

Board-level representation is a form of workplace democracy which will be strongly opposed by managers and shareholders. It brings lower-level employees into the decision-making process at the highest organizational levels. Unless reinforced with shop-floor participation, board-level representation will not enhance employee reaction to the workplace. Until corporate law is changed, board-level representation will be applied primarily in organizations which are owned by employees.

The producer co-operative will continue as an expression of democratic values, but it will not find wide acceptance in North America. For employees who share the values of and wish to explore and participate in a workplace which departs significantly from conventional practice the producer co-operative will still be an attractive alternative.

PROFIT-SHARING AND EMPLOYEE OWNERSHIP

Profit-sharing is an important yet neglected dimension of workplace democracy. Participation in the financial success of the enterprise, participation in ownership of the enterprise, and participation in decision-making are each conceptually distinct, yet each is part of the same philosophy. Profit-sharing, ownership, and democratic decision-making are mutually reinforcing.

In this sample there are five organizations with profit-sharing plans and three organizations with substantial employee ownership. Two of the firms are entirely owned by the employees.

Much of management's concern with workplace democracy centres on the belief that increased employee power will not be used responsibly in the

7 See appendix I.

pursuit of collective goals but will be used for the pursuit of narrow self-interest and as a check on managerial authority.

Profit-sharing and employee ownership are means of ensuring the responsible use of power by all parties. Profit-sharing provides a superordinate goal which can unite all employees and many stakeholders in a common endeavour.

Profit-sharing and stock bonus plans are common means of motivating senior executives. However, there is a widespread perception among managers that participation of employees in profit-sharing programs is both unnecessary and undesirable. According to prevailing beliefs, employee motivation is purchased by the going wage, and additional rewards – even when matched with increases in productivity – needlessly pamper the worker.

One of the primary virtues of profit-sharing is that it provides management with an 'excuse' to communicate regularly with employees. Frank discussion about the firm's competitive position, the amount and sources of profit, the uses to which profits will be put, and the employee's role in the creation of profits can only enhance the firm's performance and unite labour and management in a common endeavour.

Although the advocates of profit-sharing and stock purchase plans often make excessive and unrealistic claims, profit-sharing and share ownership can provide the unity of purpose guiding the resolution of differences among labour and capital, employee and employer. Profit-sharing, by diffusing ownership, also prevents aggregations of power in the hands of a few. Employee ownership, if concentrated in the hands of a single body such as a trade union, could exert significant control over an enterprise. For example, by investing $65 each to purchase one share, General Motors employees could have acquired more than one-third of General Motors voting stock in 1969. This form of ownership is more compatible with European views of workplace democracy than with the view presented in this book.

WORKPLACE DEMOCRACY AND PRODUCTIVITY

No documented evidence of organizational productivity was obtained in this sample of democratic and hierarchical organizations. Objective measures of performance are contaminated and obscured by a variety of factors including the original capitalization of the firm, the rate of depreciation of capital, the accounting practices employed by the firm, the transfer pricing policy of the parent firm, the use of profits for capital expansion or for dividend payments, and the firm's policies (short-term maximization of return, long-term growth potential, community responsibility).[8]

The European evidence concerning the relationship between employee participation and productivity is mixed. Experiments reported by Karl-Olog Faxem (1978) find no evidence for the relationship between shop-floor participation and productivity. Faxem reports that in ten firms in a variety of sectors in Sweden increased productivity resulted from improved co-ordination, joint problem-solving, and improved operating methods, but there were no increases in productivity attributable to participation. Nevertheless, Faxem reports that no experiments resulted in a simultaneous increase in employee participation and a decline in productivity.

However, Aberg (1969) estimates that approximately one-third of the increase in labour productivity in Sweden during the period 1951 to 1969 arose from employee participation in decision-making.

Although no objective data on performance were collected in this study, there is a wealth of anecdotal data from this sample on the economic performance of the democratically managed organizations. As a group the democratic organizations appear to be as productive as their hierarchical counterparts. Several of the democratic organizations are leaders in their business (e.g., Supreme Aluminium Industries, Club House Foods, Canadian Tire Corporation) while others are noted for their outstanding productivity (Lincoln Electric Limited). One firm, Tembec Forest Products, was divested by its parent because it was unprofitable; within a year of start-up under a program of workplace democracy the firm was profitable and has continued to earn a profit ever since.

Democratic decision-making is not a panacea for firms in economic difficulty. Democratic practices can create a committed and productive work-force, and such a work-force can make a substantial contribution to the performance of the organization. However, workplace democracy cannot compensate for incompetent management, and it cannot, by itself, save firms in declining industries. The Tricofil experience in St Jerome, Quebec is an example.

La société populaire Tricofil was founded in 1975 (it was formerly Regent Knitting Mills). The company employed 450 workers and was the only integrated knitting mill in eastern Canada. As a result of stiff foreign competition and a long and bitter strike, in 1972 the mill was closed by its owners and was reopened by workers. All previous managers left the com-

---

8 For example, one firm in this sample donates annually 20 per cent of pre-tax profits to the church.

pany and workers assumed all managerial responsibilities. The president of
the union local became the president of Tricofil. From 1973 until June 1977,
Tricofil was self-managing – that is, all decisions on shop-floor as well as
policy matters were made by workers. The firm, although it continued to
lose money, was regarded as a cause célèbre in Quebec. Claude Ryan
wrote, 'Tricofil s'inscrit d'emblée dans cette récherche positive de nou-
veau liens entre démocratie et économie qui est un besoin urgent de notre
civilisation.'[9]

In May 1977 a P.S. Ross report on the accounting, planning, production,
and control systems in the mill recommended that professional managers be
hired and a hierarchical management structure be imposed on the company.
Acceptance of these recommendations was tied to government financial aid.
The recommendations were accepted and five professional managers hired
and foremen placed back in the mill. Since that time the fortunes of the mill
have changed; it has recently earned a profit and appears to be on a sound
financial footing.

THE CHOICE: ADVERSARIAL OR COLLABORATIVE RELATIONS

The forms of workplace democracy studied in this book are based on
collaborative relations. There are other (non-collaborative) forms of workplace democracy, however, which afford the rank and file participation in
decision-making. Trade unionism is one such form. In North America trade
unionism is the major vehicle for worker participation in decision-making
and trade unionism will continue to be the dominant form of workplace
democracy in the future. It has served its members well, and has provided
substantial due process protection for its members.

Trade unionism is not necessarily incompatible with the collaborative
forms of employee participation studied here (three of the democratic
organizations in this sample are unionized). However, negotiations between
management and unions are too often affected by a 'we-they' perception;
much of the energy of managers and trade unionists is directed towards the
defeat of their opponent instead of towards the pursuit of common objectives.

The advocacy of collaborative methods of conflict resolution is not based
on a belief that conflict is destructive or undesirable. Conflict is desirable
because it is important to know what is good for the organization as viewed
from the perspective of each stakeholder. Mary Parker Follett observes that

9 Ryan, Le Devoir, 4 May 1976

we must 'recognize that there are two kinds of difference, the difference which disrupts and the difference which may, if properly handled, more firmly unite.'[10]

Follett's description of the difference between conflict and diversity, although written fifty years ago, shows how conflict can be used productively. 'What people often mean by getting rid of conflict is getting rid of diversity, and it is of the utmost importance that these should not be considered the same. We may wish to abolish conflict but we cannot get rid of diversity. We must face life as it is and understand that diversity is its most essential feature ... Fear of difference is dread of life itself. It is impossible to conceive conflict as not necessarily a wasteful outbreak of incompatibilities, but a normal process by which socially valuable differences register themselves for the enrichment of all concerned.'[11]

Workplace democracy exists in two forms: 'adversarial' and 'collaborative.' Adversarial workplace democracy emphasizes due process, the limitation of the rights and prerogatives of the other party and focuses on issues of disagreement rather than on issues of agreement. This form of workplace democracy relies on 'win-lose' negotiation, compromise, or domination of the other party to settle differences. Collaborative workplace democracy, on the other hand, emphasizes shared decision-making and is based on an open exchange of viewpoints within a broad framework of common understanding.

The process of arbitration does not allow an interchange of ideas and perspectives leading to integrative or creative solutions. Arbitration generates a 'low trust dynamic,'[12] positions become entrenched and what may begin as a legitimate difference of opinion often spreads to a deepening hostility towards the other party.

Compromise, like domination of the other party, does not create anything new, and therefore leads to 'conflict traps.' The integration of diverse viewpoints, built on a firm foundation of common interests, is stabilizing and settles the conflict in a manner which precludes its arising again. The process rests on a respect for the other party and an acceptance of the right of the other party to have a voice in how decisions are made. Future conflicts can then be settled within this domain of agreement.

WHAT DO WORKERS WANT?

Those who oppose workplace democracy point out that if workers really wanted to participate in decision-making, they would have negotiated this

10 Fox and Urwick 1973, 48
11 Mary Parker Follett 1924, 308
12 Fox 1974

benefit long ago. Union efforts would be marshalled, politicians beseiged, and management forced to respond. Strauss and Rosenstein, in an often-quoted article, state, 'In general, the impetus for participation has come more from intellectuals, propagandists, and politicians (sometimes all three combined) than it has from the rank-and-file workers who were supposed to do the participating.'[13]

However, the average worker is not a visionary. If asked what he wants from work, he will respond in terms of perceived practical alternatives and personal experience, not in terms of abstract ideals which have been neither experienced nor contemplated. All ideals – political democracy, universal suffrage, civil rights, and the many freedoms we enjoy – were originally the inspiration of 'propagandists' and 'politicians.' Furthermore, these advances rarely enjoyed the widespread support of those who would ultimately benefit.

Most employees do not want a direct voice in policy-making. However, they do want to know and understand what management is doing and to have confidence that their interests are being accounted for.

WORKPLACE DEMOCRACY AND THE NATURE OF WORK

There are mounting pressures in North America to improve the quality of work life for persons in semi-skilled and unskilled jobs. American hospitals, for example, are desperately short of employees willing to assume menial but essential work. The hotel industry in Toronto is unable to fill housekeeping jobs. In the past, the solution has rested on immigrant labour: Mexican and Puerto Rican labour in the United States and Jamaican labour in Canada. This use of immigrants to perform work which others are unwilling to perform will likely continue in the future and will slow down the drive towards work improvement.[14]

If work must be unpleasant and uninspiring, then participation may mitigate its undesirable effects.[15] The reasons for the unpleasant work and the constraints imposed by the technology can be discussed; participation can focus on issues which can be changed or on matters (such as productivity) which require input from different groups for effective solutions.

The proper balance between work shaped by economic imperatives and work as a source of dignity and self-worth remains one of the most perplex-

13 Strauss and Rosenstein 1970, 199
14 The use of immigrant labour to perform menial work is commonplace in Europe: 'gastarbeiters' from Turkey and Portugal in the Federal Republic of Germany, West Indians in England, and Algerians in France.
15 See chapter 6.

ing issues in modern society. Work can be made more challenging and autonomous; work need not be the uninspiring and burdensome activity it is for
so many people. However, this study has demonstrated that under programs
of workplace democracy the work itself may not change at all. The essential
point, however, is that within technological constraints it could change if
employees so desired. Workplace democracy overcomes this puzzling anomaly of the contemporary workplace: those most experienced with the daily
details of the work are prohibited from contributing to its improvement.
There is ample evidence to illustrate that when opportunities for self-
expression, challenge, and recognition are absent, the worker's productive
energies are channeled in unproductive directions. In Studs Terkel's (1972)
insightful analysis of American working people, the themes of unfulfilled
expectations, meaninglessness, and a hope that their children will not have
to endure the work which they have spent their lives performing are by no
means universal, but they recur with disturbing regularity.

In unionized organizations no program of workplace democracy will produce the desired results if it is directed against the union or threatens the
union's relationship with its members. Workplace democracy should be
jointly planned and implemented by the union and management. If the
organization is not unionized, employees of their representatives should be
involved.[16]

---

16 The letter of agreement between the UAW and General Motors illustrates the form that
joint union-management initiatives might take.

THE LETTER OF AGREEMENT BETWEEN THE UAW AND GENERAL MOTORS TO ESTABLISH A COMMIT-
TEE TO IMPROVE THE QUALITY OF WORK LIFE
In discussions prior to the opening of the current negotiations for a new collective bargaining agreement, General Motors Corporation and the UAW gave recognition to the
desirability of mutual effort to improve the quality of work life for employees. In consultation with union representatives, certain projects have been undertaken by management
in the field of organizational development involving the participation of represented
employees. These and other projects and experiments that may be undertaken in the
future are designed to improve the quality of work life, thereby advantaging the worker
by making work a more satisfying experience, advantaging the corporation by leading to
a reduction in employee absenteeism and turnover, and advantaging the consumer
through improvement in the quality of the products manufactured.

As a result of these earlier discussions and further discussions during the course of
the current negotiations for a new collective bargaining agreement, the parties have
decided that a Committee to Improve the Quality of Work Life composed of representatives of the International Union and General Motors will be established at the national
level.

This committee will meet periodically and have responsibility for:

Workplace democracy is most effective when local management and trade union officials are responsible for the program and can design it to suit their purposes and the unique requirements of their organization. This principle is easy to state but difficult to put into practice. Managers are often prisoners of an outdated ideology. In addition, this generation of trade union leaders has learned that advances in the welfare of the rank and file come only through struggle, and they have learned that power over their opponents is essential to improving the quality of work life of their members.

The experiences of the past, however, are inappropriate for the challenges of the future. The give and take of adversarial relations is enjoyed by too many managers and trade unionists. The view of 'conflict as sport' unfortunately runs deep in our society, and acceptance of other means of settling disputes and reconciling differences will not come easily.

IMPLEMENTING WORKPLACE DEMOCRACY

There are many varieties of workplace democracy found in North America. Unlike the legislated forms of employee participation in western Europe, North American forms of workplace democracy assume great diversity because they are introduced to meet the individual expectations and experiences of employers and employees and because they are tailored to the unique circumstances of each organization.

The data from this study indicate that the value system of managers in democratically managed organizations is substantially more 'theory Y' than the corresponding value system in hierarchically managed organizations. Without the appropriate value system collaborative forms of workplace

1. Reviewing and evaluating programs of the Corporation that involve improving the work environment of employees represented by the UAW.
2. Developing experiments and projects in this area.
3. Maintaining records of its meetings, deliberations, and all experiments and evaluations it conducts.
4. Making reports to the corporation and the union on the results of its activities.
5. Arranging for any outside counselling that it feels is necessary or desirable with the expenses thereof to be shared equally by the corporation and the union.

The corporation agrees to request and encourage its plant managements to cooperate in the conduct of such experiments and projects and recognizes that cooperation by its plant floor supervision is essential to success of this program.

The Union agrees to request and encourage its members and their local union representatives to cooperate in such experiments and projects and recognizes that the benefits that can flow to employees as a result of successful experimentation is dependent on the cooperation and participation of those employees and the local union representatives.

democracy are unlikely to produce many of the results found in this analysis.

Warren Bennis (1969) points out that the only viable way to change an organization is to change its 'culture.' By culture, Bennis means a way of life, a system of beliefs and values and accepted forms of interaction. Bennis also observes that changing values have a more fundamental impact on the organization than changing individuals – although one way of changing the value system of an organization is to change key individuals.

Value systems are not easily changed. The value system of the modern work organization is based on bureaucratic values; they are impersonal, task-oriented, and antithetical to humanistic and democratic principles. These values can be traced to the early part of this century, and although they have changed substantially in the intervening years, the influence of this earlier era is still apparent.

Because a shared theory Y value system is essential for collaborative workplace democracy, the successful introduction of democratic decision-making is more probable in small than in large organizations. The Scott-Bader Company in England, for example, creates a new division whenever the size of an existing division exceeds 250 employees. In Sweden Volvo deliberately designs its production facilities to employ no more than 650 people. Small size permits face-to-face exchange among all organization members and thereby facilitates interaction and the development of a shared value system. The impact of an individual or a few individuals with a democratic value system is also greater in small than in large organizations. In fact, system-wide forms of collaborative workplace democracy are unlikely to be introduced in large organizations, because established practices, traditions, and entrenched vested interests make change difficult.

The collaborative forms of workplace democracy studied here differ substantially from conventional practices in Canada. Employee expectations are determined in part by prevailing practices, and the practices in this country will continue to be authoritarian and adversarial. New ventures in employee participation in this environment promise to provide substantial benefits, but at the same time they entail considerable risks. Organization members must be given an opportunity to develop skills, an opportunity to build new relationships and an opportunity to develop trust in other stakeholders. Programs of workplace democracy are not easily reversible (that is, workplace democracy is not an addendum to the personnel manual but a thoroughgoing change in the way in which decisions are made); such programs may upset existing organizational arrangements and may require significant changes in the relationship with the union, in administrative arrangements, and in the values of employees.

Although not all of the democratic workplaces studied here allowed rank and file input into the design of the program of employee participation, 'grass roots' support is essential to the success of any program.[17] Toby Wall and Joseph Lischeron (1977) point out that the top-down manner of introduction of employee participation violates the very spirit embodied by the concept. Employees must be able to participate in the development of the system which they will be operating.

Democracy is best extended into the workplace by incremental changes to existing structures, not by the imposition of complex structures such as those in many of the democratic organizations in this study. Participation should begin on the shop floor, perhaps in the form of self-directing work groups. These changes raise the level of employee interest, involvement, and competence.[18,19]

Employee disinterest, suspicion, and perhaps outright hostility, as well as reluctance on the part of supervisory staff can be expected, unless employees are prepared for their new rights and responsibilities. Employee participation does not necessarily entail changes in the nature of work, although it should if the technology permits. If economic and technological factors constrain changes to the conditions of work, then workplace democracy may begin with consultation or joint decision-making over shop-floor matters

17　Fred Lesieur, for example, requires the support of at least 75 per cent of workers before introducing a Scanlon plan.
18　One form of shop-floor participation which is growing in popularity in North America is the 'quality control circle.' A quality control circle is a group of five to ten workers and supervisors (the leader is generally a supervisor) which meets once a week during working hours to discuss matters pertaining to product quality. Causes of substandard quality are noted, solutions developed and action steps implemented. Membership is voluntary and circles meet on a continuing basis, not just when problems occur. To function effectively in quality control circles workers must learn the techniques of statistical quality control, control charts, Pareto curves, etc. – all the techniques which have remained in the hands of management and industrial engineers.

　　Although quality control circles began in Japan in 1962, the concept has spread rapidly in North America. J.M. Juran, an authority on quality management, estimates that seven million Japanese workers have been trained in the techniques of quality control circles. In North America the concept of quality control circles provides workers with an opportunity to participate in planning and decision-making and it fosters the view that both labour and management are responsible for productivity and product quality.
19　These changes also raise employee expectations.

such as shift schedules, vacation times, and staffing of machines. As trust develops among the parties and as parties see the mutual benefits to be obtained, the participation can spread to more significant issues.[20] Participation should begin with issues on which there is likely to be substantial agreement (e.g., an alcohol abuse program), then, as trust and competence develops, move to issues which have greater potential for conflict (e.g., a productivity improvement program).

Some form of participation at the shop-floor level is essential for desirable results. If employee representatives participate in decision-making at the higher management level, there must also be a means for employees to participate on matters of more immediate relevance to their work.

Innovations are more likely to succeed when an explicit statement of intent binds labour and management. In Sweden the Employees Confederation and the LO (the national blue-collar union) signed a 'rationalization agreement' which specified that changes in production methods would be guided by four criteria: (1) increased productivity, (2) increased job satisfaction, (3) improvements in the work environment, and (4) greater job security. All innovations are to give equal weight to the four criteria and all changes are to be made in consultation with employees.

GOVERNMENT INITIATIVES

Developments in workplace democracy have proceeded further in western Europe than they have in Canada or the United States. In Europe workplace democracy is a matter of political doctrine. Examples include: legislation initiatives in the Federal Republic of Germany and in Sweden, the innovations in shop-floor democracy in Norway; and the self-management system in Yugoslavia.

Should the Canadian and American governments take the initiative in legislating workplace democracy? Government intervention is both unlikely and undesirable. Workplace democracy will not emerge as a political issue in Canada or the United States in the foreseeable future. Even the New Democratic Party – the only major socialist party in North America – will not endorse forms of workplace democracy which do not involve the trade union as a partner. Some members of the NDP would like to see a form of

20 Emery and Thorsrud's (1969) 'developmental model of industrial democracy' finds limited support in Norwegian experiments. Increased autonomy on the shop-floor has not necessarily led to increased workers participation in broader company affairs. Changes beyond the shop-floor are constrained by organizational conditions: the resistance of managers and supervisors and long-established traditions and procedures.

workers' control, but organized labour – a founding partner of the party and a significant force in the party – has opposed such moves.

Participation is not a process easily prompted by political edict. Long-standing values and perspectives must be overcome; if the adversarial process continues, workplace democracy (in the form of works councils or worker representatives on the boards of directors) will simply provide a new battleground for labour and management. The inability of legislative initiative to overcome long-standing adversarial relations is illustrated by the 1977 Bullock Committee *Report*. This attempt to impose a universal formula on all of British industry was opposed by both unions and management.

The advocacy of 'big bang' approaches to workplace democracy is unwise. Government legislation cannot create overnight a new and collaborative industrial relations system. For the most part our system has evolved gradually and sweeping changes would be disruptive. Furthermore, unlike the western European systems, the industrial relations systems in Canada and the United States protect (and value) diversity. National or sector bargaining between employers' confederations and national union bodies is commonplace in Europe and has been successful, but such an arrangement is fragile. When an agreement cannot be reached, the nation is paralysed. The 1980 national strike in Sweden rendered idle more than one-quarter of the labour force. The poisoned relations between the national leaders of the two sides spread throughout the country. Sweden's strength has become its weakness.

Canadians and Americans tend to do things by trial and error, and our manner of organizing the workplace is no exception. European innovations in the workplace are ideologically inspired and government sanctioned and often involve statutory and sweeping transfers of power. In North America workplace innovations have been more pragmatic, management initiated, and particularistic – that is, designed for specific situations and consistent with the values of the persons involved. These innovations, though small in number, are as resourceful and innovative as any of the European programs.

This is not to say, however, that there is no role for government. Governments have a significant role to play in the encouragement of profit-sharing plans and stock purchase plans. The legislation of joint union-management industrial health and safety committees and co-management of pension funds is also desirable. Governments might require that any organization which conducts business with the government have some form of significant employee participation. Government-owned operations and Crown corporations might require the same, as John Crispo (1978) has advocated.

Firms in receipt of government aid might also be required to introduce significant employee participation in decision-making.[21]

The further elaboration and refinement of labour law is part of the answer to our industrial relations problems, but it is not a complete answer. Carl Goldenberg observes, 'Legislation does not change attitudes, and laws will not by themselves solve problems flowing from the conflicts of interest that give rise to industrial disputes.'[22]

Professor Kahn-Freund of Oxford, a leading authority on labour law, also points out that 'the longer one ponders the problem of industrial disputes, the more sceptical one gets as regards the effectiveness of the law. Industrial conflict is often a symptom rather than a disease. I think we lawyers would do well to be modest in our claims to be able to provide cures.'[23]

The preoccupation of managers with economic objectives (and their reliance on authoritarian practices to achieve these objectives) has created the standard of material well-being we enjoy today. However, it has been achieved at a heavy cost. The command-and-obey system of authority and fragmented and meaningless work were appropriate in an era of widespread illiteracy, poverty, and malnutrition. These conditions have been eradicated by the material prosperity created by the work organization. However, to continue these practices is to sacrifice human dignity and the rights of citizenship as well as to leave untapped the human resources of the work-force.

As we move towards the potential that awaits, there will be many failures and much controversy. However, reforms such as those described in this book are rarely so devastating in their effects as their critics fear; and they rarely signal the millennium as their proponents hope.

Greater employee participation in decision-making is not the only solution to the problems of employee dissatisfaction at work. Job security, safe working conditions, and better pay are major concerns of working people. However, great gains could be made – not only in employee satisfaction, but also in the more effective use of human resources – by extending participation in the workplace. Democratic practices would release human talent and ingenuity which are currently held in check by unchallenging jobs, authoritarian supervision, and a workplace which places little value on employees as creative, responsible, and autonomous human beings.

---

21 Government aid to democratically managed firms include Tembec Forest Products, Tricofil, and Pioneer Chainsaw.
22 Goldenberg 1978, 7
23 Kahn-Freund in Goldenberg 1978, 7

APPENDICES

Forms of workplace democracy in Canada

The forms of workplace democracy found in North America are many and varied. Unlike European examples of workplace democracy these forms have not been influenced by legislation but have been designed to fit the desires and expectations of individual managers and employees.

The ten democratic workplaces in this sample fall into six categories: (1) board-level representation (Tembec Forest Products); (2) Scanlon plan (Hayes-Dana); (3) works council (Supreme Aluminium, Lincoln Electric, Canadian Tire, Club House Foods); (4) producer co-operatives (Les Industries du Saguenay and Harvey Transport); (5) self-regulating work groups (Laidlaw Lumber); and (6) The Group at Cox, a firm which cannot, because of its unique characteristics, be subsumed under a general construct.

The descriptions of the six categories of workplace democracy will focus on the concept of participation underlying each category; where appropriate, details on the actual functioning of the program of workplace democracy will be provided.

BOARD LEVEL REPRESENTATION

Worker representation on boards of directors remains one of the more beguiling and seductive approaches to the problem of alienation at the workplace. Worker representation on boards of directors is recognized by statute in West Germany, Sweden, Denmark, Norway, Holland, Austria, Luxembourg, and France (although in the latter country worker representatives are not permitted to vote).

The prima facie evidence suggests that board level representation can improve labour-management relations. Countries which have legislated board-level representation, such as West Germany and Sweden, enjoy the most positive and collaborative industrial relations as well as the healthiest economies among the western industrial nations. In the United Kingdom and Italy no statutory provision exists for board-level representation. These countries have the worst industrial relations records in western Europe; the labour movements in these countries are dominated by the political left and trade union leaders view their relationship with management as part of a larger class struggle.

The report of the Biedenkopf Commission (established in 1967 to examine the West German experience with board-level representation) concluded in its report published in 1970 that co-determination in West Germany had worked reasonably well. Board-level representation had satisfied the trade unions while it had not interfered with the economic and technical efficiency of the firm. The commission also concluded that the supervisory board had not been a strong instrument of control over the firm's policy because of collusion between the executive committee and the works council. The commission found no evidence of stalemate in decision-making at the supervisory board level.

The commission reported general employee satisfaction with co-determination but also reported that among workers there was little sense that co-determination had helped them personally.

Other reviews of worker representation on the boards of directors in Europe suggest that this form of participation has few significant psychological effects on rank and file employees.[1] A review of the Norwegian, Yugoslav, and West German experiences with employee representatives[2] finds no effect on rank and file employees in any of the companies studied. Tannenbaum (1974) observes that indirect forms of participation have little psychological effect on workers who do not participate directly in decision-making. There is evidence indicating that workers on the shop-floor rarely know the names of their employee representatives.[3]

Employee representation on the boards of directors is rare in Canada and the United States, and where it exists it is usually justified by employee ownership. Employee representatives sit on the boards of four of the democratically managed organizations in this sample, and in three of these four cases the practice is justified by employee ownership.[4]

1 Connaghan 1976; Crispo 1978; and Jain 1980
2 Holter 1965; Lammers 1967; and Emery and Thorsrud 1969
3 Emery and Thorsrud 1964; and Emery and Thorsrud 1969
4 The European experience with co-determination has generated a good deal of interest in Canada. However, most analyses of European-style industrial democracy have cautioned against transplanting these programs to this country (Crispo 1978).

Employee board-level representation in Canadian and American firms is effectively precluded by corporation law. Members of boards of directors are obligated by law to protect the interests of shareholders. Legislation governing the responsibilities of board members first emerged as a means of protecting shareholders from unscrupulous entrepreneurs and directors. Under current corporation law employee representation on boards of directors can be justified only through employee ownership. However, worker directors cannot be answerable to shareholders and responsible for protecting their interests, and at the same time safeguard the interests of workers. This dual responsibility would create a conflict of interest for employee representatives.

Employee board-level representation must await a change in the spirit, if not the letter, of Canadian and American laws governing the responsibilities of board members. Such a change is easy to justify. Employee representation on the boards of directors could be justified in terms of the special competence and insight which employee representatives would bring to the board of directors. To the extent that employee representatives on the board would bring forth matters of concern to employees, it could be argued that the welfare of the company would be enhanced.[5]

It might also be argued that employees as legitimate stakeholders in the enterprise have a *right* to participate in making decisions affecting the organization. The legal obligations of board members might be changed so that members are explicitly charged with the responsibility of protecting the interests of their constituents, whether they be shareholders, employees, or members of the community at large.

Blumberg (1977) argues that under such a plan the board of directors might become a 'political' institution and might become nothing more than a forum for the expression of conflicting interests. However, this conflict would be a simple recognition of the divergent interests of various organizational stakeholders. The consensus among members of boards of directors is a simple reflection of the homogeneity of the backgrounds of directors and the unity of interests they represent. Work organizations, no less than political democracies, can profit from the open expression of opinions from diverse constituencies.

At the very least, employee representatives on boards of directors will ensure that decisions made by the board take employee interests into account, especially in areas of special interest to employees, such as person-

---

5 This rationale was used to justify the appointment of former union executives to the board of Via Rail.

nel policy. Employee representatives can also communicate the views of the board to employees and explain the reasons underlying the decisions of the board.

If strong differences were to emerge between employee and shareholder interests on boards of directors, board meetings might become a ritualistic formality. Informal caucuses among members who share similar interests might mitigate the effectiveness of the board.

Board-level representation and adversarial relations
The European experience with co-determination suggests that board level representation works best in situations where labour and management have demonstrated an interest in and an ability to work collaboratively, and where issues of ownership rights and the class struggle do not colour the relationship between labour and management. Recent labour difficulties at Opel, the General Motors automobile subsidiary in West Germany, suggest that adversarial relations on the shop floor can influence relations between the union and management at board level. At Opel young militant employees have tilted the balance of power away from their more accommodating elders on the works council. Employee representatives on the board of Opel are now bringing forward shop-floor issues for resolution. Previously, worker representatives routinely approved investment decisions; now, worker representatives insist on reviewing the decisions one at a time. The absence of common ground and trust among labour and management representatives on the board has transformed the board's activities and, in this instance, has reduced the effectiveness of the board.

The difficulties created by two powerful opponents – labour and management – which do not share common ideological ground is demonstrated by the experience of several Italian firms in which union pressure on management to change a product or to delay its introduction impaired the long-run efficiency of the industry.[6] In one case trade union officials felt that the introduction of the company's product – a colour television set – would be inappropriate when the country was in the midst of a recession. They argued that this new product would tempt customers, particularly those in the lower classes, to purchase a colour television when they had more basic and pressing needs. Union influence on the industry delayed the introduction of colour television, and weakened the firm's ability to compete with foreign firms.

6 Mazzolini 1978

In another case, Alfa Romeo's introduction of the Alfa Sud, an economy car, was encouraged by the unions because this type of automobile was believed to reflect the social needs of the market more than the luxury sports cars then manufactured by the firm. The decision to market the Alfa Sud was made on ideological, not economic grounds.

Worker representation on the boards of directors of firms in North America will neither increase nor decrease conflict between labour and management. The relationship between employee and shareholder interests on the board will be determined by the values, traditions, and attitudes of the parties. The board could be another battleground for labour and management; or the board could be a forum for the resolution of differences, a recognition and confirmation of common ground, and a means for the parties to resolve minor problems before they become major problems.

Further difficulties with board-level representation
Two difficulties with board-level representation have been pointed out: the conflict of interest of employee representatives under corporation law and the possibility of conflict or stalemate between the interests of shareholders and employees. Several other difficulties are worth noting. Through board-level representation trade union representatives would have access to confidential financial information. This information might be used for wage negotiations, or if made public it might embarrass or financially endanger the firm. Board-level representation consequently strengthens the hand of labour in negotiations with management.

A collaborative mechanism cannot be grafted to a relationship that is primarily adversarial. If representatives from national or international unions are to sit on boards of directors, they may pursue broad social goals (as in Italy) and may not adequately represent the interests of employees in the firm. Similarly, the local union may wish to work collaboratively with management, while the national union may seek confrontation with management.

A clash of the policies of the national union and one of its locals is found at Tembec Forest Products. The official policy of the Canadian Paper Workers Union is not to enter into co-determination programs with management; nevertheless, the president of this union and the president of Local 233 of the union are members of the board of directors of Tembec Forest Products.

In many of the larger Canadian and American firms worker directors could not, in any important sense, be considered representatives. Let us assume that all employees in a firm of 20,000 employees have the right to be represented on the board of directors. The board of a firm of this size might have fifteen members. If one-half are to be worker directors and one-half shareholder representatives, seven directors would represent the interests of 20,000 employees. These employees would likely be geographically dispersed and would probably have little face-to-face interaction with their representatives. Board-level representation in the larger corporations would require a continuing commitment to regular communications wtih employees. Trade unions would more effectively represent the interests of workers than programs of worker representation on the board.

The future of board-level representation

Employee board-level representation can be approached from one of two basic perspectives: it provides a check on managerial power and controls or limits the rights of capital and prevents abuses; or it is consistent with the pluralist political model. That is, employee representation provides a countervailing balance against the interests of capital and management; or it provides the basis for the accommodation of the interests of all stakeholders in the organization.

The introduction of co-determination in North America through statute is likely to be vigorously opposed by management and shareholder interests. Opposition to employee representation on boards of directors is motivated in part by a fear that the rights of property owners will be compromised. The conflict between labour and capital over control of the enterprise (the familiar debate: 'is labour to be hired by capital or is capital to be hired by labour?') is not a particularly important conflict in Canada and the United States, when compared to disagreements over wages and conditions of work.

Many believe that board-level representation is the culmination of other forms of shop floor participation.[7] Proponents of this position believe that workers can be drawn successively into higher forms of participation as their skills in decision-making develop. Through a form of 'progressive socialization' workers are drawn into a wider sphere of organizational life.

The belief that participation limited to the shop-floor will eventually frustrate workers is popular, although there is little empirical evidence to support it. Emery and Thorsrud (1964) find no support for their 'developmental model of industrial democracy.' They find no evidence from European experience that shop-floor participation leads inevitably and progressively to participation on matters of greater import.

7 Hilgendorf and Irving 1976

It is clear from an examination of the firms in this sample that it is possible for workers in routine and closely supervised jobs to overcome the limitations imposed on them by their work and to become involved in organizational decision-making at higher levels. However, board-level representation by itself is not likely to have much effect on employee attitudes. Board-level representation must necessarily be an indirect form of participation, and the issues discussed are often remote from the immediate concerns of the rank and file employee. Shop-floor participation is found in this study to be far more effective in improving employee attitudes, morale, and motivation than board-level representation.

Without reinforcement on the shop-floor, board-level participation is not likely to have a demonstrable impact on employee attitudes. Board-level representation should reinforce and support shop-floor participation and should not be the beginning point for the development of participation at lower levels. The values, skills, and trust required to make board-level representation work effectively will not occur spontaneously in most organizations. When shop-floor participation is well established, participation can be extended to the board level.

Tembec Forest Products Limited: an example of board-level representation
Tembec Forest Products Limited is a bleach sulfite mill located in Temiscaming, Quebec, 350 miles north of Montreal on the Ottawa River. It offers perhaps the most celebrated example of workplace democracy in North America. Tembec is one of the few settings for workplace democracy in which a trade union was involved from the beginning and where the union is considered to be a integral part of the program. Board-level representation is the key to workplace democracy at Tembec, although there are two additional features: continuous bargaining and joint union-management committees on a variety of shop-floor matters.

The history of Tembec
Canadian International Paper Limited (CIP), which owned the mill, had allowed it to deteriorate by minimizing capital expenditures over the years prior to 1970. In May 1972 the mill was closed. The closure of the mill was a serious blow to the town; the mill was the community's only industry and the average age of the workers was forty-eight years.

An intensive lobbying effort by four former executives of CIP, community groups, and the Canadian Paperworkers Union began soon after the plant closed. There followed fifteen months of negotiations with federal and provincial governments and private capital markets. During this period the mill was left unattended and exposed to the harsh, northern Quebec winter. Although many felt that the mill would never open again, sufficient capital was acquired to purchase it from CIP and make it operational.

The mill was bought by the new firm, 'Tembec,' on 1 August 1973 and it was fully operational by January 1974. The quick reopening of the plant is a testimony to the considerable enthusiasm and team-work of former CIP employees. The sense of common purpose and the struggle to save the town and the mill helped overcome the bitterness which characterized relations between the union and the former management.

The mill (along with spare parts and seventeen homes) was purchased for $2.4 million in 1973. In 1978 the mill was appraised at a replacement value of $119 million and a fair market value of $57 million. The financial success enjoyed by the firm is due to a talented and hard-working management as well as to a loyal and committed work-force.

Financial structure
The company structure and members on the boards of directors are as follows:

Party	Ownership (per cent)	Members on the boards of directors
Founders	38.8	4
Workers	30.8	2
Towns people	8	0
Government of Quebec	9.6	2
Private investors	12.8	1

The four management founders (G.S. Petty, R.G. Stevens, G.F. Chandler, and F.B. Dottori) control their shares through a holding company named PSCD (the initials of the founders). Local 233 of the Canadian Paper Workers Union holds its equity through a holding company called ATKWA (Association des Travailleurs de Kipawa). The Government of Quebec contributed $1 million for common shares, $2.5 million for preferred shares (which have been fully redeemed) and a working capital loan of $10 million to a firm called Tembois, a wood procurement subsidiary.[8] The federal government awarded Tembec a $4 million grant from the department of regional economic expansion.

8 Fifty-one per cent of shares of Tembois are owned by Tembec and 49 per cent by Rexfor, a government resource management firm.

The ATKWA holding company ensures that employee equity is voted as a block. The ATKWA board of directors consists of seven people: four annually elected local union officials and three national union officials elected by the four local union officials.

An employee must belong to the union to work at Tembec but the employee is not required to invest in Tembec through ATKWA. Of the 550 union mill employees, approximately 400 contributed $1,000 each. Only the directors of ATKWA know which employees are shareholders. ATKWA may issue new shares if the directors so choose, and all union member shares must be owned by ATKWA. The ATKWA share price was fixed (by choice) for the first five years. Until that time, withdrawals were at the original share value. ATKWA and PSCD have agreed not to purchase the 10 per cent of Tembec's equity held by Temiscaming citizens in order to preserve their relative equity positions.

The union contributed approximately $3 million of indirect aid to the new company by forgoing competitive salaries and benefits for a period of three years. The first contract, for example, did not include a pension plan, although this benefit had previously been negotiated with CIP.

The board of directors
The board of directors of Tembec Forest Products has nine members, two of which are union representatives. The two union members are the president of Local 233, Charles Carpenter, and the president of the Canadian Paper Workers Union, L. Henri Lorrain. During their first year on the board of directors, by Quebec law the union representatives were not permitted to vote. However, in response to a request from Tembec the Quebec law was changed by an order-in-council to permit union members to vote on boards of directors of firms incorporated in that province.

Charles Carpenter reports that he was initially hesitant about accepting the position because of his lack of understanding of economic matters. However, after the first year he was conversant with the issues discussed at the board level and now participates fully in all board affairs.

Board meetings are held approximately once each month and normally last an entire day. The union representatives have become most involved in matters directly affecting employer-employee relations, although they have taken strong interest in investment policy as well. The mandate of the union representatives is to protect the financial interests of the workers. The union representatives (like all board members) have access to all financial data.

Joint union-management committees
Eight union-management committees with equal representation from union and management jointly make decisions on many matters on the shop floor. The decisions of the committees are binding on management and the union. The committees and their composition are as follows:

- The senior safety committee (made up of the plant security officer, the plant engineer, the finishing supervisor, the first and second union vice-president and the union secretary). This committee can overrule any superintendent on matters of safety.
- The job evaluation committee (consisting of the director of personnel and two management and two union representatives, one of which must be the union president)
- The hiring committee (consisting of the director of personnel, and the union president). Both must concur before any hourly employee is hired).
- The disciplinary committee (made up of the assistant director of personnel and the first vice-president of the union). The recommendations of the disciplinary committee are not binding on the mill manager. He has, however, never reversed a committee decision.
- The leave of absence committee (consisting of the director of personnel and the union president)
- The junior safety committee
- The tradesmen classification committee
- The mill cost review committee

In the pursuit of their responsibilities on these committees, union members may talk with any person in the firm to obtain information or points of view. As a result, all the changes in the plant are discussed openly between labour and management before a decision is made.

Continuous bargaining
Continuous bargaining was introduced shortly after the first contract was signed in 1974. Its purpose was to provide a means of quickly clearing up ambiguities in the new agreement. The results were so successful that the practice continues to this day. The issues subject to continuous bargaining include automation, technological change, severance pay, job classifications, and disciplinary procedures. When one party wishes to change a clause or clarify an ambiguity in the collective agreement, the clause in question is changed by each party according to its wishes. The union president and the director of personnel come to an agreement about the new wording. The

new wording then goes to the mill manager who can authorize the clause by signing an agreement (in which case it becomes part of the collective agreement and is binding on management), or he can ask that the parties work out a new clause. Before the new clause is binding on all parties it must be ratified by the rank and file. Typically one or two new clauses are ratified each month.

Other programs at Tembec

In addition to the three forms of employee participation discussed above, there are other programs worthy of note. For example, 10 per cent of after-tax earnings are distributed equally to all operating employees, according to the number of hours each employee has worked during the previous year. (Management personnel are excluded from the profit-sharing but obtain an equivalent incentive bonus.) There are fewer first-line supervisors in Tembec than under the CIP regime; in many areas supervisory responsibilities have been assumed by employees acting as 'lead hands.'

A program of improvements in working conditions is currently underway. The working conditions in the Tembec mill have been less satisfactory than those found in other bleach sulphite mills. The mill was built in 1919 and few capital expenditures were made in the last five years of the CIP operation. However, the union representatives on the board have been successful in obtaining significant funds for the improvement of employee working conditions. (The first step in the improvement of working conditions involved the preparation of two lists of priority items – one by the shop stewards and one by supervisors. The lists were exchanged and reduced to a short list of priority items.)

Future challenges for Tembec

The Tembec experience provides a number of instructive lessons. The results of the program are undeniably successful. Under CIP management an average of sixteen written grievances were filed each day. Since the reopening of the plant, there have been fewer than two written grievances per month. The number and type of grievances do not differ between shareholder and non-shareholder employees. The union president attributes the reduction in the number of grievances to the more rapid flow of information, allowing misunderstandings to be handled quickly and informally. The union president generally meets for an hour with the plant manager each day. Problems can be taken directly to the director of personnel or to the mill manager and decisions can be made immediately. Previously, company officials had to defer to head office for final decisions on many matters.

Although the mill was unprofitable before it was closed in 1972, it has made a profit every year since its opening. The company is currently embarking upon a $70 million expansion program.

At the time of data collection the 'honeymoon' between labour and management was over, and the hard realities of differing perspectives on many issues had surfaced. For example, a union proposal seeking two additional union representatives on the board is firmly opposed by management.

Although the formal structures are in place, the communication between parties is not considered to be as good as it could be. The union must take greater responsibility for educating its members, in economics, management techniques, and accounting, so that union members can fulfil their obligations as partners in the enterprise. Management and supervision (many of whom continued from the CIP days) occasionally forget that the union is a full partner in the enterprise.

The spirit of goodwill and co-operation generated by the crisis of plant shut-down in 1972 has diminished somewhat and must be renewed. The role of the local union president as a trade unionist and as a board member has proven extraordinarily difficult to manage. However, the president of the local at Tembec has handled his role and its conflicts very capably.[9]

Recently the local union president narrowly won re-election over a young challenger who charged that the president had been co-opted by management and was no longer vigorously protecting the interests of workers. Trade unionists who serve on boards of directors in Canada and the United States will inevitably face this charge. On the one hand they are expected to work collaboratively with management, while on the other hand their members expect them to protect their interests. When lay-offs occur (as in the Tembec mill shortly before the union election), the union president is open to the charge that he is colluding with management. Extraordinary skill is required to manage successfully the role conflict. It also requires a dedication to communicate regularly with constituents and to work with managers despite the inevitable disagreements on some issues.

This experiment in industrial democracy has been called a 'marriage of necessity' by Charles Carpenter, the president of Local 233 of the Canadian Paperworkers Union and a 'marriage of reason' by Real Cauchy, the director of personnel at Tembec. The evolving relationship between labour and management at Tembec will hold many valuable lessons for those who look

9 In fact, the success of the Tembec experiment in industrial democracy is in large measure due to the individuals directly involved – the mill manager, Frank Dottori; the director of personnel, Real Cauchy; and the local union president, Charles Carpenter.

to board-level representation and trade unionism as means of giving working people control over their work lives.

THE SCANLON PLAN

The Scanlon plan has been called 'the closest American equivalent to the European ideal of workers' participation in management.'[10] The Scanlon plan, named after Joseph Scanlon, a union leader in the 1930s who first proposed the concept, has relatively few applications in North America. There are an estimated 200 Scanlon plans in the United States and ten plans in Canada. The Dana Corporation currently has nineteen plants in the United States employing the Scanlon concept. The Scanlon plant studied in this sample is a division of the Dana Corporation and is the best example of the concept in Canada.

Although there are diverse applications of the Scanlon plan, each varying in details, it has three basic components: a philosophy, a participative committee system, and a financial incentive. Of the three components the philosophy is the most central. Joseph Scanlon's first application of his plan did not include a financial incentive; rather, it was an attempt to save a marginally profitable steel mill by marshalling the full efforts of labour and management. Scanlon felt that employee commitment could best be stimulated by providing information concerning company problems and by obtaining employees' ideas about ways of addressing these problems.

The Scanlon philosophy can best be characterized as 'theory Y.' That is, it is based on the belief that people are capable of self-direction, they possess creative potential, and, if given the opportunity, will contribute to the success of the organization. The association between the Scanlon plan and theory Y is not hard to understand. Douglas MacGregor was responsible for attracting Joseph Scanlon to M.I.T. in 1946. MacGregor saw the Scanlon plan as one mechanism for implementing his theory Y philosophy.

Managerial attitudes towards participative management have been found to be essential to the success of the Scanlon plan.[11] One of the great impediments to the widespread adoption of the Scanlon plan is the absence of management acceptance of the theory Y philosophy. The Scanlon plan cannot be introduced in a company where managerial practices and values are inconsistent with the Scanlon philosophy. Gibson and Lefcowitz examined cases where the Scanlon plan has failed and point out that failure occurs in

10 Strauss 1978, 24
11 Wallace 1971; Ruh, Wallace, and Frost, 1973

companies where 'a basically autocratic management did not really want participation, and where the members of a work union were unwilling to accept the responsibility inherent in participation ... there was a lack of mutual trust and willingness to focus on production problems rather than each other's motivations ... Since most of the workers were primarily oriented to the outside, they had little motivation to participate fully in the operation of the plan or to accept the responsibility of participation.'[12]

The second component of the Scanlon plan – a system of participative committees – provides a collaborative mechanism in which workers and management share technical and financial information. The Scanlon plan offers an effective means of releasing the productive potential of this generation of highly educated and sophisticated workers.

Fred Lesieur, the leading contemporary proponent of the Scanlon plan, describes the functions of the committees: 'To discuss ways and means of eliminating waste, easier and better ways of doing the job, the departmental schedules for that month, and anything else that might pertain to the work going through the department that month.'[13]

The typical Scanlon plan calls for two levels of committees – both of which meet monthly. The 'departmental production committees' consist of two or more employees and two or more management members. The employee representatives are usually elected but may also be appointed by union leadership. These committee members normally do not hold positions in grievance or safety committees. The management representatives (usually the foreman, chief engineer, office manager of the department) are appointed by plant management.

The departmental production committees typically meet for one hour once a month on company time. Each committee records suggestions which have been submitted during the month by employees in that department and record what action, if any, has been taken on past suggestions. Each committee is responsible for processing all suggestions brought before it. Each also discusses production problems, purchase of new machinery, profit margins on specific products, and other matters affecting the profitability of the enterprise. These committees do not deal with matters covered by the collective agreement, such as grievances, wages, and conditions of work.

Management reserves the right of final judgment on suggestions presented to the production committees. The committees are expected to explain to employees the reasons for not accepting particular suggestions.

12 Gilson and Lefcowitz 1957, 296
13 Lesieur 1958, 46

This is deemed essential to maintain continuing interest in submitting suggestions.

The second level of committee – the 'screening committee' – meets once a month, usually as soon as the production figure for the previous month are available. Membership consists of senior executives from various departments of the company, the senior officer of the union local, and elected employee representatives. The chairman of this committee is drawn from senior management ranks. This committee is charged with the responsibility of discussing and handling any suggestions which have not been resolved by the production committees. This committee may act as a 'court of higher appeal' for employees whose suggestions were turned down at the level of the production committee. Although most suggestions are handled at the production committees, some suggestions which involve the company as a whole or which involve major capital expenditures are forwarded to the screening committee. Typically, no votes are taken at the screening committee. Management reserves the right to make final decisions on all matters.

The screening committee also reviews the firm's performance during the previous month. The size of the Scanlon bonus, factors contributing to the size of this bonus, matters pertaining to new capital investment, new products, and competitive challenges are also discussed. At the screening committee meeting, management also communicates data on the company's competitive position – sales figures, new products, competitors' products, and long-run production problems.

The third component of the Scanlon plan is performance measurement and a bonus based on productivity improvements. Joseph Scanlon felt that individual incentives 'put the worker in business for himself.' Individual incentives pitted the employee against the larger interests of the company and produced inequities in wages, both of which led to poor morale.

Scanlon proposed a system of rewards based on individual skill and supplementary rewards based on the success of the enterprise to be shared among all employees. The calculation of bonus payments varies widely in Scanlon plants. The most commonly used method considers the 'sales value of production ratio.' This is a ratio of labour costs to the sales value of production (net sales plus or minus inventory changes) in the current period compared to the ratio in a prior base period. The bonus comes from improvement in this ratio from one period to the next. Each month part of the bonus is set aside in a reserve fund to cover possible deficit months (months in which the ratio is less favourable than in the base month). The amount set aside each month depends on the volatility of the ratio in previous months.

Typically, the company share of any bonus is 25 per cent. The remaining 75 per cent is distributed to all employees (up to and including the president or plant manager) each month as a percentage of the employee's gross income during that period. At the end of the Scanlon year, the amount set aside (after reconciling monthly deficits and surpluses) is divided in the same manner as the monthly bonuses are.

The following table is taken from the *Hayes-Dana Scanlon Handbook*. It illustrates how the Scanlon bonus is calculated in this particular plant.

HOW THE BONUS IS CALCULATED

In the base period October 1968 through June 1969, the payroll cost of making each dollar's worth of sales was .25 cents. This was known as the base ratio and was used as the measurement for our monthly performance. In 1971, this single measurement was changed to a dual measurement to permit a more equitable distribution of payroll to sales.

Today the payroll cost of making each dollar's worth of gasket sales is .2196 cents and .2710 cents for each dollar's worth of ring sales. This is now the ratio against which our performance each month is measured.

For Example:

If the net sales for gaskets was	$260,000
and there was an inventory factor decrease of	20,000
Then adjusted gasket sales for month come to	240,000
Allowed payroll for gaskets ($240,000 × .2196)	52,704
If the net sales for rings was	290,000
and there was an inventory factor increase of	10,000
Then adjusted ring sales for month come to	300,000
Allowed payroll for rings ($300,000 × .2710)	81,300
If payroll had been average this month,	
The total actual would have come to	$134,004
However, if the actual payroll for this month came to	113,804
This would mean an improvement	20,200

Bonus Pool

Set aside 25% as reserve ($20,200 × .25)	5,050
Which leaves for immediate distribution	15,150
The total employee's share (75%) of pool is ($15,150 × .75)	11,363
The Company share (25%) is ($15,150 × .25)	3,787
This is your bonus percentage paid $11,363 ÷ 113,804	10%

Your bonus is figured on your total eligible pay for the month before any deductions. This would include base pay, overtime, Holiday and Vacation pay, if any.

This total eligible pay is multiplied by the monthly bonus percent.

For example, if your monthly eligible pay was $500.00 and the monthly bonus percent was 10%, your bonus would be $50.00. ($500.00 × 10% = $50.00)

Strengths and weaknesses of the Scanlon plan
The Scanlon plan is the one form of workplace democracy which has proved to be successful in unionized operations; the role and power of the trade union is not challenged by the Scanlon plan. The union president, as a member of the screening committee, can veto any changes which infringe on the terms of the collective agreement. In addition, by sharing productivity gains with union members, the Scanlon plan allays the inevitable union suspicions over the goal of increasing productivity.

The co-operative spirit and the willingness of workers to accept technological change must be considered to be the chief advantages of the Scanlon plan. Under this plan, management need not 'open its books' to the union, although the Scanlon philosophy argues for an open and honest exchange between parties. In cases where management is fearful about 'opening the books' to the union, Scanlon consultants can provide their own independent audit to determine the monthly ratios.

The Scanlon plan, however, is not without its difficulties. It cannot survive without continuing technological improvements. The failure to pay a bonus is the most frequent cause of failure of the Scanlon plan.[14]

In many plants a plateau of interest is reached after the more obvious shortcomings and inefficiencies of the workplace have been corrected. Long-term success with the Scanlon plan requires continuing vigilance and 'feeding of the plan' to maintain interest.

Union stewards, who may not be members of the screening committee, may feel circumvented by the Scanlon plan. First-line supervisors can feel bypassed by worker representatives on the production and screening committees. The union head also faces considerable conflict; he is both an advocate for his members and a problem-solver with management. Not all union officials are able to reconcile these conflicting pressures.

The existing power positions of the union president and the plant manager are not affected by the Scanlon plan. Each retains control over his responsibilities according to the collective agreement. Contract disputes are handled through the usual collective bargaining procedures, not by Scanlon committees.

Under a Scanlon plan union officials approach the bargaining table with much more information on the company's position than would be so under conventional arrangements. Similarly, under an effectively running Scanlon plan management has better insight into the union's problems. The plan consequently can foster more collaborative labour-managment relations.

14 Driscoll 1978

There are few successful Scanlon plans in firms with more than 500 employees. In large organizations there are greater difficulties of mobilizing enthusiasm for the plan and demonstrating its financial effects.[15]

Evidence suggests that the Scanlon plan appears to work best in small companies (with fewer than 500 employees); in batch manufacturing technologies with a flexible technology, so that employee suggestions can make a difference in productivity; in firms with established union-management co-operation; in firms with an elastic demand curve so that increased production does not lead to lay-offs (alternative work should be available if productivity improvements lead to lay-offs); and in firms in which a simple and easily understood measure of performance can be calculated. The measure should be responsive to variations in the quality of work; the measure should be reasonably stable from one period to another; the measure should be adaptable to technological changes; and the company's output should be measurable for relatively short periods (such as each month).

The Scanlon plan does not work under conditions of high capital to labour ratio, in volatile consumer markets, and under conditions of rapid changes in raw material costs. The Scanlon plan promises to be most successful in firms with high volume production of standard parts (e.g., the automobile component industry) and in highly competitive industries where employee insight into technological problems may be essential for survival.

Scanlon plan success is correlated with positive management attitudes towards employee participation and with the degree of employee participation. The objective of the Scanlon plan is deceptively simple: to increase the productivity of the plant. However, the key to its success is the quality of the participation allowed employees.

The Scanlon plan is a proven and effective means of giving employees a voice in the management of the enterprise and of improving the firm's economic performance. The Scanlon plan is one form of workplace democracy which is explicitly participative in the manner in which it is introduced. Fred Lesieur (1958), for example, polls employees to obtain their attitude towards the Scanlon plan before he proceeds to introduce the plan. Lesieur will not proceed with a plan if employees, after being informed of the plan and how it might affect them, decide against it.

The Rucker plan
Closely allied to the Scanlon plan is the Rucker plan of group incentives. Like the Scanlon plan, the Rucker plan is a program designed to develop cost reductions and to improve profits through day-to-day employee participa-

15 However, White (1979) finds no correlation between size and success of the Scanlon plan.

tion and group incentives. The plan, first proposed by Allan W. Rucker, employs monthly bonuses, like the Scanlon plan, with reserves set aside to be reconciled after the annual financial audit.

Unlike the Scanlon plan, however, the Rucker plan employs as a measure of productivity the output of 'value added by manufacture' for each dollar of input of 'payroll costs.' The value added by manufacture is the difference between sales income from the goods produced and the costs of materials, supplies, and outside services consumed in the production and delivery of that output. Payroll costs include all employment costs. Flexible bonus programs may be designed using this measure of productivity for any group of plant and office employees.

The Hayes-Dana plant: the Scanlon plan in operation
The Scanlon plan in the Hayes-Dana plant in St Thomas, Ontario follows the conventional design. There are five production committees, one for each of five 'zones' in the plant. The production committees meet once a month. The screening committee consists of five elected employee representatives (elected from production committee members) and includes the president of the union. There are also five appointed management representatives, one of whom acts as chairman. This committee also meets once a month.

Following a one-year trial period 93 per cent of the bargaining unit voted to retain the Scanlon plan on a permanent basis. As in most plans, the committee operates on a consensus basis – that is, no votes are taken.

Recently, two additional committees have been formed. An 'operating committee,' consisting of three union and three management representatives is empowered to suggest and implement any changes in the Scanlon plan. For example, any changes in product mix or other conditions which might affect the equity of the program may require that the ratio be changed.

A 'task force' (a group of employees which meets with management during working hours) was also created to discuss problems which are particularly intractable. Members of a task force are charged with the responsibility of looking into the problem and reporting back to the screening committee through their zone representatives. Task forces have been found to be an effective means of mobilizing broader support and participation in the Scanlon plan.

WORKS COUNCILS

The European experience with the works council (a body of elected employee representatives who have co-decision-making rights with management) has prompted interest in the concept in North America. In Europe the works council is designed to complement employee board-level representation. In countries where collective bargaining is conducted at the national level the works council gives employees an opportunity to participate on shop floor matters. Consequently, the works council strengthens trade unionism in Europe. In North America, however, the works council has been proposed as an alternative to trade unionism.

The three firms with works councils, which are examined in this study, are not unionized. It is difficult to imagine a works council in this country operating in parallel with a trade union. The works council – North American style – is based on a collaborative, rather than on adversarial relationship between labour and management, and the works council assumes many of the responsibilities of a trade union.

Much of the interest in works councils in Canada was stimulated by the Connaghan Report (1976). Charles Connaghan, after reviewing the West German model of industrial democracy, suggested that the works council might be a means of improving labour-management relations in Canada. However, he cautioned that the form of the works council would have to be altered to suit the Canadian industrial relations system.

In this section a brief description of the works councils in West Germany as defined by the New Works Constitution Act is presented followed by a brief description of four varieties of works councils. These four examples vary in their terms of reference, in their purposes, and in the degree of employee participation.

Works councils in West Germany
The works councils in West Germany provide a means for all employees, whether members of trade unions or not, to have voice in making decisions which affect them. By law, the works council cannot interfere with either trade unions or employee associations in the pursuit of the protection of their members' interests. In general, West German trade unionists regard their right to participate in day-to-day decision-making with management as more central than the strike weapon in the protection of their members' interests.

Under the New Works Constitution Act, the works council has the right of co-determination on all matters affecting employment. That is, employee representatives have equal say with management on matters such as setting rates of pay (wages are negotiated nationally but firms are free to pay above the minimum negotiated wage); vacations, health / safety matters, job transfers, job classifications, and dismissals. The employer is obligated by law to inform and consult the works council on changes to plant, equipment, working procedures, and methods.

The size of the works council is determined by the number of employees in the firm who are eligible to vote (all employees who are at least eighteen years of age). In firms with five to twenty members, employees are allowed one representative on the works council; in firms with 300 to 600 employees, the works council will have nine employee representatives; and in firms of 3,000 to 4,000 employees, there will be twenty-three employee representatives. Employee representatives are elected for three-year terms and may be re-elected. Typically, the works council meets at least once a month.

Canadian Tire Corporation

The Canadian Tire distribution centres in Toronto have a form of works council called the 'employee-management committee,' which provides a forum for labour-management consultation and participation on a broad range of issues. The committee consists of eighteen members: fourteen elected employee representatives, each of whom represents fifteen to thirty employees in a particular work area; and four senior management personnel – the president of the corporation, the vice-president of industrial relations, the vice-president of distribution, and the personnel manager in the distribution centre. The employee representatives are elected for two-year terms. The employee-management committee meets once a month during regular work hours.

The elected representatives prepare an agenda for the meeting. In principle, any issue affecting the firm or employees can be discussed. Wages, benefits, health / safety matters, working conditions, employee complaints, grievances in the final stage, suggestions for improving productivity, and criticism of supervision are among the issues discussed at recent committee meetings.

No votes are taken in the committee. The committee operates on a collaborative basis and consensus on issues is sought. In many cases elected representatives are charged with handling local issues with supervisors. Issues not satisfactorily resolved on a face-to-face basis with supervision are brought before the committee.

Minutes of the meeting are posted in the plant. On the shop-floor spans of control are broad. Foremen act as co-ordinators and exercise little direct supervision over workers.

Recently, management decided that three shifts were necessary at the warehouse to meet commitments to their stores. This decision was made by management; the elected representatives planned the type of shift, its implementation, and the means of determing shift assignments.

The company also has a profit-sharing plan. One trustee is elected from the group of employee representatives to govern the profit-sharing plan (with two others). The profit-sharing plan has been very successful and has been a significant determinant of the collaborative relationship between management and employees.

Lincoln Electric of Canada Limited
Lincoln Electric of Canada (a subsidiary of Lincoln Electric Limited of Cleveland, Ohio) has one of the most famous and successful works councils in this country. The council, called the 'advisory council,' provides a forum for the discussion of all matters concerning the welfare of the company and its employees. No major policy changes are undertaken in the firm without discussion in the advisory council. All matters – including new products, health / safety, working conditions, sales and financial matters, appeals of merit ratings, appointment of supervision – are brought before the council.

The council consists of eight elected employee representatives (one elected representative from each department or group of departments), one elected foreman representative, and the president of the firm. The president acts as chairman of the council. Representatives are elected for one-year terms and cannot serve two consecutive terms. The representatives are charged with the responsibility of keeping people in their departments informed of council activities. The advisory council meets once a month on company time and minutes of the council are posted.

Like Canadian Tire, Lincoln Electric operates a successful profit-sharing plan. One-half of Lincoln Electric employees are shareholders; collectively they own 20 per cent of the equity in Lincoln Electric of Canada. The profit-sharing bonus normally equals 50 per cent of regular salary which is set at the prevailing wage rate for the industry.[16]

Supreme Aluminium Industries
Perhaps the best known Canadian firm with a works council is Supreme Aluminium Industries Limited in Toronto. The council is called the Supreme Association for Effective Results (SAFER). The SAFER governing body consists of eighteen members; twelve are elected from among the non-supervisory work-force; four are elected from supervisory ranks (two from the first-line supervision and two from middle management); and two representatives

16 Normally, their U.S. counterparts earn a bonus equal in size to their regular salary.

are appointed by the president from senior management ranks. Elected representatives hold office for a term of two years and no one may be elected for more than two consecutive terms. One-half of the SAFER body is elected each year.

All members have an equal vote on matters brought before the governing body. After a discussion of any issue, a vote is held. The vote may be open or secret, at the option of the chairman. The meeting is governed by *Robert's Rules of Order.*

The chairman of the governing body can be any member of the SAFER governing body or any employee in the firm with at least two years seniority. The appointment of the chairman is confirmed annually by the governing body. In addition to the eighteen members, the personnel department appoints two members, one of whom acts as recording secretary; neither may vote. All employees in the firm have an elected representative, with the exception of senior management and the sales force (members of the sales force are located in sales offices outside of the plant). Elections to the SAFER council are conducted by the governing body.

The SAFER governing body is responsible 'for all matters which directly concern people.' This includes job classifications, the establishment of salary schedules, annual wages increases, hours and conditions of work, the final decision on grievances, lay-offs, assignment and transfer of people to jobs, operating speeds, and methods of production. In addition, management reports on sales figures, profits, production, and new products.

The SAFER governing body must meet at least four times a year; in practice, it meets six to ten times per year. Meetings are usually of four hours' duration, on company time (if not, employees are paid for attending).

Management reserves the right to make decisions in three areas: hiring, suspending, or discharging employees (subject to the grievance procedure and subject to the final and binding decision of the governing council); the determination of the earnings of supervisors, salesmen, and managers; and the determination of the nature and variety of production. Although management reserves the right to make final decisions in these three areas, it is obligated to make decisions only after consultation with the SAFER governing body, the chairman of the governing body, or with the elected representatives of employees affected by the decision.

The responsibilities of elected representatives include being 'on call' to answer the questions of their constituents, to consult with managers on plans which may affect their constituents, to defend the interests of their constituents, and to keep their constituents fully informed of all developments which might affect them.

Emphasis is on direct, face-to-face problem-solving. In cases where agreement cannot be reached on this basis the question comes before the governing body for a final decision. Jeff Davidson, the industrial relations manager, has described the SAFER governing body in the following way to newly elected employee representatives.

The governing body is in effect an 'industrial parliament' (employee government) which operates in a very similar manner to our municipal, provincial, and federal governments. We elect representatives to make decisions for us in all areas of the business which affect us. Those representatives are accountable to us. We ask them to take our views into account, make decisions for us, and advise us of their decisions. We may not always be pleased with their decisions as individuals, but we do expect them to take the good of all employees into account. Just as in public life, petitions can be taken and candidates voted out of office when their decisions are unpopular to the majority of their constituents. For this reason, it makes sense that all employees weigh very carefully whom they will nominate and elect, because in the end, the choice will affect them very substantially.

In society, we elect members of parliament to decide our taxes and to make and administer our laws. In Supreme, we elect SAFER representatives to decide our wages and benefits, to make and administer our annual contract or agreement, to represent our interests, protect our rights as people and in accordance with the agreement, and to ensure that our interests and views are considered in decision making which affects us as employees. So, working conditions, work processes, changes in these areas, and personal treatment, are very much in SAFER's territory. Just as our governments make and try to fairly enforce the rules of society, so SAFER makes and tries to fairly enforce the rules of industrial life at Supreme Aluminium.[17]

The democratic values underlying the workplace democracy at Supreme Aluminium are reflected in article 3 – Purpose, taken from the constitution of the SAFER governing council: 'In the search for a better way of industrial life in which mutual trust, respect and understanding will be the goal, all employees (supervisory and non-supervisory) will work together to share information and responsibilities and thus through consultation and involvement by all concerned there will be created a democratic atmosphere in which decisions affecting the employees will be made by employees.'[18]

This ethic is further reflected in a profit-sharing plan and a stock purchase plan for employees. Thirty per cent of pre-tax profits are distributed in equal

17 Memo to SAFER representatives, 30 March 1978
18 The constitution and by-laws of Supreme Association for Effective Results 1977, 5

dollar amounts each year to all employees. One-third is paid in cash; one-third is placed in a diversified portfolio DPSP; and one-third is placed in a DPSP which consists entirely in Supreme Aluminium shares.[19]

Multiple management

One of the more unusual forms of works council found in North America is the multiple management concept, pioneered at McCormick and Company of Baltimore. There are roughly 100 firms in North America with multiple management boards. Multiple management was created by Charles McCormick, who upon assuming the presidency of McCormick and Company at the age of thirty-six felt he needed assistance in managing the company and enlisted the co-operation of employees by allowing them to participate in decision-making.[20]

Underlying the concept of multiple management is a strong democratic philosophy. For example, Charles McCormick reports

The Multiple Management plan is built on a firm concept of putting people first. The plan operates through a combination of auxiliary management boards, participation, sponsorship (every new recruit is assigned to a senior manager, much like the 'god-father' system in Japan – author's note), merit rating, and two-way communication between all employees and management. A major aim is to eliminate one-man rule in business and to train and develop young executives in accordance with their merit, rather than their age. The real secret of its success is participation; it offers administrative outlets for our basic needs as workers.[21]

In McCormick and Company there are four boards – a senior board (the equivalent of a board of directors), a junior board, a factory board, and a sales board. Members of each board are assigned the responsibility of bringing forward proposals to improve the operation. The boards are charged explicitly with the responsibility of studying the company operation and of suggesting ways in which it might be improved. The boards are designed to bring new perspectives into the management structure; to provide recognition of outstanding employees; to provide promotion opportunities in addition to the normal channels; to provide a training ground for employees; to

19 See chapter 8 for a description of DPSP.
20 There is a interesting parallel with Lincoln Electric. Lincoln, as a young man of 31 years assumed control of Lincoln Electric and involved his workers because he felt he needed their advice.
21 McCormick 1973, 15

break down departmental interests by emphasizing common interests; and to emphasize team accomplishment rather than individual competition.

In McCormick and Company, McCormick appointed the first members to each board, but thereafter new members were selected by existing members by means of a merit rating system. The boards elect their own officers and they govern themselves. Any proposal brought forward from a board must have the unanimous endorsement of all members of the board before it is sent to the senior board for consideration.

The junior board represents office employees, personnel and administrative employees, and office management. It consists of twenty members. There are two types of members of the junior board: regular and associate. An associate member cannot vote or hold office and becomes eligible for consideration for regular membership after completion of four three-month terms within a twenty-four-month period.

The factory board, consisting of twenty members (both regular and associate) represents factory management. This board considers matters pertaining to working conditions, employee suggestions, and improving the relationship between the company and its employees.

The sales board consists of fifteen members and is concerned with sales, advertising, and merchandising matters.

The senior board (of directors) receives the reports and suggestions of the three other boards. All proposals brought forward to the senior board must have the unanimous endorsement of all members of the junior board. All members of the senior board are recruited from members of the other boards. Final selection is made by shareholders, with no limit to the number of reappointments.

The senior board, in turn, must give unanimous approval before a proposal is given to line management for action. Approximately 80 per cent of proposals of the junior boards are adopted by the senior board. All major company decisions must pass through the relevant board. Meetings of the boards take place at least every two weeks and members are paid for time spent on board activities.

In McCormick and Company in Baltimore there are ten junior boards in the area of factory, sales, and corporate office. Any employee in middle or junior management who shows managerial potential can be elected by his peers to one of these junior boards. At six-month intervals members of the boards evaluate each other on six factors: originality, judgment, achievement, forcefulness, stability, and human relations. The 20 per cent of current board members receiving the lowest evaluations are rotated off the board and new members are elected from a list of candidates compiled by the membership committee of the board. Individuals rotated off the board may be re-elected later if justified by their performance.

The executive committee of the junior boards is made up of the three highest rated regular members at each semi-annual rating (excluding the chairman and secretary).

The multiple management board concept is an effective means of involving management personnel in organizational decision-making, although in many firms the rank and file worker cannot participate. Watson (1974) reports that increasingly, firms employing multiple management boards are spending less time on routine operational procedures and more time on corporate planning, policy matters, and comprehensive projects involving interdepartmental co-ordination. Watson also reports a shift away from direct involvement in day-to-day employee affairs such as benefits and working conditions. This trend is unfortunate in non-unionized firms because these matters may not be attended to in a manner which allows employee participation.

The most essential condition for the success of multiple management is the management philosophy. Harry K. Wells, president and chief executive officer of McCormick and Company, observes,

McCormick is bound together – is motivated – and thrives – because of our Multiple Management Philosophy.

Multiple Management is at once a system of management and of management development – as well as a philosophy of people – a philosophy which recognizes and appreciates the dignity of the individual, and understanding of human relations and of human relationships, participation at all levels of employment, recognition, and lastly – a sharing of rewards for success. Multiple Management is operational every day through our board systems, through our personnel policies, through our benefit programs, through profit sharing and genuine concern for all connected with the business – employees, customers, and stockholders alike.[22]

Club House Foods
The program of multiple management at Club House Foods (a Canadian subsidiary of McComick and Company) is somewhat simpler than the McCormick and Company model. Club House employs 136 people and has one management board. The board consists of six regular members (four senior and two middle managers); six associate members (mostly from middle-management ranks and some recently promoted); and eight 'orien-

22 H.K. Wells, quoted in Metzger 1975b, 26

tees' (at the time of the survey, five from management and three from the rank and file). The orientees are permitted to observe and participate in some board activities.

This board can examine any facet of the company's operation except wages and benefits. Annual wage increases are handled through a survey of comparable firms in the immediate area. As in McCormick and Company, board members evaluate each other semi-annually on the six criteria. The five highest-ranking members form a membership committee to choose the remaining regular and associate members and orientees.

PRODUCER CO-OPERATIVES

The producer co-operative, like other forms of workplace democracy, has not enjoyed widespread acceptance in Canada, despite a long history in both the United States and Europe. The best-known early examples were the Rochdale Pioneers in the United Kingdom (who established co-operative mills in 1844 for the purpose of breaking the monopoly of the corn millers) and Robert Owen's experiment at New Lanark on the Clyde. Producer co-operatives were established in the United States as early as 1791. Several hundred worker-run factories were established in the United States during the New Deal, but most disappeared soon afterward. Today clusters of producer co-operatives can be found in the Pacific north-west of the United States and in the provinces of Quebec and Saskatchewan.

Unlike their European counterparts Canadian and American producer co-operatives did not develop from a political / ideological base; most evolved for purely pragmatic reasons – the economic benefit of members, maintaining employment, saving a company town, or keeping employees off welfare rolls. Perhaps Sidney and Beatrice Webb's (1894; 1902) disapproval of the concept of producer co-operatives weakened the link between the concept of worker-ownership and the political left. The Webbs' advocacy of collective bargaining and their support of consumer co-operatives rather than producer co-operatives removed the ideological base from the movement.

Because of the absence of an ideological base, producer co-operatives have taken a variety of organizational forms in North America. The labels 'industrial co-operative,' 'expanded employee ownership,' 'worker co-operative,' and 'labour-managed firm,' have been used to describe variants of producer co-operatives. The term 'producer co-operative' in general defines an economic enterprise owned collectively by employees. Ultimate control of the enterprise is exercised by employees.[23]

The classic producer co-operative represents a significant departure from conventional practice. Following Jones (1978), a classic producer co-operative is defined in terms of the following five attributes:

1 It is autonomous, that is, it is not a subsidiary of another firm.
2 Workers are able to become members of the enterprise, usually by nominal holdings of share capital.
3 Formal provision exists for direct and indirect participation in decision-making by worker-members at all levels.
4 Worker-members, by virtue of their functional role as workers, share in the income remaining after payment of all other costs of production.
5 The co-operative principles of 'one member – one vote' and 'limited return on capital' apply.

The fifth attribute is the most restrictive; few North American enterprises qualify as classic producer co-operatives if these two principles apply.

The co-operative creed is illustrated in the 1966 Statement of the Congress of the International Co-operative Alliance. The six co-operative principles of this statement are as follows.

1 Membership of a co-operative society should be voluntary and available without artificial restriction or any social, political, racial, or religious discrimination, to all persons who can make use of its services and are willing to accept the responsibilities of membership.
2 Co-operative societies are democratic organizations. Their affairs should be administered by persons elected or appointed in a manner agreed by the members and accountable to them. Members of primary societies

---

23 Producer co-operatives are to be distinguished from consumer co-operatives. In the latter profits are distributed to customers as a dividend on purchases instead of to shareholders as a dividend on shares. Producer co-operatives produce a product or provide a service and members involved in a productive role in the organization are considered as members. Surplus is distributed to the members, not to customers.

The term 'producer co-operatives' has been used to define a group of employers or single owners. The term producer co-operative will be used here to define enterprises owned by all or a substantial majority of employees. The essence of the producer co-operative, therefore, is significant employee ownership of the enterprise.

should enjoy equal rights of voting (one member, one vote) and participation in decisions affecting their societies. In other than primary societies the administration should be conducted on a democratic basis in a suitable form.

3 Share capital should receive only a strictly limited rate of interest.

4 The economic results arising out of the operations of a society belong to the members of that society and should be distributed in such a manner as would avoid one member gaining at the expense of others. This may be done by decision of the members as follows: (a) by provision for development of the business of the co-operatives, (b) by provision of common services, or, (c) by distribution among the members in proportion to their transactions with the society.

5 All co-operative societies should make provision for the education of their members, officers, and employees, and of the general public, in the principles and techniques of co-operation, both economic and democratic.

6 All co-operative organizations, in order to best serve the interest of their members and their communities, should actively co-operate in every practical way with other co-operatives at local, national, and international levels.

The goals of the classic producer co-operative include education in co-operative principles, social welfare, as well as the creation and maintenance of jobs for its members. The classic producer co-operative is more ideologically and politically oriented than other varieties of producer co-operatives found in North America. Many members of classic producer co-operatives perceive the organization as a socialist enclave within a corrupt and exploitative capitalist system. The creed of democratic control, collective decision-making, and worker liberation from the domination and exploitation of market relationships lies behind most classic producer co-operatives.

Producer co-operatives differ from one another in many respects: the procedures by which workers become members; structures permitting participation in the management of the enterprise; procedures for determining the distribution of surplus; whether or not employment of non-member labour is permitted; whether the co-operative contributes to the welfare of the larger community; and relationships with co-operative banks and financial institutions. Ownership may be direct or indirect through a trust; membership may or may not provide voting rights; stock ownership may or may not be compulsory for membership.

Among the forms of producer co-operatives found in North America, relatively few offer a high degree of rank and file participation in decision-making. Many are organized along conventional lines, although employees as shareholders exercise ultimate control over the organization. Seventeen of the twenty-five producer co-operatives in Quebec studied by Vaillancourt (1975) were of this kind. Similarly, none of the six employee-owned enterprises studied by Hammer and Stern (1980) was based on the 'one member – one vote' standard of the classic producer co-operative.

Vanek (1975) distinguishes between the pure 'worker-managed' firm and the pure 'labor-managed' firm. Both permit complete control of an autonomous enterprise by all employees on the basis of equal votes. In the 'worker-managed' firm no charge is made for the use of capital. Investment is financed by retained earnings, which cannot be recovered by individual worker members. In the 'labor-managed' firm, on the other hand, a fixed scarcity reflecting return is paid for capital.[24]

Vanek considers most North American producer co-operatives to be imperfect forms of worker participation. They are controlled by capital and often involve less than the entire work force. Ideally, all control, management, and income reside in the hands of those who actually work in the enterprise according to the 'one member – one vote' principle.

Challenges for the producer co-operative
The classic producer co-operative is rarely found in North America. This form of organization faces a number of serious challenges. The success of the classic producer co-operative rests on the acceptance of values which are not widely shared in the larger community. Work organizations cannot be closed systems, insensitive to the cultural and economic conditions which surround them. The importance of environmental support for the survival of producer co-operatives may explain the clustering of co-operatives in particular regions and industries in North America.

In western Canada farm machinery co-operatives (co-operative ownership of farm machinery) and 'agripools' are commonplace. Agripools are co-operatives in which members rent land to the co-operative but retain ownership. Members farm all of the land and share wages and profits made by the co-operative.

One of the most favourable social environments for co-operatives in North America is found in the province of Quebec. In Quebec farming co-operatives control 40 per cent of the market (fishing 45 per cent, milk

24 Vanek observes that most economic failures of producer co-operatives result from the reliance on internal financing through retained earnings and the failure to charge a scarcity reflecting price for the use of capital.

products 80 per cent, and meat packing 30 per cent). Co-operatives are also common in the logging industry. Further, 57 per cent of French-speaking adults are members of caisses populaires (co-operative savings and loan associations) and approximately 1.4 per cent of the working population of Quebec works in co-operatives. Support for the co-operative movement has come from many quarters in Quebec society – the political left, the labour movement, the Parti Québécois, the Catholic church, municipal-provincial governments, and political idealists.

The co-operative ethic is often difficult to maintain in the North American economic environment. The Vermont Asbestos Group, for example, was recently purchased by 200 employees from G.A.F. Corporation and survived for three years as a co-operative. However, during that period, the book value of a share rose from $50 to $2,103. Employees voted to sell their shares to a private owner.

In Canada employees in two employee-owned enterprises have voted to sell their shares to a private owner and thereby to terminate their control over the firm. At Byers Transport in Edmonton, Alberta employees realized a very substantial financial gain by selling their shares. According to the firm's charter, unanimous agreement of employee-owners was required before an offer of purchase could be accepted. This unanimous agreement was obtained.

At Pioneer Chain Saw in Peterborough, Ontario employee-owners, when faced with an offer of purchase, voted to sell their shares. They preferred a financial gain to co-owning and co-managing the company.

In the classic producer co-operative the individual worker can never recover his investment (except in unusual circumstances). Consequently, in order to recover their equity founding members have an incentive to sell the co-operative.

Vaillancourt observes,

Collective norms of social organization are not encouraged in the capitalist market system. Rather, people are taught to be competitive and to analyze situations from their own individualistic self-interest. A worker production cooperative demands that these orientations be abandoned and that people inside the cooperative work together collectively. Such a collective is difficult to build and maintain because of the fact that the daily face-to-face relationships encountered in the society are essentially competitive and based on personal interest. The contradictions between behaviour expected inside the cooperative and behavior expected outside in the world at large is sometimes too great to overcome. If the cooperative is to survive in the capitalist, competitive world, it must at the same time sustain harmonious internal relationships and a competitive posture in external relationships.[25]

One important principle in the larger society violated by the classic producer co-operative is the right of ownership. Ownership of property implies the right of use, the right of disposal, and the right of benefits from the use or disposal of the property (subject to the rights of others who have standing in law). Although these rights are never absolute in our society and although the domain of individual freedom and control over property has been subject to increasing limitations over time, the classic producer co-operative significantly abridges contemporary standards of the rights of ownership. These ownership rights are limited in the classic producer co-operative, because the owner of capital cannot draw unlimited return from invested capital. The surplus is distributed in proportion to participation in production, not in proportion to ownership of capital.

Shares cannot be withdrawn in the classic producer co-operative. Members of the co-operative are trustees, and cannot benefit from the surplus. The surplus is to be re-invested or to be used for the benefit of the community at large. Members of the co-operative have the right to employ the assets of the co-operative (which they or their predecessors have built up) and they have an obligation to pass the accumulated surplus on to future generations. Upon dissolution of the co-operative members are entitled to take out only as much as they have put in (in some cases allowing for inflation). Any surplus goes to charity or is given to another co-operative.

The conventions and practices in the larger society often make it difficult for the classic producer co-operative to survive while upholding its principles. Among the difficult questions to be faced by the producer co-operative are the following. During periods of economic downturn, should worker-members be laid off? Can the producer co-operative hire and pay for managerial talent? Can managers be found who share the ideology of the co-operative yet who possess the requisite managerial skills? Will salary differentials reflecting differences in contribution among members be permitted? Will the co-operative be able to finance technological improvements through retained earnings? Can the co-operative accumulate capital at the same rate as the entrepreneurially managed organization?

Many proponents of the classic co-operative model have expressed disappointment in those producer co-operatives which have 'degenerated' into

25 Vaillancourt 1975, 27

simple profit-making businesses, indistinguishable from private enterprises. Many co-operatives close membership by raising the cost of membership or by taking on hired labour. Many co-operatives also limit employee participation in decision-making. These tendencies are not surprising, however, given the pressures from the larger economic environment.

In co-operatives where financing comes from retained earnings only investments with very high rates of return will be undertaken, and the co-operative will be at equilibrium in a position of underinvestment.

In North America producer co-operatives often face hostile capital markets. In Canada, however, the Desjardins Co-operative Movement does provide support for co-operative endeavours (e.g., to the Canadian Co-operative Implements Limited and to Tricofil). Proponents of the co-operative movement suggest that the inhospitable economic environment dominated by market relationships has impaired the economic efficiency of producer co-operatives.

In the classic co-operative all workers are members. However, in many North American co-operatives, membership is based on stock ownership rather than on participation in the productive process. In these cases two classes of worker may emerge: the worker-owner and the non-worker-owner. When the capitalized value of individual shares becomes very high, new members cannot afford to join the co-operative. Workers then hire other workers without admitting them to the co-operatives.[26]

Retiring members who cash their shares (if this procedure is allowed) can create liquidity problems for the co-operative. Care must be taken during the planning of a co-operative to provide a means for the ready selling of shares without placing undue financial pressure on the co-operative. Employees who join a producer co-operative or who wish to create one must make trade-offs between ownership, savings, and their retirement security. Often workers have no savings available to invest in an enterprise and must borrow or invest their pension funds in the new enterprise.

Evidence for the effectiveness of producer co-operatives
On the basis of available evidence little can be said about the comparative effectiveness of producer co-operatives and conventional capitalist enterprises. Few producer co-operatives have survived over the years, although some appear to have performed better than their capitalist counterparts in the short run. The two producer co-operatives in this study (Harvey Trans-

26 See Russell, Hochner, and Perry, 1977; refuse collectors in San Francisco are an example.

port and Les Industries du Saguenay) are economically viable and profitable enterprises.

The most complete documentation of the effects of employee ownership comes from a study by Richard Long of Byers Transport. Long examined behavioural and financial outcomes in the firm before and after it had been purchased by employees. He reports that the change to employee ownership resulted in more employee influence at the organizational, departmental, and job levels. He found that employee-owners tended to view their organizational lives more positively and to be more committed, involved, and integrated into the firm than non-employee-owners.[27]

Managers and workers cite many advantages of employee ownership: monetary gain, satisfaction of working for oneself, improved motivation of staff, and improved communication between management and workers.

Long also reports increases in output. Damage claims in the firm declined by 60 per cent; the quantity of work performed by freight handlers improved by 75 per cent; turnover declined by 30 per cent; and the profits of the firm have increased.

The participation paradox

The co-operative is based on the principle of ownership and not directly on the principle of governance. That is, 'who owns' is not necessarily the same as 'who governs.' Table A-1 presents four combinations of ownership and control.

Evidence from this study suggests that employee ownership is not necessarily associated with employee participation in decision-making. Ownership entails the right to appoint members to the board, although in many producer co-operatives, this right is not exercised. The two producer co-operatives in this sample fall into cell 2 of the table. Authoritarian leadership styles have frequently been observed in producer co-operatives.[28] There are many well-known American examples of employee-owned firms which do not permit participation: the Chicago-Northwestern Railroad, the Kansas City Star, and the Milwaukee Journal. Several observers have also commented that workers – even worker-owners – do not necessarily want democratic management.[29] They prefer to let management run the business.

27 Strict comparisons, however, are impossible because employees who have purchased shares might have already been more committed to the organization than their counterparts who did not purchase shares (Long 1978).
28 Shirom 1972
29 Pateman 1970; Dahl 1970; and Strauss 1963

TABLE A-1
Organizations classified by degree of
employee ownership and control

Degree of employee ownership	Degree of employee control	
	high	low
High	1	2
Low	3	4

Dachler and Wilpert (1978) raise the question 'Under what organizational, group, and individual conditions does participative structure lead to participative process?' It is clear that the day-to-day decision-making process need not correspond to the formal organization structure, although congruence theory postulates a close relationship between the two. Participation in the human relations tradition would be found in organizations in cell 3. Organizations whose members are protected by a strong union would also be found in cell 3. Several of the firms in this sample would also fall in cell 3 (e.g., The Group at Cox) while some firms, such as Supreme Aluminium Industries, would fall in cell 1.

Hammer and Stern (1980), in a study of a furniture factory purchased by employees, found that workers perceived management as the true owners of the firm, and did not perceive themselves as equal partners with management. The workers also preferred a hierarchical rather than an egalitarian distribution of power.

However, Russell, Hochner, and Perry (1977), in a study of worker-owned and conventionally managed refuse collection firms in San Francisco state that worker-owners, compared to non-worker-owners in other organizations report greater participation, more total influence, and more equal distribution of influence in their firms.

Workers must feel that their control of the enterprise is legitimate (the prevailing North American ideology is not congenial with this notion) and that they have the expertise required to co-manage the business. The workers in the two producer co-operatives in this sample were satisfied with their rights of ownership – the right to dividend income, the right of appointment of the members of the board, and the right of access to financial data. The relationship between labour and management was sufficiently positive that the workers allowed management to run the enterprise on a day-to-day basis.

Summary
Employee ownership promises to be one vehicle for the democratization of workplaces in the future. However, the form will not be the classic producer co-operative; ownership will take the form of stock purchase plans offered by conventionally managed firms through ESOPs, and by firms purchased by employees (such as Tembec Forest Products Limited) to maintain employment. Pressure will be placed on governments to support financially employees who purchase firms divested by a parent corporation, and trade unions will increasingly be called upon to underwrite investments which guarantee jobs for their members. In cases where government support is offered to firms about to be purchased by employees it is not unreasonable to expect the governments to insist on significant employee ownership and / or participation in the management of the enterprise. The government of the province of Quebec was instrumental in the creation of Tembec Forest Products Limited, although it opposed the union's request for labour parity on the board of directors of the firm, because it was not confident that the firm could be managed profitably through parity co-management.

However, the increasing willingness to experiment with new forms of work organization and the spreading of the democratic ethic into work organizations will mean that producer co-operatives will undoubtedly flourish in the future.

SELF-DIRECTING WORK GROUPS

Direct participation at the work group level on the shop floor is the most popular form of workplace democracy in Canada and the United States. The concept of self-directing (autonomous) work groups represents a substantial departure from conventional management practice, but among the varieties of employee participation examined in this study it is the most consistent with prevailing ideology and practice. Ownership rights and the control of organizational policy are not questioned by the concept; further, the concept offers many advantages to the worker which cannot be attained by membership in a trade union.

Shop-floor democracy through job design has received considerable attention from both the academic community and the mass media. The celebrated labour-management conflict at Lordstown, Ohio was not sparked by a demand for worker control and was not an assault on private property; it was a revolt against the monotony, subordination, and inflexibility of the assembly line. Self-directing work groups – even in the most rigid technologies – offer promise of eliminating the boredom and alienation of the shop-floor by involving employees directly in making decisions pertaining to their work activities.

Davis and Taylor identify four characteristics of self-directing behaviour in the workplace: self-regulation of the content and structure of the job; self-evaluation of job performance; self-adjustment to changes required by the work technology; and participation in determining the production goals of the group.[30] In self-directing work groups responsibility for planning, co-ordinating, directing, and evaluating work activities is achieved by a direct participative process.

Susman (1976) observes that self-directing work groups are permitted three types of decisions: self-regulating decisions – which are intrinsic to the production process itself (e.g., maintaining performance standards); self-governing decisions – that is, decisions about the process through which decisions will be made by work group members; and decisions in areas where independence and judgment can be exercised – the timing of work breaks, lunch, shift scheduling, holidays, and work assignments.

Although the process is limited to the shop-floor, it has implications for the larger organization and requires simultaneous changes in other aspects of the organization. Shop-floor democracy requires changes in supervision, reporting relationships, wage payment, work rules, and job descriptions.

The concept of self-directing work groups viewed participation as a process employed in the design or redesign of jobs as well as an outcome of job design itself. The rationale for increased employee participation on the job is based on the belief that the workers themselves are closest to the production process and often possess skills and knowledge about the job not possessed by others. In addition, the cost of self-direction and self-co-ordination is less than the cost of external direction and co-ordination.

In self-directing work groups, members develop their own norms about appropriate behaviour. Groups contain more potential for checks and balances, understanding, compassion, and justice than traditional supervision does.[31]

Although the terms 'autonomous,' 'self-directing,' and 'self-regulating' are used to describe decision-making activities, work groups on the shop floor are never fully autonomous or fully self-directing. Susman points out 'what

30 Davis and Taylor 1979, xiv-xvi
31 Walton 1972

determines whether a unit at any level is autonomous is not the kind of decisions that are made; there is no check list one can consult. Autonomy is determined by whether the unit can make decisions for the unit as a whole and thus allow the unit to maintain certain critical performance standards at steady-state levels.'[32] Members of self-directing work groups remain part of the larger organization and are bound by its policies and procedures.

Socio-technical design

Socio-technical systems theory provides the underlying theoretical rationale for participation through job design.[33] Socio-technical job design is based on the principle of 'joint optimization.' This principle endeavours to optimize the functioning of a productive system – which has both social and technical subsystems – by satisfying both the task requirements and the psychological and social needs of the job incumbent. The optimal socio-technical system is characterized by meaningful work, responsibility, control over the work process, work which allows the completion of an entire operation, and work which allows opportunities to interact with others.

Socio-technical systems theory highlights a significant oversight of traditional job design: the needs for variety, autonomy, and challenge of the person performing the job. This perspective is often difficult for managers and engineers to accept. They have been trained to know the problems and solutions; allowing workers to participate is seen as an admission that their understanding of the job is incomplete.

Socio-technical systems theory also emphasizes the latent talents and abilities of workers which are often ignored in conventional job design. The research evidence employing socio-technical job design by Cummings and Molloy (1977) demonstrates that performance improvement is the most consistent outcome of autonomous work group experimentation. While attitudinal effects are also positive, they are weaker. Research evidence also demonstrates that machinery design can add variety, autonomy and responsibility to routine, machine-paced jobs.

Socio-technical systems theory has become the dominant perspective employed by those concerned with the human factors in job design. Support for socio-technical theory comes largely from case studies, not from research which employs standardized research instruments. In fact, empirical support for the central postulate of this theory – productivity is maximized when the social and technical subsystems are jointly optimized – has never been

32 Susman 1976, 119
33 Rice 1958; Emery 1969; Trist and Bamforth 1951

FIGURE A-1 Strategies for accommodating the social and the technical
           subsystems of work

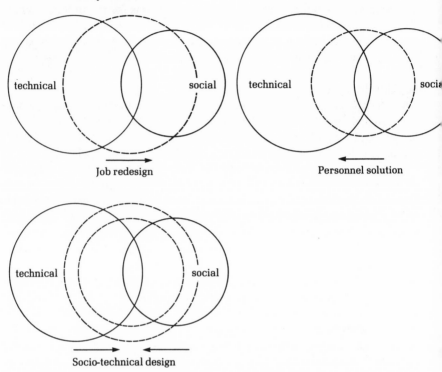

empirically confirmed. The original studies of productivity of coal mines
makes only one reference to productivity: 'though the more highly mechan-
ized faces studied in the present research had achieved a steady state, their
level of productivity was not impressively greater than that found on conventional long-walls and was substantially below the level theoretically
possible.'[34] Trist and his colleagues found that technical systems designed
without accommodating the human and social systems did not approach the
potential that justified their introduction to the coal face. However, this is
not to say that productivity is greatest when the social and technical systems
are jointly optimized. This proposition remains to be empirically tested.

The support for this proposition is largely anecdotal and impressionistic.
Walton, for example, points out, 'I believe that the average effectiveness of

34 Trist et al. 1963, 95. This passage was brought to my attention by Harvey Kolodny.

these innovative work systems is higher than the average of more conventionally organized but otherwise comparable plants. Certainly, however, the poorly managed innovative plants are less effective than the better managed conventional ones. I cannot offer proof that these assumptions are valid, but the mixed experiences of the companies I have discussed illustrate my observations.'[35]

The socio-technical strategy is illustrated schematically in figure A-1. It is compared with two other strategies – job redesign and selection and placement practices. Orthodox job redesign (Herzberg 1966) endeavours to achieve an accommodation between the technical and social subsystems by changing the technical system. Schematically, this procedure involves moving the technical area towards the social.

The traditional personnel solution endeavours to obtain overlap between the social and technical systems by moving the social subsystem towards the technical. In other words, people are hired or trained to accommodate a fixed technical system. The socio-technical strategy endeavours to move both the social and technical systems to a point of joint accommodation.

Techniques of job redesign
Recent interest in job redesign has focused on the process of 'enriching' work. One of the more obvious ways of enriching work is to extend the work cycle, so that each worker is allowed to complete an entire unit of work. However, this approach may require the rebuilding of the entire technology and may involve significant training costs.

The extension of work cycles appears to have its limits. Swedish evidence indicates that the optimum work cycle is twenty to twenty-five minutes for light assembly, and forty-five to sixty minutes for heavy assembly. It is becoming clear from accumulating evidence that optimum cycles (that is, cycles which do not adversely affect productivity) must be assessed for each case. In work technologies which do not permit the extension of the work cycle job rotation may be possible.

The most common form of job rotation involves an exchange of jobs among workers for a defined period of time. At Laidlaw Lumber, for example, workers rotate jobs every two hours. A second form of job rotation is 'rolling work' whereby the worker moves from one work station to the next, following a product as it moves through the production system. Evidence from Sweden, however, suggests that many workers do not like the movement and the adjustment to new tasks as they shift from one work

35   Walton 1979, 93

station to another. In general, the results of job rotation from Sweden are disappointing.[36]

Job rotation can also be part of a training program to increase an individual operator's skills and ability to stand in for absent workers. This form of job rotation often occurs spontaneously in work groups given the responsibility for production; when work builds up at one station, some workers voluntarily shift from their tasks to assist others (as in The Group at Cox).

In addition to extending the work cycle or rotating jobs, work may be enriched by integrating production and auxiliary tasks; production workers can be made responsible for preventive maintenance, repair of machinery, and quality control. However, in some technologies an operator cannot possess all the specialized skills; or quality control equipment may be expensive and, therefore, not available at all work stations. The integration of production and auxiliary tasks may also conflict with trade union jurisdictions.

Jobs can also be enriched by providing the worker with greater autonomy. The worker is given more authority over day-to-day work decisions and is given the responsibility and resources necessary to exercise this authority. Often, in order to provide the worker with greater autonomy, it is necessary to free him from the rhythms of the machine. 'Buffer' inventories or 'looser' methods of getting materials to work stations are common means of freeing the worker from the machine.

Central to the design or redesign of jobs are group factors. For example, it is easier to create a cohesive group responsible for a facet of production when positions 'with the grain' rather than 'across the grain' are combined. That is, groups should be formed along the direction of production and should not combine similar machine functions on different production lines. When groups are formed in this way, mutual assistance is facilitated. It is easier for workers to keep track of productivity and to cope with the inevitable disruptions when the group is located along the flow of the production than when every member is performing the same task on different lines.

The sense of membership in a team and co-operation among team members are often enhanced by group payment. Typically, payment to individuals is based on competence, seniority, and the number of jobs the individual is trained to perform.

One important advantage of job redesign forms of workplace democracy is their applicability to entire production systems (as in Laidlaw Lumber) as well as to individual work groups within larger organizations. The concept

36 Agmen, Hansson, and Kensson 1976

of the 'factory within a factory' in which subgroups function independently of one another in the larger organization has been proposed as a means of improving productivity and employee morale. Each factory within the larger factory would be a small unit and everyone could become involved on a first-hand basis in the operation of each unit. Each subfactory would possess all the resources necessary to perform its work.

Although the concept of a factory within a factory is an appealing one, it does have certain limits. First, it is unlikely that in small operations, production units could contain all the necessary skill and resources to complete their work. For example, sophisticated maintenance or quality control equipment may be too expensive for all subunits to purchase. Secondly, complete separation leads inevitably to duplication or to 'slack resources,' especially for specialized personnel who may not be fully occupied in any one subfactory. It is unlikely that the workers or supervision in each subunit would be fully conversant with all specialties required to manufacture a product.

Job redesign and individual differences

Critics of job redesign observe that a relatively small percentage of workers want more challenging and more autonomous work. They point out that if workers did want enriched work, they would pursue this objective through collective bargaining. They point to evidence from surveys of employee attitudes that indicate that challenging work is typically ranked lower than the conventional concerns of wages, benefits, and working conditions.

However, most workers take the nature of job and the work technology itself as a given, while they do not consider wages, benefits, and conditions of work as given. Since most workers have not experienced enriched work and since few can imagine what it would be like, it is not surprising that job redesign has not emerged as a priority of labour on the bargaining table. It is time to move beyond the debate over whether or not workers really want enriched work. The workplace should be designed to make challenge, autonomy, and variety available to those workers who want enriched work.

Trade unions and job enrichment

The creation of self-directing work groups can disturb collectively bargained policies. Within self-directing groups jobs are shared, distinctions between task and craft boundaries are blurred, and supervisory and non-supervisory tasks are combined. Consequently, it is important when considering job redesign to involve trade unions in the process.

Many problems of job redesign encounter difficulties around the issue of pay. 'The match in the gasoline is pay.'[37] Employees whose responsibilities have been increased through job redesign often demand greater pay. The enrichment of jobs means that pay rates for trade classifications must be renegotiated or altered. The concern with pay becomes especially acute in firms which remove supervisory positions and consequently block promotion opportunities for workers who wish to advance further in the organization. These problems require a good deal of trust and goodwill between parties.

Despite these difficulties, shop-floor participation through self-regulating groups remains an attractive form of workplace democracy. Many forms of indirect workplace democracy are remote from the immediate concerns of the rank and file employee, and only a small minority of workers is involved in these forms of participation. Unlike other forms of workplace democracy participation through job redesign can be undertaken in a small unit in the organization on an experimental basis. As employee and management competence increases, the job redesign can be undertaken in other units of the enterprise. Changes need not be wholesale and changes need not necessarily question management's right to manage.

Laidlaw Lumber
Laidlaw Lumber is a waferboard manufacturer in Thunder Bay, Ontario. The work technology is continuous process. Much of the work is physically demanding (lifting logs) and semi-skilled; and the work technology places severe constraints on the freedom of workers.

The entire shop-floor is organized into self-directing work groups. Each group, consisting of five to six members, makes all decisions directly affecting the group, including: distribution of work among team members (this issue is subject to team consensus); temporary reassignment of tasks to cover for absent employees; selection of team operators to serve as co-ordinators; screening, selecting, and hiring of new recruits; discipline within the group; resolution of conflicts among group members; training of new group members; solving of technical problems; maintenance of equipment and machine repair (usually performed by millwrights in other firms); counselling of members who do not meet team performance standards (e.g., tardiness and absenteeism); and participation with management on the purchase of new machines, tools, and machinery design.

---

37 Walton 1977, 428

Only one level of management exists between workers and the general manager. Managers at this level are called 'shift co-ordinators,' and they are responsible for giving teams information on the types of product to be run during the shift.

The salary of production workers depends on skills and training. There are three basic rates of pay: the starting rate, the team rate, and the plant rate. The plant rate is given to employees who have mastered all jobs in the plant. Anyone can train on any job, given team approval. Only several workers in this particular operation have attained this level of competence.

The spirit of co-operation and autonomy pervades the organization, even in the offices which are run along conventional lines. Rank and file employees in this firm attained the second highest score of all firms in this study on outcomes such as loyalty, motivation, satisfaction, and commitment. This finding is surprising, given the nature of the work technology and the unpleasant and hazardous nature of the work.

THE GROUP AT COX – A RADICAL DEPARTURE

The Group at Cox, located in Stoney Creek, Ontario designs and manufactures systems for dental offices and clinics. Since its beginning in 1966 The Group at Cox has experienced a sales growth of approximately 60 per cent per year and is the only firm of its size to break into this highly competitive market, which is dominated by several American multinationals. The Group at Cox now leads the industry in some design and service areas.

Wilson Southam, the general manager and co-founder of The Group at Cox, sought to invest his venture capital in an enterprise which met four criteria: (1) the enterprise would be sufficiently small to permit experimentation with and implementation of new forms of work organization; (2) the enterprise would operate in the 'helping field,' such as health or education; (3) the enterprise would operate in a sector which permitted successful competition with multinational firms from a Canadian base; and (4) the clientele would be sophisticated, and the business would be user-centred, innovative, and systems-oriented.

The workplace democracy at The Group at Cox involves a combination of board-level representation, a works council, and self-directing work groups. This program of employee participation is a significant departure from conventional practice. The decision-making rights of employees in the company are the most extensive of the ten democratic organizations in this study and probably the most extensive of any industrial organization in this country. The workplace democracy at The Group at Cox is based on an explicit philosophy which supports and defines the decision-making structures within the firm. This philosophy is presented below.

BASIC CREDO OF THE GROUP AT COX – INDIVIDUALS

01 I have a right to work for GOALS which I have participated in creating.

02 I have a right to work with a COMMUNITY of my peers and to participate with that Community in setting the standards for that work.

03 I have a right to join with people from various Communities in forming a work TEAM whose output is seen by team members as a meaningful part in the production of useful goods and services and, as a team, we will have the right to set productivity targets and co-ordinate the work.

04 I have the right to be IN CHARGE of some aspect of meaningful and responsible work which is separate from my daily direct work and is of value in terms of our goals.

05 I have a right to participate in creation of, or change to, the POLICY of the Group at Cox which affects me – a right which extends to knowing and believing that Policy will be by unanimous consent of those affected.

06 I have a right to elect a REPRESENTATIVE who will work with other Elected Representatives and delegates of the shareholders to ensure that Policy and its interpretation will stay within the spirit of this Credo.

07 I have a right to APPEAL to this group of Elected Representatives and Delegates for help whenever I believe that my rights are being threatened and a further right to a period of employment protection when the representatives support my view.

08 I have a right to be present when I am discussed as an individual by Co-Ordinators and a right of free access to PANEL meetings where decisions are being taken which affect me in my life at Cox.

09 I have a right to elect separate representatives to a MEMBERS Panel which will co-ordinate all social, athletic or spiritual activities which may, from time to time, occur at Cox and a further right to insist that this elected panel will control all such activities in a way that ensures that the 'company' will stay out of my private life.

10 I have a right to participate in creating and maintaining an environment at Cox which is consistent, within the available means, with my freedom to pursue HEALTH, safety and personal growth at work.

11 I have a right to share on an equal basis with other Members of the Group at Cox in a percentage of the PROFITS once I have qualified under the profit sharing agreement.

12 I have a right to be related to and otherwise treated as EQUAL to other members
of the Group at Cox, with the exception of my total annual salary which will be
set by a participatory process, providing my actions are perceived by my peers as
helping the group achieve its goals.

Decision-making structures

The decision-making structures in the firm are based on 'communities,'
'teams,' and 'small groups.' Communities consist of persons who have the
same professional or craft skill; in cases where people do not have a profession or craft communities consist of persons who perform similar work.
Communities are composed of four to twelve employees. Members of a
community are responsible for the quality of work performed by the community. Members of a community decide on acceptable quality criteria and
collectively possess the right of veto over all quality decisions. No one in
the firm can give a community member any order with respect to product
quality.

Community co-ordinators are appointed by the general manager after
consultation with community members. They are responsible for integrating the activities performed by community members. Co-ordinators have no
formal authority and must rely on persuasion and collaboration in their
work. They receive no extra compensation for their responsibilities.

Members of communities are also members of multi-community teams.
A team normally consists of two to four members who work together on a
particular product. For example, the 'module sub-assembly team' consists of
members from several communities – the 'cabinetry assembly community,'
the 'cabinet hardware community,' and the 'cleaning and packing community.' Team members set production targets which are reviewed annually.
Team leaders are appointed by the general manager after consultation with
team members.

Members of a 'small group' are those who belong to the same community
and team. A small group has complete control over its work space, including
cleaning, decorating, and the work itself.

Six 'resource co-ordinators' are appointed by the general manager. They
meet approximately ten times per year and handle operational problems,
establish priorities, and make technical decisions. They have no formal
authority over group members. They cannot give orders, and like community co-ordinators, they must operate through persuasion and collaboration.
They serve as resources ('servants') and assist in planning and co-ordinating
the activities of the various communities and teams.

Finally, employee representatives elected for one-year terms are assigned the responsibility of protecting the interests of their constituents. There are five elected representatives, one for approximately every ten people. Any employee (except officers of the company as defined in the company's Act) can be a representative; and anyone can vote for a representative. The elected representatives meet monthly to discuss policy, salary, and other matters brought to their attention.

The general manager is the only person in the firm who can fire another employee. However, the firing can be appealed to the elected representatives. Their decision is final and binding on the general manager. The general manager must justify the firing to the elected representatives; he is obliged to explain all factors (except those of a personal nature) entering into his decision. If his decision is appealed, the general manager can bring forward all information entering into his decision if he wishes.

The board of directors of The Group at Cox consists of ten members. Five are 'inside' and five are 'outside' the firm. Of the two major shareholders one is inside and one is outside. The board of directors' meeting is the only meeting in the company which all employees cannot attend.

Town hall meetings

'Town hall meetings' are held once or twice a year, as needed. All employees are invited to the town hall meeting (on paid time). The purpose of the meeting is to discuss the firm's performance, sales, new products, and competitive challenges. In addition, personnel policy is discussed and then established at these meetings.

Before any decision is made consensus is necessary. No decision is taken in the firm unless everyone affected by the decision agrees with it. (All decisions have been unanimous, although occasionally an employee has abstained from voting. Under these conditions considerable peer pressure tends to move the group towards consensus.)

At the town hall meetings, a meeting co-ordinator is picked at random. During the meeting, there are four 'modalities.' The most frequently used mode is the 'right to know' mode. In this mode, one topic without restriction is suggested by everyone present. The first individual speaks on the topic of his or her choice, and the discussion continues until consensus is reached. The next individual, proceeding around the table, addresses the topic of his or her choice. Normally, all topics are covered within an hour and a half. This modality allows everyone the opportunity to discuss any topic and swift movement between topics. Brief minutes are kept – one or two sentences per topic.

The second mode – the 'information' mode – can be requested by any member to get information. This mode allows the transmission of information without interruption.

The third mode – the 'how to' mode – is essentially a brainstorming process in which evaluation is held until all ideas have been presented. Any evaluation then tends to be supportive and is offered to assist individuals in gaining a greater understanding of the potential of various ideas.

The fourth mode is the 'integrative' mode and can be used by the meeting co-ordinator to cut off discussion and impose a decision. It is seldom used and only in cases which require an immediate decision. Any issue settled in this fashion can be raised again at a future meeting.

A good deal of information is exchanged among employees at these meetings. In addition, in the intervening periods there is a weekly newsletter, 'This Week at Cox,' in which weekly events, items of human interest, and the firm's performance are presented. A bulletin board called 'The Owning Centre' permits the immediate transmission of memos, production schedules, and letters from clients.

Work

As mentioned earlier, members of communities and teams make important decisions concerning the quality and standards of work. Some of the production work could be automated, but the production process emphasizes craft skills in order to maintain employee interest in the work, and in order to ensure a product of high quality. Buffer zones between work stations allow the small groups to vary the pace of work according to the wishes of team members.

All employees in the firm engage in both direct labour (that is, making a product or performing a service) and indirect labour (supportive and resource work for a community or team).

Members of communities and teams 'float' to other communities and teams as needed in order to meet production or quality standards. Decisions on floating are made voluntarily by the parties concerned. No one can be forced to float from one group to another, and no group must accept a floater. In practice, the intersection of communities and teams and the floating of members into other communities and teams is intended to prevent group members from being isolated in one type of work.

There is neither piece-work nor measurement of individual productivity. Individual management and individual incentives are downplayed. The 'labour ticket' used to determine labour input on a particular product is coded only by 'small group' and not by individual name. Consequently, an individual cannot be measured by anyone outside of the small group. There are no quality control inspectors in the company.

The merit pay and recruitment process

Two issues – recruiting and the determination of employee salaries – are subject to peer review. The recruiting process begins when members of a community decide they can no longer fulfil their commitments without additional help.

The recruiting process has four stages. The first stage, 'pre-screening,' involves two people (the secretary-treasurer of the firm, and one person from the community) meeting with the applicant for the purpose of establishing the applicant's competence. The applicant is told about the philosophy at The Group at Cox and is encouraged to spend time in the firm talking with employees.

If the applicant is interested in pursuing further employment opportunities at The Group at Cox, the second stage begins with the applicant's return to talk with employees and, if desired, to examine the records of the firm. The applicant is invited to check with external sources on the viability of the firm and its future.

In the third stage the applicant is interviewed by six group members: two people from the community, two people from a closely related community, and two people from the group at large. These six persons make a decision on hiring the applicant by unanimous consent. Any member may abstain from voting.

In the fourth and final stage an offer is extended to the applicant. At this point salary is discussed as well as other operational concerns. The first three months of employment are probationary; the new recruit is paid by the hour and, unlike regular employees, is given work direction.

Annual salary increases are also determined by a participative process. Everyone in the firm is paid a salary (except new employees); the general manager, the resource co-ordinators, and the elected representatives meet annually to set the total amount available for wage increases in the coming year. They also agree to set a high and a low wage increase. A wage survey of other companies in the area is used to determine the pay increases (the wages at The Group at Cox are lower than comparable wages in other firms.)

Each employee ranks in order all employees with whom he works and whose performance he knows well enough to evaluate. There are six such groups in the firm (four in production and two in the office). Each employee ranks other members of the group (employees do not rank themselves), places his signature on the rank ordering for the particular group, and sends the rank ordering to the firm's accountant to be tabulated. This voting is conducted twice a year.

The general manager, the resource co-ordinators, and the elected representatives then combine the six sets of rankings into a single list. At this step, the ranking of an employee in his group cannot be changed. That is, when the lists are combined, the employee ranked first in one of the six groups must be ranked above all other members in his particular group in the final grading, and the same holds for the other positions. (Originally, members of the group voted on their own rank ordering, but many were uncomfortable with this procedure and it was subsequently changed.)

The general manager is permitted to give merit pay to those employees who are involved in work which may not be visible to other members of the company or who may conduct difficult tasks which may not be recognized by other members of the company.

An employee who improves his rank order from the previous evaluation (e.g., his mean ranking changes from 2.4 to 2.1) is called a 'jumper' and receives a merit increase. An employee whose rank order is lowered is called a 'hold back' and receives no merit pay. An employee who 'jumps' from one ranking to the next gets half of the merit pay and receives the other half if this position is held in the next voting. A 'hold back' receives a smaller increase. This procedure allows someone (who may not want to work so hard as in the past) to continue to contribute to the firm without facing pressure to maintain or improve performance. In The Group at Cox salary of such an individual would drift downward until it stabilized at a level acceptable to the employee.

Power

In The Group at Cox power is viewed as manipulative and antithetical to personal freedom and interpersonal trust. All employees at The Group at Cox have rights which protect them from the unilateral power of other employees. An employee can be fired for using power over another. Anyone who feels subjected to 'managerial power' by another can appeal to his elected representative. If the appeal is upheld, the person filing the appeal is automatically granted six months' employment security.

There are only special circumstances in which it is legitimate for employees to discuss another employee in that person's absence. Any employee has complete access to information in his personnel file, and any person has the right to be present when he is being discussed. Even the power of the general manager is checked; his decision to fire an employee is subject to the binding decision of the group of elected representatives.

Anyone affected by a decision in The Group at Cox must agree with the decision before action is taken. That is, consensus is essential among all those persons affected by a particular decision. As much time as necessary is allocated to achieve consensus.

The personal lives of employees are kept entirely separate from work lives. A sports program and other social activities are handled by a separate group of elected persons. Participation in social activities is strictly voluntary. Some social activities are conducted during company time. For example, employees play soccer in a field behind the plant on company time. The firm was successful on appeal in obtaining workmen's compensation for a worker injured during a soccer game. The firm's philosophy is based on teamwork, and it is felt that team sports contribute to this spirit.

The Group at Cox offers no employee benefits beyond those required by law. This practice is based on a belief that benefit packaging is a form of employee manipulation. It interferes with an employee's right to use his pay as desired, and to grow and benefit from his own successes.

The hours of work are flexible (everyone works between 10:00 a.m. and 2:00 p.m.). The firm has a profit-sharing plan, although, to date, all profits have been reinvested in the firm (a decision made by employees). Everyone in the firm is referred to by his or her first name.

The future at The Group at Cox
The workplace democracy at The Group at Cox is rather complex, yet it succeeds. As the firm grows it will inevitably face pressures to streamline some of its decision-making structures and processes. As the average age and seniority of members of The Group at Cox rise, they may become less willing to experiment with new arrangements.

Although each employee has a remarkable degree of influence over the workplace, peers exert some pressure on each other. Persons who adapt best to this system are group-oriented, tolerant of ambiguity, self-starting, and able to interact easily and successfully with other group members.

The general manager has deliberately removed himself from the day-to-day operations of the firm and from group meetings to allow them to function and evolve on their own. Despite the highly participative nature of this firm, it has nevertheless been highly dependent upon its founder and general manager. In recent years he has assumed a higher profile within the company, because some employees interpreted his absence as an expression of disinterest in the firm.

The system is currently evolving in the direction of providing the general manager with the opportunity to exercise his authority more directly and frequently. Peer pressure has not been entirely successful in stimulating workers who are not carrying their own weight.

Perhaps the most remarkable feature of The Group at Cox has been the emphasis on evolving new forms of work organization which guarantee significant decision-making rights to all employees while at the same time struggling to survive in a highly competitive market. Although this survey was undertaken in the firm at a point when its survival was not assured and when morale was at a low ebb, on a composite measure of outcomes (including job satisfaction, alienation, commitment, and loyalty to the firm) rank and file members at The Group at Cox scored highest of all companies in this sample. Today, with its future more assured, morale has improved substantially.

Methodology

Allport (1937) identifies two fundamental approaches to the study of human behaviour: the ideographic and the nomothetic methods. Ideographic laws are derived from the study of a single case; nomothetic laws are derived from the study of populations of cases. The study of a single case is justified when each case (person, group or organization) is believed to operate according to its own laws; that is, relationships between variables are believed to vary from case to case. If individual cases are governed by laws unique to each, the study of populations cannot identify ideographic laws, since the diverse laws governing each will be masked by the analysis of large populations.

The study of workplace democracy has been dominated by the ideographic strategy. This strategy has been justified by the relative scarcity of cases available for study as well as by the belief that the development of nomothetic laws will eventually follow from a study of individual cases.

Both the ideographic and the nomothetic approaches to science have merit, and one cannot be held superior to the other under all circumstances.

The ideographic approach to organizational behaviour is based on the proposition that all organizations are unique. Although organizations do have unique characteristics, they also have qualities and dimensions in common with one another. If we consider each organization to be unique, then generalization of results obtained from one organization or one sample of organizations to another organization or sample is not valid; according to this perspective all organizational research should be of single organizations.

Information about single organizations can always be obtained from nomothetic studies by disaggregating the data. The opposite, however, is rarely possible. Aggregating individual case studies is possible only in the unlikely event that data in the individual organizations were obtained through the use of identical procedures and measures.

Susman (1976) in defence of the ideographic strategy argues that the practitioner cannot apply nomothetic laws to his own organization because he knows nothing about the configuration of variables in his organization and how they might compare to the configuration of the variables in the typical organization described by nomothetic research. This criticism is valid, but the ideographic and nomothetic strategies have complementary strengths and weaknesses. The ideographic approach is useful for generating hypotheses, gaining insight into the workings of complex phenomena and allowing the researcher to gain familiarity with a research setting. The nomothetic approach permits statistical analysis, an exploration of the generality of relationships among phenomena, and facilitates comparison between studies.

The fundamental weakness of the ideographic approach is apparent in Susman's analysis of autonomous workgroups. He asserts that only changes in the job or changes in the conditions under which work is performed will have any influence on worker attitudes; the introduction of indirect participation in the workplace will not have so great an effect. This proposition can be verified only by systematic comparisons of samples of organizations in which changes in the work have been made and organizations in which changes in the extent of indirect participation have been made. No comparison of separate case studies can test Susman's proposition. Clearly an in-depth analysis of individual organizations combined with a systematic and large-sample comparative analysis unite the strengths of the two approaches.

Research on workplace democracy is still in its infancy and suffers from many of the shortcomings of ideographic research. Among these shortcomings are:

- absence of a unifying theoretical framework to guide analysis; an overemphasis on unstructured observation and anecdotal evidence;
- a corresponding absence of comparability of data across organizational settings;
- non-standardized measurement and a corresponding absence of statistical analysis;
- difficulties of replicating studies and generalizing findings to other settings;
- a preoccupation with single forms of participation such as Scanlon plans, autonomous work groups, or employee ownership; that is, research

focuses on phenotypically similar organizations and not on genotypic commonalities;
- lack of variety of systems studied; that is, comparisons among participative organizations have not examined the full range of forms which participation can take.

The research strategy employed in this study differs from existing research strategies on workplace democracy in two key respects: (1) this research is comparative – that is, the study is based on a matched sample of democratic and hierarchical organizations; and (2) the data are obtained by both case analysis, with detailed descriptive data, and standardized research instruments.

RESEARCH INSTRUMENTS

Three operationally independent methods were used to collect data from the 1,000 respondents: (1) a personal twenty-seven-item interview with each respondent; (2) a 177-item questionnaire completed at the workplace by each respondent; and (3) direct field observations of each respondent at the workplace.

A semi-structured interview was conducted with the chief executive officer, the personnel / industrial relations manager and the union or employee association president in each organization. In addition, company documents and collective agreements were examined to measure the amount of participation in decision-making permitted organizational members at various hierarchical levels.

THE INTERVIEW

Before completing the questionnaire, each potential respondent was interviewed by a member of the field staff. The interview typically lasted ten minutes. The respondent was informed of the general nature of the study, that is, that it was a 'quality of work life' survey of Canadian working people. The respondent was told that participation in the study was voluntary, that individual responses would be anonymous, and that a summary report of the group responses would be given to the company for all employees to see.

Each respondent was then shown a seven-point scale (ranging from strongly disagree to strongly agree) on a 5 inch by 20 inch cardboard display. The nature of the scale was explained and ten statements were read to the respondent. The respondent indicated the extent to which he agreed or disagreed with each statement by selecting one of the seven points on the scale.

This procedure enabled the interviewer to determine the extent to which the individual understood the concept of an ordinal scale and whether or not the individual could complete the questionnaire without assistance. In cases where the respondent could not comprehend the questions or the meaning of the scale, the individual was replaced by random selection. Fifty such potential respondents were replaced. In other cases where the respondent understood the nature of the scale but had some difficulty understanding the questions a proctor was provided to read all questions to the respondent. There were twenty-five such cases.

During the interview data on eleven characteristics of the individual, such as union membership, size of the work group, nature of work (white-collar / blue-collar; direct / indirect), were also obtained.

The interview served as a 'warm-up' to the questionnaire. The interview begins with relatively simple items and proceeds to increasingly more difficult items. The interview items are presented in appendix III.

The items include some general reactions to the workplace and measures of growth need strength. A pretest of the Hackman and Oldham (1975) measures of growth need strength revealed that many workers could not understand the questions and needed assistance. Consequently, the measures of growth need strength were obtained by interview.

The split-half reliability of the interview corrected by Spearman-Brown is 0.83.

QUESTIONNAIRE

Upon completion of the interview, each respondent was given a questionnaire. Proctors were available at all times to assist respondents. The questionnaire typically required thirty to forty-five minutes to complete. The questionnaire is presented in appendix III.

The questionnaire is a broad-based organizational assessment instrument which covers the four concepts of congruence theory: values, structure, process and outcomes.

Because both the attention span of respondents and company co-operation place limits on the number of items which a researcher can measure, future tests of congruence theory and workplace democracy might employ partially overlapping samples of questions from randomly selected subsamples of respondents. That is, no one respondent would be asked all questions; rather, groups of respondents would be asked different subsets of questions. Subsets of respondents could be asked questions on which they would serve as 'knowledgeable informants' (e.g., top management on administrative structure; union representatives on worker attitudes towards management).

Some of the measures in the questionnaire are well defined, have been validated in past research, and are of known and acceptable reliability (e.g., the job satisfaction items). Other measures are at a relatively early stage of development (e.g., the values items) and will require further refinement and development in future research.

The questionnaire items were obtained from the Michigan Organizational Assessment Package (1975); Hage and Aiken (1969); Likert (1961); Tannenbaum (1974a) and Nightingale and Toulouse (1977). Only the values items (question 23 in the questionnaire) had not been used in previous research. These items were obtained from a larger sample of sixty-seven items pretested on two samples of students (of size fifty).

There are English, French, and Italian versions of the questionnaire and interview. The French and Italian versions were obtained through a double-blind back translation procedure. French- and Italian-speaking interviewers and proctors were available in all organizations in which employees preferred to complete the questionnaire in their mother tongue.

The split-half reliability of the questionnaire corrected by Spearman-Brown is 0.83.

FIELD OBSERVATIONS

The physical attributes and psychological qualities of the work were assessed by direct field observation. The job observation guide (see appendix III) is based on the Michigan Organizational Assessment Package (1975), Turner and Lawrence (1965), and Jenkins et al. (1975). Field observations for production workers typically required twenty minutes each, while interviews / observations for supervisory and managerial respondents typically required forty-five minutes each. Interviews / observations were necessary for managers and supervisors and others whose rhythms of work did not permit reliable observation in a twenty-minute period. Over 450 job titles are represented in this sample.

The three field observers in the study were trained over a five-day period. Direct observations of managers and production workers for half-hour observation periods were followed by half-hour discussion periods. The convergence of the field observation data with engineering and time study data provided an external check on the validity of the measures. In addition, the convergence between different sources of data was examined. Items which were ambiguous were dropped and others added; scales were changed and wording was changed, until the reliability of the instrument reached an acceptable level.

The split-half reliability of the field observation instrument corrected by Spearman-Brown is 0.84. The test-retest reliability of the observation instrument is 0.80. (One hundred observations were repeated by another member of the field observation team. One-half of the observations were completed at the same time by both observers, one-half at different times.)

Field observations provide an objective measure of task attributes. Most research employs self-report measures of work and is consequently subject to 'halo responsing,'[1] 'Socratic effects,'[2] and 'priming effects.'[3]

The advantages of field observation sources of data have been pointed out by Haynes and Zander (1953); and Webb et al. (1966). The use of 'objective' (field observation) measures is important for concepts with 'an objective reality' (such as the characteristics of tasks). 'Subjective' questionnaire measures must be employed for concepts with no objective referent (such as attitudes, opinions, perspectives, feelings, and values).

MANAGEMENT / UNION INTERVIEW

In-depth, semi-structured interviews with the chief executive officer, the personnel / industrial relations manager, and the union / employee association president were also conducted in each firm (see appendix III). Detailed notes on company operation and performance were taken. This information provides a more detailed perspective on the data collected from questionnaires and interviews. Descriptions of the ten democratic organizations based on these sources are provided in appendix I.

---

1 Nightingale and Toulouse 1977
2 Salancik and Pfeffer 1977
3 Weyer 1974

Research instruments and measures

INTERVIEW SCHEDULE

Name of interviewee: _____

Code number: _____

Hierarchical level: (a) levels above: _____
                    (b) levels below: _____
                                     _____

Nature of work: (a) white / blue-collar: _____
                (b) direct / indirect: _____
                (c) lead hand: _____

Number of persons in work group: _____

Number of persons reporting directly to interviewee: _____

Union member: _____

Employee (union) representative: now: _____
                                 in past: _____

Sex: _____

INTERVIEW

I shall read some statements to you and I would like you to indicate the extent to which you *agree* or *disagree* with each (hand a copy of the scale).

1. I often do extra work on my job which is not required.

2. When the management of this company says something, you can really believe it's true.

3. Management has no interest at all in the welfare of those who work here.

4. I would like to move to a higher-level position in this company.

5. My union (elected) representative does not know how I feel about things.

6. I am told frequently by my superior about how well I am doing in my job.

7. I often meet socially with the people I work with.

8. Have you taken any courses or training to upgrade your job in the past year? (yes or no).

9. Did you vote in the last provincial or federal election? (yes or no).

10. Did you vote in the last employee association (union) election? (yes or no).

1	2	3	4	5	6	7
strongly disagree	disagree	slightly disagree	neither agree nor disagree	slightly agree	agree	strongly agree

GROWTH NEED STRENGTH SCALE

Respondent code number: _____

Job A			Job B	
A job where the wage is very good			A job where there is considerable opportunity to be creative and innovative	
1	**2**	**3**	**4**	**5**
strongly prefer A	slightly prefer A	neutral	slightly prefer B	strongly prefer B

A job where you are often required to make important decisions			A job with many pleasant people to work with	
1	**2**	**3**	**4**	**5**
strongly prefer A	slightly prefer A	neutral	slightly prefer B	strongly prefer B

A job in which greater responsibility is given to loyal employees who have the most seniority			A job in which greater responsibility is given to those who do the best work	
1	**2**	**3**	**4**	**5**
strongly prefer A	slightly prefer A	neutral	slightly prefer B	strongly prefer B

A very routine job

A job where your co-workers are *not* very friendly

1	2	3	4	5
strongly prefer A	slightly prefer A	neutral	slightly prefer B	strongly prefer B

A job in which there is a real chance for you to develop new skills and advance in the organization

A job which provides lots of vacation time and an excellent fringe-benefit package

1	2	3	4	5
strongly prefer A	slightly prefer A	neutral	slightly prefer B	strongly prefer B

A job which offers little or no challenge

A job which requires you to be completely isolated from co-workers

1	2	3	4	5
strongly prefer A	slightly prefer A	neutral	slightly prefer B	strongly prefer B

QUESTIONNAIRE

This questionnaire is part of a major survey of Canadian working people. The study is directed by Professor Donald V. Nightingale of Queen's University, and is supported by The Canada Council.

The purpose of the survey is to learn how Canadians feel about different aspects of their work, fellow employees and the companies that employ them. Ultimately, this information will be used to understand better those factors that contribute to the quality of working life of people like yourself.

In no case will any individual's responses be separated or studied alone, and in no case will any of the completed questionnaires be available to your company. We will report only group data, and hence can assure complete confidentiality. Also, please do not write your name anywhere on this questionnaire.

Your cooperation is very much appreciated.

1 Here are some statements about you and your job. How much do you agree or disagree **with each?** (Check one box on each line across.)

	Strongly Disagree	Disagree	Slightly Disagree	Neither Agree nor Disagree	Slightly Agree	Agree	Strongly Agree
a I get a feeling of personal satisfaction from doing my job well.	☐	☐	☐	☐	☐	☐	☐
b I work hard on my job.	☐	☐	☐	☐	☐	☐	☐
c All in all, I am satisfied with my job.	☐	☐	☐	☐	☐	☐	☐
d What happens to this organization is really important to me.	☐	☐	☐	☐	☐	☐	☐
e I often think about quitting.	☐	☐	☐	☐	☐	☐	☐
f I don't care what happens to this organization as long as I get my pay cheque.	☐	☐	☐	☐	☐	☐	☐
g I feel badly when I do a poor job.	☐	☐	☐	☐	☐	☐	☐

2 The following are statements that may or may not describe your work group. How much do you agree or disagree **with each statement?** (Check one box on each line across.)

	Strongly Disagree	Disagree	Slightly Disagree	Neither Agree nor Disagree	Slightly Agree	Agree	Strongly Agree
a I have confidence and trust in my co-workers.	☐	☐	☐	☐	☐	☐	☐
b In my group, everyone's opinion gets listened to.	☐	☐	☐	☐	☐	☐	☐
c There is constant bickering in my work group.	☐	☐	☐	☐	☐	☐	☐
d I feel I am really part of my work group.	☐	☐	☐	☐	☐	☐	☐
e I look forward to being with the members of my work group each day.	☐	☐	☐	☐	☐	☐	☐
f If we have a decision to make, everyone is involved in making it.	☐	☐	☐	☐	☐	☐	☐
g We tell each other the way we are feeling.	☐	☐	☐	☐	☐	☐	☐

3 Please indicate how satisfied you are with each of the following aspects of your job.
(Check one box on each line across.)

How satisfied are you with . . .	Very Dissatisfied	Dissatisfied	Slightly Dissatisfied	Neither Satisfied nor Dissatisfied	Slightly Satisfied	Satisfied	Very Satisfied
a fringe benefits	☐	☐	☐	☐	☐	☐	☐
b the friendliness of the people you work with	☐	☐	☐	☐	☐	☐	☐
c the amount of freedom you have on your job	☐	☐	☐	☐	☐	☐	☐
d your chances for getting a promotion	☐	☐	☐	☐	☐	☐	☐
e the chances you have to learn new things	☐	☐	☐	☐	☐	☐	☐
f the respect you receive from the people you work with	☐	☐	☐	☐	☐	☐	☐
g the chances you have to accomplish something worthwhile	☐	☐	☐	☐	☐	☐	☐
h the chances you have to take part in making decisions	☐	☐	☐	☐	☐	☐	☐
i the amount of pay you get	☐	☐	☐	☐	☐	☐	☐
j the amount of job security you have	☐	☐	☐	☐	☐	☐	☐
k the opportunity to develop your skills and abilities	☐	☐	☐	☐	☐	☐	☐

4 All in all, how satisfied are you with the work you are doing? (Check one box.)

☐ very satisfied

☐ quite satisfied

☐ neither satisfied nor dissatisfied

☐ quite dissatisfied

☐ very dissatisfied

5 Please indicate whether you agree with each of the statements as descriptions of your direct supervisor. (Check one box on each line across.)

My supervisor . . .

	Strongly Disagree	Disagree	Slightly Disagree	Neither Agree nor Disagree	Slightly Agree	Agree	Strongly Agree
a helps subordinates with their personal problems	☐	☐	☐	☐	☐	☐	☐
b encourages subordinates to participate in important decisions	☐	☐	☐	☐	☐	☐	☐
c is always fair with subordinates	☐	☐	☐	☐	☐	☐	☐
d demands that people give their best effort	☐	☐	☐	☐	☐	☐	☐
e is someone I can trust	☐	☐	☐	☐	☐	☐	☐
f leaves it up to me to decide how to go about doing my job	☐	☐	☐	☐	☐	☐	☐
g defends subordinates to 'higher ups'	☐	☐	☐	☐	☐	☐	☐
h is concerned about me as a person	☐	☐	☐	☐	☐	☐	☐
i is competent	☐	☐	☐	☐	☐	☐	☐
j feels each subordinate is important as an individual	☐	☐	☐	☐	☐	☐	☐
k evaluates my performance accurately	☐	☐	☐	☐	☐	☐	☐

6 Now, some questions about groups in this company. (Check one box on each line across.)

	Strongly Disagree	Disagree	Slightly Disagree	Neither Agree nor Disagree	Slightly Agree	Agree	Strongly Agree
a In general, different groups here work well with each other.	☐	☐	☐	☐	☐	☐	☐
b The amount of conflict that exists between groups here makes this an unpleasant place to work.	☐	☐	☐	☐	☐	☐	☐
c No matter how well we do, other groups always criticize us.	☐	☐	☐	☐	☐	☐	☐

7 How much influence do the following groups or persons have on what happens in this plant? (Check one box on each line across.)

	Very Little Influence	Little Influence	Some Influence	Quite a Lot of Influence	A Very Great Deal of Influence
a plant manager and his executive board	☐	☐	☐	☐	☐
b all other managers and supervisors	☐	☐	☐	☐	☐
c workers as a group	☐	☐	☐	☐	☐
d employee (union) representatives	☐	☐	☐	☐	☐
e you, personally	☐	☐	☐	☐	☐

8 How much influence should the following groups or persons have on what happens in this plant? (Check one box on each line across.)

	Very Little Influence	Little Influence	Some Influence	Quite a Lot of Influence	A Very Great Deal of Influence
a plant manager and his executive board	☐	☐	☐	☐	☐
b all other managers and supervisors	☐	☐	☐	☐	☐
c workers as a group	☐	☐	☐	☐	☐
d employee (union) representatives	☐	☐	☐	☐	☐
e you, personally	☐	☐	☐	☐	☐

9 Do **employees participate in making important decisions relating to their work?** (Check one box.)

☐ not at all
☐ they never participate, but they are sometimes asked for their opinions and suggestions
☐ they jointly decide about many important things concerning their work
☐ they jointly decide about all important things concerning their work

10 Should **employees participate in making important decisions relating to their work?** (Check one box.)

☐ not at all
☐ they should never participate, but they should sometimes be asked for their opinions and suggestions
☐ they should jointly decide about many important things concerning their work
☐ they should jointly decide about all important things concerning their work

5

11 How much do you agree **or** disagree **with the following statements?** (Check one box on each line across.)

	Strongly Disagree	Disagree	Slightly Disagree	Neither Agree nor Disagree	Slightly Agree	Agree	Strongly Agree
a I have a lot of say over how decisions are made	☐	☐	☐	☐	☐	☐	☐
b I seldom have decisions forced on me	☐	☐	☐	☐	☐	☐	☐
c I can modify decisions made by other people	☐	☐	☐	☐	☐	☐	☐
d I feel that I am my own boss in most matters	☐	☐	☐	☐	☐	☐	☐
e Whatever situation arises, we have procedures to follow in dealing with it	☐	☐	☐	☐	☐	☐	☐
f The company keeps a written record of everyone's job performance	☐	☐	☐	☐	☐	☐	☐
g Going through proper channels is constantly stressed	☐	☐	☐	☐	☐	☐	☐
h Written orders from higher up are followed without question	☐	☐	☐	☐	☐	☐	☐
i Employees are constantly checked on for rule violations	☐	☐	☐	☐	☐	☐	☐
j Employees are often permitted to use their own judgement as to how to handle various problems	☐	☐	☐	☐	☐	☐	☐
k A person can make his own decisions here without checking with anybody else	☐	☐	☐	☐	☐	☐	☐
l People here feel as though they are constantly being watched to see that they obey all the rules	☐	☐	☐	☐	☐	☐	☐
m Even small matters have to be referred to someone higher up for a final answer	☐	☐	☐	☐	☐	☐	☐
n Changes here always seem to create more problems than they solve	☐	☐	☐	☐	☐	☐	☐
o When changes are made in this organization, the employees usually lose out in the end	☐	☐	☐	☐	☐	☐	☐
p If we made a few changes here, this could be a much better place to work	☐	☐	☐	☐	☐	☐	☐

12 **When you do what your immediate superior requests you to do on the job, why do you do it?**
(Pick the 3 most important and put in the three boxes.)

a I respect his competence and judgement

b He can give special help and benefits

c He's a nice guy

d He can punish or penalize me

e It is my duty

f It is necessary if the organization is to function properly

☐ ☐ ☐

3 most important

13 **How much do you** agree or disagree **with each of the following statements.** (Check one box on each line across.)

	Strongly Disagree	Disagree	Slightly Disagree	Neither Agree nor Disagree	Slightly Agree	Agree	Strongly Agree
a I think each of us can do a great deal to improve world opinion of Canada.	☐	☐	☐	☐	☐	☐	☐
b There is very little we can do to prevent prices from going higher.	☐	☐	☐	☐	☐	☐	☐
c People like me cannot influence the course of events; only people in high positions can have such influence.	☐	☐	☐	☐	☐	☐	☐
d The world in which we live is basically a friendly place.	☐	☐	☐	☐	☐	☐	☐
e Today it is practically impossible to find real friends because everyone thinks only of himself.	☐	☐	☐	☐	☐	☐	☐
f It is not possible to rely on others.	☐	☐	☐	☐	☐	☐	☐
g The trouble with the world today is that most people really don't believe in anything.	☐	☐	☐	☐	☐	☐	☐
h Nowadays it is hard to know right from wrong.	☐	☐	☐	☐	☐	☐	☐
i It's hardly fair to bring children into the world with the way things look for the future.	☐	☐	☐	☐	☐	☐	☐

7

14 How frequently do you speak to persons in the following groups about work matters? (Check one box on each line across.)

	Very Often	Often	Sometimes	Rarely	Never
a your co-workers	☐	☐	☐	☐	☐
b your superiors	☐	☐	☐	☐	☐
c your subordinates (for managers only)	☐	☐	☐	☐	☐

15 How frequently do you speak to persons in the following groups about non-work matters? (Check one box on each line across.)

	Very Often	Often	Sometimes	Rarely	Never
a your co-workers	☐	☐	☐	☐	☐
b your superiors	☐	☐	☐	☐	☐
c your subordinates (for managers only)	☐	☐	☐	☐	☐

16 What do workers communicate to their superiors? (Check one box.)

☐ they communicate all relevant information accurately

☐ they communicate mainly what their superiors like to hear

☐ they communicate only what their superiors like to hear

☐ they distort all information

17 How accurate is the information you receive from: (Check one box on each line across.)

	Very Accurate	Accurate	Inaccurate	Very Inaccurate
a your supervisor	☐	☐	☐	☐
b your peers (others at the same job level)	☐	☐	☐	☐
c your subordinates (for managers only)	☐	☐	☐	☐

8

18 In organizations, conflict between groups is often dealt with in different ways. Below is a list of methods which might be used to resolve conflict. How frequently are each of these methods used to resolve conflict in this organization? (Check one box on each line across.)

	Never	Sometimes	Often	Almost Always
a When problems arise, people usually ignore them	☐	☐	☐	☐
b When problems arise, everybody involved works together to solve them	☐	☐	☐	☐
c People try at all costs to avoid offending others	☐	☐	☐	☐
d Supervisors are generally asked to resolve conflicts between subordinates	☐	☐	☐	☐
e People openly discuss problems with co-workers	☐	☐	☐	☐

19 Below are listed some words and phrases which ask you how you feel about your present life in general. For example, if you think that your life is very interesting, put a mark in the box right next to the word "interesting". If you feel that your life is very boring, put a mark in the box right next to the word "boring". If you feel somewhere in between, put a mark where you think it belongs. (Check one box on each line across.)

HOW DO YOU FEEL ABOUT YOUR PRESENT LIFE IN GENERAL?

a Boring	☐	☐	☐	☐	☐	☐	☐	Interesting
b Enjoyable	☐	☐	☐	☐	☐	☐	☐	Miserable
c Easy	☐	☐	☐	☐	☐	☐	☐	Hard
d Useless	☐	☐	☐	☐	☐	☐	☐	Worthwhile
e Friendly	☐	☐	☐	☐	☐	☐	☐	Lonely
f Full	☐	☐	☐	☐	☐	☐	☐	Empty
g Discouraging	☐	☐	☐	☐	☐	☐	☐	Hopeful
h Tied Down	☐	☐	☐	☐	☐	☐	☐	Free
i Disappointing	☐	☐	☐	☐	☐	☐	☐	Rewarding
j Brings out the best in me	☐	☐	☐	☐	☐	☐	☐	Doesn't give me much of a chance
k Successful	☐	☐	☐	☐	☐	☐	☐	Not successful
l Important	☐	☐	☐	☐	☐	☐	☐	Not important

20 How is your health these days? (Check one box.)

☐ very good ☐ good ☐ fair ☐ poor ☐ very poor

21 During the last six months, did you have trouble with any of the following? (Check one box on each line across.)

	Very Often	Often	Sometimes	Seldom	Never
a sleeplessness	☐	☐	☐	☐	☐
b stomach complaints	☐	☐	☐	☐	☐
c nervousness	☐	☐	☐	☐	☐
d headache	☐	☐	☐	☐	☐
e rapid heart beat	☐	☐	☐	☐	☐
f heart condition	☐	☐	☐	☐	☐
g ulcer	☐	☐	☐	☐	☐
h unusual loss of appetite	☐	☐	☐	☐	☐
i dizzy spells, fainting	☐	☐	☐	☐	☐
j unusual number of colds	☐	☐	☐	☐	☐
k sudden outbursts of perspiration	☐	☐	☐	☐	☐

22 To what extent do you feel responsible for the success of: (Check one box on each line across.)

	Not at All	A Little	Somewhat	Quite a Bit	Very Much
a your own work group	☐	☐	☐	☐	☐
b your department	☐	☐	☐	☐	☐
c the whole plant	☐	☐	☐	☐	☐

23 Below are listed a number of statements. There are no right or wrong answers to these statements. We are interested only in your opinion about each statement. (Check one box on each line across.)

	Strongly Disagree	Disagree	Neither Agree Nor Disagree	Agree	Strongly Agree
a A group of people who are equal will work a lot better than one with a boss over it.	☐	☐	☐	☐	☐
b Everyone should have an equal chance and an equal say in most things.	☐	☐	☐	☐	☐
c Things work best when people concern themselves with their own welfare and let others take care of themselves.	☐	☐	☐	☐	☐
d Generally speaking, men work hardest when they're free from pressure from their superiors.	☐	☐	☐	☐	☐
e Anyone who trusts everyone else is asking for trouble.	☐	☐	☐	☐	☐
f Many people really don't know what is best for them.	☐	☐	☐	☐	☐
g A person shouldn't delegate a decision to his subordinates when he is competent to make it himself.	☐	☐	☐	☐	☐
h If you want people to do a job right, you should explain things to them in great detail.	☐	☐	☐	☐	☐
i If you give the average person a job to do and leave him to do it, he will finish it successfully.	☐	☐	☐	☐	☐
j Most people work best under close supervision.	☐	☐	☐	☐	☐
k Most people today try to work as little as possible.	☐	☐	☐	☐	☐
l Very few people today are taking advantage of unemployment insurance.	☐	☐	☐	☐	☐
m Most people in this country put in a fair day's work for their wages.	☐	☐	☐	☐	☐
n Almost all people are basically hard-working and honest	☐	☐	☐	☐	☐
o The average person will rarely express his opinion in a group when he sees that others disagree with him.	☐	☐	☐	☐	☐
p Most people would cheat on their income tax, if they had a chance.	☐	☐	☐	☐	☐

24 Now we would like to ask a few additional questions.

How old are you?_____

How many years have you been working in your present position?_____

How many years have you been working in this organization?_____

What is your annual salary (including overtime and bonus)?_____

How many years of school did you finish?_____

11

Thank you for your interest. Your comments on this questionnaire are welcome.

JOB OBSERVATION GUIDE

COMPANY: _____

RESPONDENT'S NAME: _____

RESPONDENT'S CODE NUMBER: _____

OBSERVER: _____

TIME OF OBSERVATION: _____

1. For each of the following statements, check the number indicating how much you agree with this statement as a description of the employee's job.

	strongly disagree	disagree	slightly disagree	slightly agree	agree	strongly agree
a) The work area is clean.	1	2	3	4	5	6
b) The work area is very hot (or cold, depending on the season).	1	2	3	4	5	6
c) The work requires physical effort.	1	2	3	4	5	6
d) The work requires high concentration and attention.	1	2	3	4	5	6
e) The job is dangerous and / or unhealthy.	1	2	3	4	5	6

2. How much *variety* in work pace is there on the job?

1	2	3	4	5	6	7
Always the same for 95 per cent of the working time			More than one work pace, but variations only at long intervals			Varies considerably; job does not define the work pace.

3. How much *change* in physical location is there?

1	2	3	4	5	6	7
Sits or stands at the same place for 95 per cent of the working time		Moves in a fixed work place; does not have to sit or stand all the time, but fixed working position			Moves most of the time to different working positions; no predetermined position	

4. How much *autonomy* is there in the job? That is, to what extent does the job permit the individual himself to decide how to go about doing the work?

1	2	3	4	5	6	7
Very little; the job gives him almost no personal 'say' about how and when the work is done.		Moderate autonomy; many things are standardized and not under his control, but he can make some decisions about the work.			Very much; the job gives him almost complete responsibility for deciding how and when the work is done.	

5. How much does the job involve the individual producing an *entire product or an entire service*?

1	2	3	4	5	6	7
The job involves doing only a small part of the entire product or service; it is also *worked* on by others or by automatic equipment, and he may not see or be aware of much of the work done on the product or service.		The job involves doing a moderate sized 'chunk' of the work; while others are also involved, his contribution is significant.			The job involves producing the entire product or service from start to finish; the final outcome of the work is clearly the result of his work.	

6. How *intellectually demanding* is the job?

1	2	3	4	5	6	7
Not at all; the job is very routine and does not require any mental effort.		Moderately			Extremely; the job is very non-routine and involves a lot of 'thinking-through' or pro-blem-solving.	

7. To what extent does the job require the use of sophisticated or complex skills or knowledge?

1	2	3	4	5	6	7
Very little; no skills are required which the average person would not already have.		Moderate; some skills are required, but they would not be difficult for the average person to obtain in a short time (three months).			Very much; highly complex or sophis-ticated skills are needed to do the job.	

8. To what extent does the job require the individual to *work closely with other people* (either 'clients,' or people in related jobs within the organizations?).

1	2	3	4	5	6	7
Very little; dealing with other people is not at all neces-sary in doing the job.		Moderately; some dealing with others is necessary.			Very much; dealing with other people is an absolutely essential and cru-cial part of doing the job.	

9. How much *uncertainty* is there in the job?

1	2	3	4	5	6	7

Very little; the individual almost always knows what to expect and is frequently surprised by something happening unexpectedly on the job.

Moderate uncertainty

Very much; the individual is almost never sure what is going to happen; unexpected things frequently happen.

10. How close is supervision?

1	2	3	4	5	6	7

Immediate supervisor always or almost always present

Immediate supervisor nearby

Immediate supervisor rarely or never present

11. How is work quality determined?

1	2	3	4	5	6	7

Determined by machines or by factors beyond the person's control

Equal mixture of person and machines

Determined largely by person

12. Please indicate how true each of the following statements is as a description of the job you are observing.

	false	more false than true		more true than false	true		
a) Just doing the work required by the job gives the individual many chances to assess how well he is doing.	1	2	3	4	5	6	7
b) The job lets the individual do a variety of different things.	1	2	3	4	5	6	7
c) The job requires a high level of skill.	1	2	3	4	5	6	7

	false	more false than true		more true than false		true
d) The job requires a high level of mental effort.	1	2	3	4	5	6	7
e) The job allows the individual to determine his own pace.	1	2	3	4	5	6	7
f) The individual has enough freedom as to how he does the work.	1	2	3	4	5	6	7
g) The individual has to co-operate directly with other people in order to do his job.	1	2	3	4	5	6	7
h) The job is so simple that virtually anybody could handle it with little or no initial training.	1	2	3	4	5	6	7
i) The individual has to depend on the work performed by others in order to get the materials of information he needs to do his work.	1	2	3	4	5	6	7
j) The individual has a lot to say over what happens on his job.	1	2	3	4	5	6	7
k) The job requires that the individual constantly repeat the same actions.	1	2	3	4	5	6	7
l) The job allows the individual to make many decisions on his own.	1	2	3	4	5	6	7

13. Please indicate how much you agree or disagree with each of the following statements as a description of the job you are watching.

	strongly disagree	disagree	slightly disagree	neither agree nor disagree	slightly agree	agree	strongly agree
a) The individual working on the job does tasks which are clearly defined.	1	2	3	4	5	6	7

	strongly disagree	disagree	slightly disagree	neither agree nor disagree	slightly agree	agree	strongly agree
b) The individual working on this job is free from conflicting demands which others may make of him.	1	2	3	4	5	6	7
c) The job requires the individual to be prepared to handle surprising or unpredictable situations.	1	2	3	4	5	6	7
d) The job denies the individual any chance to use his personal initiative or discretion at work.	1	2	3	4	5	6	7
e) The job is highly predictable and rarely presents the individual with surprising or unpredictable situations.	1	2	3	4	5	6	7

14. Once you have completed observing and rating the job, but before you leave the area where the individual works, fill out the following information.

How confident are you of the accuracy of your ratings of this job?

1	2	3	4
Not at all confident; I was not at all able to rate the job I observed accurately.	Somewhat confident; my ratings are only partially descriptive of the job I observed.	Moderately confident; my ratings provide a fairly accurate description of the job I observed.	Very confident; my ratings accurately describe the job I observed.

Ask the individual how typical the sequence you observed is of the work which is normally done?

1	2	3
Not at all typical; he usually does a very different type of work.	Somewhat typical; he often does similar work, but this observation period did not completely cover his job.	Very typical; he usually does work of the type observed.

Was this a validated observation, that is, did another observer make this observation with you?
1 Yes   2 No

EMPLOYEE (UNION) REPRESENTATIVE INTERVIEW

1. How would you characterize the relationship between management and employees?
2. How often do you talk with your constituents?
3. What are the major concerns of your constituents?
4. Tell me about your job as an employee representative.
5. What would you like to see changed in this company?
6. What are the major problems you face? Do you like your role as employee representative?
7. Does this company operate the way it claims? (Do you have the influence you are supposed to have?)

PERSONNEL MANAGER INTERVIEW

1. Describe the grievance procedure.

2. Can you give us some recent examples of written grievances? (e.g., work areas, issues.)

3. What percentage goes to arbitration?

4. What percentage of these does the company win?

5. What would you estimate the annual cost of grievances to be?

6. Have there been strikes, lock-outs or slow-downs in the past three years? If so, state duration, number of workers involved, estimated cost of lost production etc.

7. Can you give us data on
   a) absenteeism
   b) lateness   for all
   c) grievance-filing persons in
   d) accidents   our sample
   e) performance ratings

8. Can you give us company data on
   a) absenteeism
   b) turnover
   c) accidents
   d) visits to the infirmary or to company nurse

9. Why was the participation program started? When? What problems? How long before it was working properly? What role did key personalities have? How many of the key personalities are still around?

10. Describe the work force – frequency, distribution of age, sex, education, ethnic background, seniority, income.

11. How do wages in this company compare to wages for comparable work in other companies in this area?

12. Who owns this company? What percentage is owned by different groups?

13. What issues are discussed in (the participative body)?

14. How would you characterize the relationship between management and employees in this company? (friendly-hostile; co-operative-competitive, etc.)

15. What would you like to see changed in this company?

MEASURES

		Number of items	Coefficient alpha
Values			
Participation potential	23c, 23f, 23o	3	0.33
Motivation of average person	23i, 23k, 23in	3	0.31
Honesty of average person	23l, 23n, 23p	3	0.25
Leadership qualities	23d, 23g, 23h, 23j	4	0.41
Trust in people	23e	1	–
Equality	23a, 23b	2	0.51
Structure			
Rule emphasis	11e, 11f	2	0.39
Surveillance	11i, 11l	2	0.62
Opportunities for initiative	11j, 11k	2	0.51
Hierarchy of authority	11g, 11h, 11m	3	0.53
Democratic / hierarchical structure (see chapter 5)		tauB = 0.73	
Process			
Intergroup conflict	6a, 6b, 6c	3	0.61
Conflict resolution policies			
problem-solving	18b, 18e	2	0.48
ignoring	18a	1	
smoothing	18c	1	
forcing	18d	1	
Relations among group members			
openness	2b, 2g	2	0.45
cohesiveness	2a, 2d	2	0.55
friendliness	2c, 2e	2	0.39
participativeness	2f	1	
Participativeness of the organization	9	1	
Influence over decision-making	8a, 8b, 8c, 8d, 8e	5	0.74
Communication re: work	14a, 14b, 14c	3	0.59
Communication re: non-work	15a, 15b, 15c	3	0.70
Supervisory style	5a, 5b, 5e, 5f, 5h, 5j	6	0.86

		Number of items	Coefficient alpha
Outcomes			
Mental health	19a, 19b, 19d, 19e, 19f, 19g, 19i, 19j, 19k, 19l,	10	0.91
Physical health	20	1	
Alienation	13a, 13b, 13c, 13d, 13e, 13f, 13g, 13h, 13i	9	0.89
Stress	21a, 21b, 21c, 21d, 21e, 21g, 21h	7	0.73
Behavioural outcomes			
job upgrading	8 on interview	1	
voting in political elections	9 on interview	1	
voting in union elections	10 on interview	1	
Satisfaction			
pay	3i	1	
fringe benefits	3a	1	
job security	3j	1	
participation	3h	1	
freedom on the job	3c	1	
opportunities			
promotion	3d	1	
learn new things	3e	1	
develop skills	3k	1	
accomplishment	3g	1	
respect from co-workers	3f	1	
social relations	3b	1	
Intrinsic job satisfaction	3c, 3d, 3e, 3h, 3k, 3g	6	0.84
Job satisfaction	1c, 4	2	0.73
Attitudes towards management	2, 3 on interview	2	0.55
Commitment to organization	1d, 1e, 1f	3	0.70
Negative reactions to change	11n, 11o, 11p	3	0.72
Social interaction			
outside workplace	7 on interview	1	
Characteristics of tasks (from job observation guide)			
Variety	2, 3, 12b, 12k	4	0.85
Task completion	5	1	
Autonomy	4, 12e, 12f, 12j, 12l, 13d	6	0.94

		Number of items	Coefficient alpha
Skills	6, 7, 12c, 12h	4	0.93
Novelty	13a, 13c, 13e, 9	4	0.89
Intellectual demands	11, 12d, 1d	3	0.74
Required interaction	8, 12g	2	0.91
Conflicting demands	13b	1	
Physical conditions	1a, 1b, 1c, 1e	4	0.85
Feedback	12a	1	
Task enrichment	measures 1 through 5	19	0.82
Growth need strength	6 measures on interview	6	0.80

References

Aberg, Y. 1969. 'Produktion och produktwiteri Svenge, 1861–1965.' *Uppsala Lang-titsutredningen och teknikfaktorn Industriforbundets Tidskrift* 5, 1971, 15–19

Agmen, S., R. Hansson, and K.G. Kensson. 1976. *The Volvo Kalmar Plant: The Impact of New Design on Work Organization.* Trans. by David Jenkins. Stockholm: The Rationalization Council SAF-LO

Aiken, M., and J. Hage. 1966. 'Organization alienation: A comparative analysis.' *American Sociological Review* 31, 497–507

Allport, G.W. 1937. *Personality: A Psychological Interpretation.* New York: Holt-Rinehart

Antonides, H. 1980. *Industrial Democracy: Illusion and Promise.* Toronto: Christian Labour Association of Canada

Argyris, C. 1962. *Interpersonal Competence and Organizational Effectiveness.* Homewood, Ill.: Irwin-Dorsey

– *Integrating the Individual and the Organization.* New York: John Wiley and Sons

Barnard, C.I. 1938. *The Functions of the Executive.* Cambridge, Mass.: Harvard University Press

Bass, B.M. and V.J. Shackelton. 'Industrial democracy and participative management: a case for a synthesis.' *Academy of Management Review* 4, 393–404

Bell, D. 1976. *The Cultural Contradictions of Capitalism.* New York: Basic Books

Bendix, R. 1956. *Work and Authority in Industry.* New York: John Wiley and Sons

Bennis, W.G. 1969. *Organization Development: Its Nature, Origins and Prospects.* Reading, Mass.: Addison-Wesley

– 1975. 'Tied down.' *Yale Alumni Magazine,* 18–20

Bernstein, P. 1974. 'Run your own business.' Working papers

– 1976. 'Necessary elements for effective worker participation in decision-making.' *Journal of Economic Issues* 10, 490–525

Bierstedt, R. 1950. 'An analysis of social power.' *American Sociological Review* 15, 730–8

Blades, L.E. 1967. 'Employment at will vs. individual freedom: on limiting the abusive exercise of employer power.' *Columbia Law Review* 67, 1405

Blau, D.M. and W.R. Scott. 1962. *Formal Organizations.* San Francisco: Chandler

Blau, P. 1964. *Exchange and Power in Social Life.* New York: Wiley and Sons

Blauner, R. 1964. *Alienation and Freedom.* Chicago: University of Chicago Press

Bliss, M. 1974. *A Living Profit: Studies in the Social History of Canadian Business, 1883–1911.* Toronto: McClelland and Stewart

Blumberg, P. 1968. *Industrial Democracy.* London: Constable

Blumberg, P.I. 1977. 'Implications of representation trend for U.S. corporations.' *Harvard Business Review* 55, 46

Bolweg, J.F. 1979. 'Industrial democracy and job design.' In L.E. Davis and J.C. Taylor, eds, *Design of Jobs.* Santa Monica: Goodyear Publishing

Bonjean, C.M., R.J. Hill, and S.D. McLemore. 1967. *Sociological Measurements: An Inventory of Scales and Indices.* San Francisco: Chandler

Brown, N. 1979. 'An operational model of participation for use in academic libraries.' Working paper, Guelph, Ontario

Browning, G.J., M.F. Farmer, H.D. Kirk, and C.D. Mitchell. 1961. 'On the meaning of alienation.' *American Sociological Review* 26, 780–1

Bruyn, S.T. and L. Nicolaou-Smokovitis. 1977. 'A theoretical framework for studying worker participation: The psychosocial contract.' Paper presented at Second International Conference on Participation, Worker's Control and Self-Management, Paris, Sept. 7

Burns, T. and G.M. Stalker. 1961. *The Management of Innovation.* London: Tavistock Publications

Burnstein, M., N. Tienhaara, P. Hewson, and B.B. Warrander. 1975. *Canadian Work Values: Findings of a Work Ethic Survey and a Job Satisfaction Survey.* Ottawa: Information Canada

Cammett, J.H. 1967. *Antonio Gramsci and the Origins of Italian Communism.* Stanford: Stanford University Press

Chapple, E.D. and L. Sayles. 1961. *The Measurement of Management.* New York: Macmillan

Child, J. 1973. 'Strategies of control and organizational behavior.' *Administrative Science Quarterly* 18, 1–17

Clarke, A. 1979. 'Industrial democracy. A Canadian case study 82173 Canada Limited.' MA thesis, Carleton University

Clegg, H. 1951. *Industrial Democracy and Nationalisation.* London: Blackwell

– 1960. *A New Approach to Industrial Democracy*. London: Blackwell

Cole, G.D.H. 1920. *Guild Socialism Restated*. London: Leonard Parsons

Connaghan, C.J. 1976. *Partnership or Marriage of Convenience? A Critical Examination of Contemporary Labour Relations in West Germany with Suggestions for Improving the Canadian Labour-Management Relationships Based on the West German Experience*. Ottawa: Department of Labour

Conot, R. 1974. *American Odyssey: A Unique History of America Told Through the Life of a Great City*. New York: Morrow

Conte, M. and A.S. Tannenbaum. 1977. 'Employee ownership.' Report to the Economic Development Administration, United States Department of Commerce

Cooper, M.R., B.S. Morgan, P.M. Foley, and L.B. Kaplan. 1979. 'Changing employee values: Deepening discontent?' *Harvard Business Review* 57, 117–25

Couch, C.J. 1966. 'Self-identification and alienation.' *Sociological Quarterly* 7, 255–64

Crispo, J. 1978. *Industrial Democracy in Western Europe: A North American Perspective*. Toronto: McGraw-Hill

Cummings, T.G. and E.S. Molloy. 1977. *Improving Productivity and the Quality of Work Life*. New York: Praeger

Current Economic and Industrial Relations Indicators, 1979, Kingston: Industrial Relations Centre, Queen's University

Czikszentmihalyi, M. and R. Graef. 1979. 'Feeling free.' *Psychology Today* 13, 84–99

Dachler, P. and B. Wilpert. 1978. 'Conceptual dimensions and boundaries of participation in organizations: a critical evaluation.' *Administrative Science Quarterly* 23, 1–39

Dahl, R. 1970. *After the Revolution: Authority in a Good Society*. New Haven: Yale University Press

Dalton, M. 1959. *Men Who Manage*. New York: Wiley

Davis, L.E. 1971. 'Job satisfaction research: The post-industrial view.' *Industrial Relations* 10, 176–93

– 1979. 'Job design: future directions.' In L.E. Davis and J.C. Taylor, *Design of Jobs*. Santa Monica: Goodyear Publishing

Davis, L.E. and A.B. Cherns, eds. 1975. *Quality of Working Life: Problems, Prospects and State of the Art*. Vol. 1. New York: Free Press

Davis, L.E. and C.S. Sullivan. 1980. 'A labour-management contracted quality of working life.' *Journal of Occupational Behaviour* 1, 29–41

Davis, L.E. and J.C. Taylor. 1979. *Design of Jobs*. Santa Monica: Goodyear Publishing

Dean, D.G. 1961. 'Alienation: Its meaning and measurement.' *American Sociological Review* 20, 753–8

Derber, M. 1970. *The American Idea of Industrial Democracy, 1865–1965.* Urbana, Ill.: University of Illinois Press

Dornbusch, S.M. and W.R. Scott. 1975. *Evaluation and the Exercise of Authority.* San Francisco: Jossey-Bass

Dowling, J.B. 1978. *Organizational Legitimation: The Management of Meaning.*, PHD thesis, Stanford University

Driscoll, J.W. 1978. 'A change strategy for union-management cooperation: the Scanlon plan.' Working paper, M.I.T., Cambridge, Mass. May

Drucker, P.F. 1976. *The Unseen Revolution: How Pension Fund Socialism Came to America.* New York: Harper and Row

Dunnette, M. 1976. *Handbook of Industrial and Organizational Psychology.* Chicago: Rand McNally

Economic Council of Canada. 1976. *People and Jobs: A Study of the Canadian Labour Market.* Ottawa: Economic Council of Canada

Emery, F.E. 1969. 'Characteristics of socio-technical systems.' Document No. 527. London: Tavistock Institute of Human Relations

Emery, F.E. and E. Thorsrud. 1964. *Form and Content in Industrial Democracy.* London: Tavistock

– 1969. *New Designs for Work Organization.* Oslo: Tannum Press

Etzioni, A. 1961. *A Comparative Analysis of Complex Organizations.* New York: Free Press

Faxem, K.-O. 1978. 'Does employee participation in decision making contribute to change and growth?' Stockholm: Swedish Employers Confederation

Fayol, H. 1916. *Administration Industrielle et Générale.* Trans. by Storrs. London: Sir Isaac Pitman and Sons, 1949

Fenn, D.H. and D. Yankelovich. 1972. 'Responding to the employee voice.' *Harvard Business Review* 50, 83–91

Festinger, L. 1954. 'A theory of social comparison processes.' *Human Relations* 7, 117–40

Finn, E. 1973. 'Industrial democracy and recent union demands.' In G. Hunnius, G.D. Garson, and J. Case, *Workers Control: A Reader Labor and Social Change.* New York: Random House

Flanagan, R., G. Strauss, and L. Ulman. 1974. 'Worker discontent and work place behavior.' *Industrial Relations* 13, 1–23

Follett, M.P. 1924. *Creative Experience.* London: Longmans, Green

Fox, A. 1974. *Beyond Contract: Work, Power and Trust Relations.* London: Faber and Faber

Fox, E.M. and L. Urwick. 1973. *Dynamic Administration: The Collected Papers of Mary Parker Follett.* New York: Hippocrene Books

French, J.R.P. 1964. 'Laboratory and field studies of power.' In E. Boulding, ed., *Power and Conflict in Organizations*. London: Tavistock

French, J.R.P. and B.H. Raven. 1960. 'The bases of social power.' In D. Cartwright and A. Zander, eds, *Group Dynamics: Research and Theory*. Second ed. New York: Row, Peterson, 607–23

Friedland, S. 1971. 'Stock options and company performance.' In *Incentive Through Profit Sharing: The Harold Victor Lush Essays on Profit Sharing*. Vol. 1. Downsview: York University

Friedlander, F. and H. Pickle. 1968. 'Components of effectiveness in small organizations.' *Administrative Science Quarterly* 13, 289–304

Friedman, G. 1961. *The Anatomy of Work*. New York: Free Press

Garnier, M.A. 1972. 'Changing recruitment patterns and organizational ideology: The case of a British military academy.' *Administrative Science Quarterly* 17, 499–507

Geyer, F. 1972. *Bibliography Alienation*. Second ed. Amsterdam: Netherlands University

Gilbreth, F.B., and E.G. Carey. 1948. *Cheaper by the Dozen*. New York: Thomas Y. Crowell

Gilson, T.Q. and J.M. Lefcowitz. 1957. 'A plant-wide productivity bonus in a small factory: Study of an unsuccessful case.' *Industrial and Labour Relations Review* 10, 284–96

Godfrey, D. and M. Watkins, eds. 1970. *Gordon to Watkins to You – A Documentary: The Battle for Control of Our Economy*. Toronto: New Press

Goldenberg, H.C. 1978. 'Facing human facts in industrial relations.' Address Delivered at the Annual Industrial Relations Seminar. Queen's University, Kingston, Ont., Oct. 22–27

Gordon, F.M. 1978. 'Marx's concept of alienation and empirical sociological research.' Discussion paper. Cambridge, Mass.: A Group For Work Democracy

Gorz, A. 1967. *A Strategy for Labor*. Boston: Beacon Press
– 1973. *Socialism and Revolution*. Garden City: Anchor Press

Gouldner, A.W. 1955. *Patterns of Industrial Bureaucracy*. London: Routledge and Kegan Paul
– 1960. 'The norm of reciprocity: A preliminary statement.' *American Sociological Review* 25, 161–78

Graen, G.B. 1968. 'Testing traditional and two-factor hypotheses concerning job satisfaction.' *Journal of Applied Psychology* 52, 366–71

Grand'Maison, J. 1975. *Une Tentative d'Autogestion*. Montréal: Les Presses de l'Université de Montréal

Greenberg, E.S. 1975. 'The consequences of worker participation: A clarification of the theoretical literature.' *Social Science Quarterly* 56, 191–209

Gulick, L. and L. Urwick, eds. 1937. *Papers on the Science of Administration*. New York: Institute of Public Administration, Columbia University

Haas, J.E., R.H. Hall, and N.J. Johnson. 1966. 'Toward an empirically derived taxonomy of organizations.' In R.V. Bowers, ed., *Studies on Behavior in Organizations*. Athens: University of Georgia Press, 157–80

Hackman, J.R. and E.E. Lawler. 1971. 'Employee reactions to job characteristics.' *Journal of Applied Psychology* 55, 259–86

Hackman, J.R. and G.R. Oldman. 1975. 'Development of the job diagnostic survey.' *Journal of Applied Psychology* 60, 159–70

Hage, J. and M. Aiken. 1969. 'Routine technology, social structure and organizational goals.' *Administrative Science Quarterly* 14, 366–76

Hammer, T.H. and R.N. Stern. 1980. 'Employee ownership: Implications for the organizational distribution of power.' *Academy of Management Journal* 23, 78–100

Hartmann, H. 1975. 'Codetermination today and tomorrow.' *British Journal of Industrial Relations* 13, 57

Herzberg, F. 1966. *Work and the Nature of Man*. Cleveland, Ohio: World Publishing

Hespe, G. and G. Wall. 1976. 'The demand for participation among employees.' *Human Relations* 29, 411–28

Heynes, R.W. and A. Zander. 1953. 'Observation of group behavior.' In L. Festinger and D. Katz, eds, *Research Methods in the Behavioral Sciences*. New York: Dryden Press, 381–417

Hilgendorf, E.L. and B.L. Irving. 1976. 'Workers' experience of participation: The case of British Rail.' *Human Relations* 29, 471–505

Hobbes, T. 1651. *Leviathan, or the Matter, Forme and Power of a Commonwealth, Ecclesiasticall and Civil*. London: A. Crooke

Hochner, A. 1978. 'Worker ownership and the theory of participation.' PHD. thesis, Harvard University

Hoffer, E. 1952. *The Ordeal of Change*. New York: Harper and Row

Holter, H. 1965. 'Attitudes towards employee participation in company decision-making processes.' *Human Relations* 18, 297–321

Hopp, M.A. 1976. 'The development of rating scales to measure behaviors associated with work alienation and their perceived causes.' Report to the U.S. department of labor

House, R.J. and L. Wigdor. 1967. 'Herzberg's dual-factor theory of job satisfaction and motivation: A review of the evidence and a criticism.' *Personnel Psychology* 20, 369–89

Hoxie, R.F. 1915. *Scientific Management and Labor*. New York: Appleton-Century-Crofts

Hulin, C.L. and M.R. Blood. 1968. 'Job enlargement, individual differences and worker responses.' *Psychological Bulletin* 69, 41–55

Hunnius, G., G.D. Garson, and J. Case. 1973. *Worker's Control: A Reader on Labor and Social Change*. New York: Random House

Indik, B.P. 1972. 'Toward an effective theory of organization behavior.' In J. Turner, A Filley, and R.J. House, eds, *Studies in Managerial Process and Organizational Behavior*. Glenview, Ill.: Scott-Foresman

Jahoda, M. 1958. *Current Concepts of Mental Health*. New York: Basic Books

Jain, H. 1980. *Worker Participation: Success and Problems*. New York: Praeger

Jaques, E. 1964. *Time-span Handbook*. London: Heinemann Educational Books

Jenkins, D. 1973. *Job Power: Blue and White Collar Democracy*. Garden City, N.Y.: Doubleday

Jenkins, G.D., D.A. Nadler, E.E. Lawler, and C. Cammann. 1975. 'Standardized observations: An approach to measuring the nature of jobs.' *Journal of Applied Psychology* 60, 171–81

Johnson, F., ed. 1973. *Alienation: Concept, Term and Meanings*. New York: Seminar Press

Jones, D.C. 1978. 'Producer cooperatives in industrialized western economies: An overview.' *Annals of Public and Cooperative Economy* 49(2), 149–61

Kanter, R.M. 1977. *Men and Women of the Corporation*. New York: Basic Books

Kasl, S. 1973. 'Work and mental health.' In *Work in America*. New Haven: Yale University Press, 11–12

Katz, D. and B.S. Georgopoulos. 1971. 'Organizations in a changing world.' *Journal of Applied Behavioral Science* 7, 342–70

Katz, D. and R.L. Kahn. 1966. *The Social Psychology of Organizations*. New York: John Wiley and Sons

Kelly, L. 1975. 'Absenteeism.' Industrial Relations Centre, Queen's University

Kelso, L. and M. Adler. 1958. *The Capitalist Manifesto*. New York: Random House

– 1961. *The New Capitalists*. New York: Random House

Kelso, L. and P. Hetter. 1967. *Two-Factor Theory: The Economics of Reality*. New York: Vintage Books

Kendall, W. 1968. 'Social contract.' In *International Encyclopaedia of the Social Sciences* 14, 376–81. New York: Macmillan

Kirby, M.J.L. 1980. 'New employee attitudes and demands: The challenge for corporate objectives in the 1980's.' Special supplement. Montreal: The Institute for Research on Public Policy

Kirsch, B.A. and J.J. Lengermann. 1972. 'An empirical test of Robert Blauner's ideas on alienation in work as applied to different type jobs in a white collar setting.' *Sociology and Social Research* 56, 180–94

Kochan, T., D. Lipsky, and L. Dyer. 1974. 'Collective bargaining and quality of work life: The views of union activists.' Proceedings of 27th Annual Meeting, Industrial Relations Research Association, 150–62. San Francisco, 28–29 December

Kwoka, J.E. 1976. 'The organization of work: A conceptual framework.' Social Science Quarterly 57, 632–43

Lakoff, S.A. and D. Rich, eds. 1973. Private Government: Introductory Readings. Glenview, Ill.: Scott Foresman and Co.

Lammers, C.J. 1967. 'Power and participation in decision-making in formal organizations.' American Journal of Sociology 73, 201–16

Landsberger, H.A. 1958. Hawthorne Revisited. Ithaca, N.Y.: New York State School of Industrial and Labor Relations, Cornell University

Leavitt, H.J. 1972. Managerial Psychology. Third ed. Chicago: University of Chicago Press

Lesieur, F.G., ed. 1958. The Scanlon Plan: A Frontier in Labor-Management Cooperation. Cambridge, Mass.: Technology Press, M.I.T. and New York: Wiley, joint publishers

Likert, R. 1961. New Patterns of Management. New York: McGraw-Hill

– 1968. The Human Organization: Its Management and Value. New York: McGraw-Hill

Lindblom, C.E. 1977. Politics and Markets. New York: Basic Books

Locke, J. 1948. The Second Treatise of Civil Government and A Letter Concerning Toleration. I.W. Gough, ed. Oxford: Blackwell

Long, R.J. 1978. 'The effects of employee ownership on organizational identification, employee job attitudes and organizational performance: A tentative framework and empirical findings.' Human Relations 31, 29–48

Maslow, A.H. 1954. Motivation and Personality. New York: Harper and Row

Mayo, E. 1931. The Human Problems of Industrial Civilization. New York: Viking Press

– 1945. The Social Problems of Industrial Civilization. Cambridge, Mass.: Harvard University Press

Mazzolini, R. 1978. 'The influence of European workers over corporate strategy.' Sloan Management Review 19, 59–81

McCormick, C.P. 1973. The Power of People: Multiple Management Up to Date. Baltimore: McCormick and Company

McGregor, D. 1960. The Human Side of Enterprise. New York: McGraw-Hill

McGuire, W.J. 1968. 'A syllogistic analysis of cognitive relationships.' In M.J. Rosenberg, C.I. Hovland, W.J. McGuire, R.P. Abelson, and J.W. Brehm, eds, Attitude, Organizations, and Change. New Haven: Yale University

Meissner, M. 1971. 'The long arm of the job: A study of work and leisure.' Industrial Relations 10, 239–60

Metcalf, H.C. and L. Urwick. 1942. *Dynamic Administration. The Collected Papers of Mary Parker Follett*. New York: Harper and Row

Metzger, B. and B. Colletti. 1971. *Does Profit Sharing Pay? A Comparative Study of the Financial Performance of Retailers With and Without Profit Sharing Programs*. Evanston, Ill.: Profit Sharing Research Foundation

Metzger, B.L. 1975a. *Profit Sharing in 38 Large Companies: A Piece of the Action for 1,000,000 Participants*. Vol. 1. Evanston, Ill.: Profit Sharing Research Foundation

– 1975b. *Sharing a Business: Prescription for Growth*. Evanston, Ill.: Profit Sharing Research Foundation

– 1977. 'Inflation, productivity and profit sharing.' Article. Evanston, Ill.: Profit Sharing Research Foundation

Metzger, B.L. and B. Diekman. 1975. *Profit-Sharing: The Industrial Adrenalin*. Evanston, Ill.: Profit Sharing Research Foundation

Michels, R. 1962. *Political Parties: A Sociological Study of the Oligarchical Tendencies of Modern Democracy*. New York: Free Press

Michigan Organizational Assessment Package: Progress Report II. 1975. Ann Arbor: Institute for Social Research, University of Michigan

Middleton, R. 1963. 'Alienation, race and education.' *American Sociological Review* 38, 973–7

Miles, R.E. 1965. 'Human relations or human resources?' *Harvard Business Review* 43, 148–63

– 1975. *Theories of Management: Implications for Organizational Behavior and Development*. New York: McGraw-Hill

Milgram, S. 1965. 'Some conditions of obedience and disobedience to authority.' *Human Relations* 18, 57–76

Mogenson, A.H. 1963. 'Works simplification: A program of continuous improvement.' In H.B. Maynard, *Industrial Engineering Handbook*. New York: McGraw-Hill

Mooney, J.D. and A.C. Reiley. 1931. *Onward Industry*. New York: Harper and Row

– 1939. *The Principles of Organization*. New York: Harper and Row

Morse, N.C. and R.S. Weiss. 1955. 'The function and meaning of work and the job.' *American Sociological Review* 20, 191–8

Mulder, M. 1971, 'Power equalization through participation.' *Administrative Science Quarterly* 16, 31–8

Neal, A.C. 1963. 'Dimensions of alienation among manual and non-manual workers.' *American Sociological Review* 28, 599–608

Neal, A.C. and S. Rettig. 1967. 'On the multi-dimensionality of alienation.' *American Sociological Review* 27, 54–64

Neal, A.C. and M. Seeman. 1964. 'Organizations and powerlessness: A test of the mediation hypothesis.' *American Sociological Review* 29, 216–26

Nettler, G. 1957. 'A measure of alienation.' *American Sociological Review* 22, 670–7

Nightingale, D.V. 1980. *Profit Sharing and Employee Ownership: A Review and Appraisal.* A Report to the Employment Relations Branch of Labour Canada. Kingston: Queen's University

Nightingale, D.V. and J.M. Toulouse. 1977. 'Toward a multilevel congruence theory of organizations.' *Administrative Science Quarterly* 22, 264–80

O'Toole, J. 1979. 'The uneven record of employee ownership.' *Harvard Business Review* 57, 185–97

Palmore, E. 1969a. 'Physical, mental and social factors in predicting longevity.' *The Gerontologist* 9, 103–8

– 1969b. 'Predicting longevity: A follow-up controlling for age.' *The Gerontologist* 9, 247–50

Parsons, T. 1960. *Structure and Process in Modern Society.* New York: Free Press

Parker, S. 1971. *The Future of Work and Leisure.* New York: Praeger

Pateman, C. 1970. *Participation and Democratic Theory.* London: Cambridge University Press

Pearlin, L. 1962. 'Alienation from work.' *American Sociological Review* 27, 314–26

Perrow, C. 1979. *Complex Organizations: A Critical Essay.* Second ed. Glenview, Ill.: Scott-Foresman

Policy Paper #18. 1979. Public Service Alliance of Canada, Quebec City Convention, 30 July–3 August

Pondy, L.R. and D.M. Boje. 1976. 'Bringing mind back in: Paradigm development as a frontier problem in organization theory.' Unpublished manuscript, Urbana, Ill.: University of Illinois, Organizational Behavior Group

Presthus, R.U. 1958. 'Toward a theory of organizational behavior.' *Administrative Science Quarterly* 3, 48–72

Ratner, D.L. 1970. 'The government of business corporations: Critical reflections on the role of "one share, one vote".' *Cornell Law Review* 1, 1–56

Rawls, J. 1971. *A Theory of Justice.* Cambridge: Harvard University Press

Report of the Royal Commission Inquiry into Labour Disputes. 1968. Ottawa: Queen's Printer

Reuther, W. 1966. 'Remarks at press conference.' Quoted in B. Metzger, *Profit Sharing in Perspective,* Evanston, Ill.: Profit Sharing Research Foundation. 143–4

Rhodes, A.L. 1961. 'Authoritarianism and alienation: The F-scale and the Srole scale as predictors of prejudice.' *Sociological Quarterly* 2, 193–202

Rice, A.K. 1958. *Productivity and Social Organization: The Ahmedabad Experiment.* London: Tavistock Publications

Ritzer, G. 1975. 'Sociology: A multiple paradigm science.' *American Sociological Review* 40, 156–67

Roethlisberger, F.J. and W.J. Dickson. 1939. *Management and the Worker*. Cambridge, Mass.: Harvard University Press

Rogers, C.R. 1961. *On Becoming a Person: A Therapist's View of Psychotherapy.* Boston: Houghton Mifflin Company

Rosow, J. 1974. *The Worker and the Job: Coping With Change.* Englewood Cliffs, N.J.: Prentice Hall

Rotter, J.B. 1966. 'Generalized expectancies for internal versus external control of reinforcement.' *Psychological Monograph* 80, (whole, No. 609), 1

Rousseau, D.M. 1977. 'Technological differences in job characteristics, employee satisfaction and motivation: A synthesis of job design research and sociotechnical systems theory.' *Organizational Behavior and Human Performance* 19, 18–42

– 1978. 'Characteristics of departments, positions and individuals: Context for attitudes and behavior.' *Administrative Science Quarterly* 23, 521–38

Rousseau, J.J. 1962. *The Social Contract.* New York: Hafner. First published 1762

Roy, S.K. 1973. 'Participative management in public industry: Organizational groundwork necessary.' In C.P. Thakur and K.C. Sethi, eds, *Industrial democracy: Some issues and experiences.* New Delhi, Shri Ram Centre for Industrial Relations and Human Resources

Ruh, R.A., R.L. Wallace, and C.F. Frost. 1973. 'Management attitudes and Scanlon Plan.' *Industrial Relations* 12, 282–8

Russell, R.A., A. Hochner, and S.E. Perry. 1977. 'San Francisco "Scavengers" run their own firm.' Working paper. Belmont, Mass.: Institute for New Enterprise Development

Salancik, G.R. and J. Pfeffer. 1977. 'An examination of need satisfaction models of job attitudes.' *Administrative Science Quarterly* 22, 427–56

Schein, E.H. 1965. *Organizational Psychology.* Englewood Cliffs, N.J.: Prentice-Hall

Schrank, R. 1978. *Ten Thousand Working Days.* Cambridge, Mass.: M.I.T. Press

Seashore, S.E. 1977. 'Participation in decision making: Some issues of conception, measurement and interaction.' Paper presented to the 37th Annual Meeting of the Academy of Management, Orlando, Fla, 14–17 August

Seeman, M. 1959. 'On the meaning of alienation.' *American Sociological Review* 24, 783–91

– 1967. 'On the personal consequences of alienation in work.' *American Sociological Review* 32, 273–85

– 1971. 'The urban alienations: Some dubious theses from Marx to Marcuse.' *Journal of Personality and Social Psychology* 19, 135–43

– 1972. 'Alienation and engagement.' In A. Campbell and P.E. Converse, eds, *The Human Meaning of Social Change.* New York: Russell Sage Foundation, 467–527

Selznick, P. 1948. 'Foundations of the theory of organizations.' *American Sociological Review*, 13, 25–35

– 1949. *TVA and the Grass Roots*. Berkeley: University of California Press

– 1957. *Leadership in Administration*. Evanston, Ill.: Row, Peterson and Co.

Seybold, J.W. 1976. 'Work satisfaction as a function of the person-environment interaction.' *Organizational Behavior and Human Performance* 17, 66–75

Sheldon, O. 1923. *The Philosophy of Management*. London: Sir Isaac Pitman and Sons

Shephard, H.A. 1965. 'Changing interpersonal and intergroup relationships in organizations.' In J.G. March, ed., *Handbook of Organizations*. Chicago: Rand McNally and Co.

Sheppard, H.L. and N.Q. Herrick. 1972. *Where Have All the Robots Gone? Worker Dissatisfaction in the 70's*. New York: Free Press

Shirom, A. 1972. 'The industrial relations systems of industrial cooperatives in the United States, 1880–1935.' *Labor History* 13, 533–55

Simon, H.A. 1957. *Administrative Behavior*. New York: Free Press

Slater, P.E. and W. Bennis. 1964. 'Democracy is inevitable.' *Harvard Business Review* 42, 51–9

Slote, A. 1969. *Termination: Closing at the Baker Plant*. Ann Arbor, Mich.: Institute of Social Research

Srole, L. 1956. 'Social integration and certain corollaries: An exploratory study.' *American Sociological Review* 21, 709–16

Steers, R.M. and D.G. Spencer. 1977. 'The role of achievement motivation in job design.' *Journal of Applied Psychology* 67, 472–9

Stern, R.N. and T.H. Hammer. 1978. 'Buying your job: Factors affecting the success or failure of employee acquisition attempts.' Working paper. Cornell University

Stogdill, R.M. 1966. 'Dimensions of organization theory.' In J.D. Thompson, *Approaches to Organizational Design*. Pittsburgh: University of Pittsburgh Press

Stone, E.F. 1976. 'The moderating effect of work-related values in the job scope-job satisfaction relationship.' *Organizational Behavior and Human Performance* 15, 147–67

Stone, E.F., R.T. Mowday and L.W. Porter. 1977. 'Higher-order need strengths as moderators of the job scope-job satisfaction relationship.' *Journal of Applied Psychology* 67, 468–73

Strauss, G. 1963. 'Some notes on power-equalization.' In H.J. Leavitt ed., *The Social Science of Organizations: Four Perspectives*. Englewood Cliffs, N.J.: Prentice-Hall

– 1974. 'Workers' attitudes and adjustments.' In J.W. Rosow, ed., *The Worker and the Job: Coping with Change*. Englewood Cliffs, N.J.: Prentice-Hall

- 1978. 'Quality of worklife and participation as bargaining issues.' Paper presented at M.I.T. Conference on Industrial Democracy in Europe, July 18–20
Strauss, G. and E. Rosenstein. 1970. 'Workers' participation: A critical view.' Industrial Relations 9, 197–214
Streuning, E.L. and A.H. Richardson. 1965. 'A factor analytic exploration of the alienation, anomia, and authoritarian domain.' American Sociological Review 30, 768–76
Susman, G.I. 1976. Autonomy at Work: A Sociotechnical Analysis of Participative Management. New York: Praeger
Tannenbaum, A.S. 1968. Control in Organizations. New York: McGraw-Hill
- 1974a. 'Systems of formal participation.' In G. Strauss, R.E. Miles, C.C. Snow, and A.S. Tannenbaum, eds, Organizational Behavior: Research and Issues. Belmont, Calif.: Industrial Relations Research Association
Tannenbaum, A.S., B. Kavcic, M. Rosner, M. Vianello, and G. Wieser. 1974b. Hierarchy in Organizations: An International Comparison. San Francisco: Jossey-Bass
Taylor, F.W. 1903. Shop Management. New York: Harper and Row
- 1911. The Principles of Scientific Management. Harper and Row
- 1947. Scientific Management: Comprising Shop Management, The Principles of Scientific Management and Testimony Before the Special House Committee. New York: Harper and Row
Taylor, J.C. 1979a. 'Job design criteria twenty years later.' In L.E. Davis and J.C. Taylor, eds, Design of Jobs. Santa Monica: Goodyear Publishing
- 1979b. 'Job satisfaction and quality of working life: A reassessment.' In L.E. Davis and J.C. Taylor, eds, Design of Jobs. Santa Monica: Goodyear Publishing
Terkel, S. 1972. Working: People Talk About What They Do All Day and How They Feel About What They Do. New York: Pantheon
Thompson, J.D. 1956. 'Authority and power in "identical" organizations.' American Journal of Sociology 62, 290–301
- 1967. Organizations in Action. New York: McGraw-Hill
Thompson, V. 1961. Modern Organization. New York: Knopf
Thurman, J.E. 1977. 'Job satisfaction: An international overview.' International Labour Review 117, 249–67
Trist, E.L. and K.W. Bamforth. 1951. 'Some social and psychological consequences of the Longwall method of coal getting.' Human Relations 4, 3–38
Trist, E.L., G.W. Higgins, E. Murray, and A.B. Pollock. 1963. Organizational Choice. London: Tavistock Publications
Trower, E. 1973. 'Collective Bargaining and Industrial Democracy.' In G. Hunnius, G.D. Garson, and J. Case, eds, Workers Control: A Reader on Labor and Social Change. New York: Random House

Tudor, B. 1972. 'A specification of relationships between job simplicity and powerlessness.' *American Sociological Review* 37, 596–604

Turner, A.N. and P.R. Lawrence. 1965. *Industrial Jobs and the Worker: An Investigation of Requisite Task Attributes*. Harvard University, Division of Research, Graduate School of Business Administration

Urwick, L. 1938. *Scientific Principles of Organization*. New York: American Management Association

– 1944. *The Elements of Administration*. New York: Harper and Row

U.S. department of health, education and welfare. *Work in America: Report of a Special Task Force to the Secretary of Health, Education and Welfare*. Cambridge, Mass.: M.I.T. Press

Vaillancourt, P.M. 1975. 'Quebec worker production cooperatives.' Paper presented to the annual meeting of the Canadian Political Science Association, Edmonton, June

Vanek, J. 1971. *The Participatory Economy: An Evolutionary Hypothesis and a Strategy for Development*. Ithaca, N.Y.: Cornell University Press

– 1975. *Self-management: Economic Liberation of Man*. Harmondsworth: Penguin

Walker, K.F. 1974. *Workers' Participation in Management – Problems, Practice and Prospects*. Geneva: International Institute for Labour Studies

Wall, T. and J.A. Lischeron. 1977. *Worker Participation: A Critique of the Literature and Some Fresh Evidence*. London: McGraw-Hill

Wallace, R.L. 1971. 'A comparative study of attitude scores of managers toward employees and toward selected leadership policies in groups of firms which have either discontinued or retained cost reduction sharing plans.' Unpublished doctoral dissertation, Michigan State University

Walton, R. 1972. 'How to counter alienation in the plant.' *Harvard Business Review* 50, 70–81

– 1977. 'Work innovation at Topeka: After six years.' *Journal of Applied Behavioural Science* 13, 422–33

Walton, R.E. 1974. 'Innovative restructuring of work.' In J.M. Rosow, ed., *The Worker and the Job: Coping With Change*. Englewood Cliffs, N.J.: Prentice-Hall, 145–76

– 1979. 'Work innovations in the United States.' *Harvard Business Review* 57, 88–98

Walton, R.E. and R.B. McKersie. 1965. *Behavioral Theory of Labor Negotiations*. New York: McGraw-Hill

Wanous, J.P. 1974. 'Individual differences and reactions to job characteristics.' *Journal of Applied Psychology* 59, 616–22

Warr, P. and T. Wall. 1975. *Work and Well-being*. Baltimore: Penguin

Watson, K.B. 1974. 'The maturing of multiple management.' *Management Review* 63, 4–14

Ways, M. 1979. 'The virtues, dangers and units of negotiation.' *Fortune*, 15 January, 86–90

Webb, E., D.T. Campbell, R.D. Schwartz, and L. Sechrest. 1966. *Unobtrusive Measures: Nonreactive Research in Social Sciences*. Chicago: Rand McNally

Webb, S. and B. Webb. 1894. *The History of Trade Unionism*. London: Longmans, Green

– 1902. *Industrial Democracy*. London: Longmans, Green

Weber, M. 1947. *The Theory of Social and Economic Organization*. Glencoe, Ill.: Free Press

Weick, K. 1969. *The Social Psychology of Organizing*. Reading, Mass.: Addison Wesley

Westley, W.A. and M.W. Westley. 1971. *The Emerging Worker: Equality and Conflict in the Mass Consumption Society*. Montreal, London: McGill-Queen's University Press

Weyer, R.S., Jr. 1974. *Cognitive Organization and Change: An Information Processing Approach*. Potomac, Md: Erlbaum

White, J.K. 1979. 'The Scanlon plan: causes and correlates of success.' *Academy of Management Journal* 22, 292–312

Whitehorn, A. 1979a. 'Alienation and industrial society: A study of workers' self-management.' *Canadian Review of Sociology and Anthropology* 16, 206–17

– 1979b. 'Yugoslavia: A case study of self-managing socialism?' In Andre Liebich, ed., *The Future of Socialism in Europe*. Montreal: ICES

Wilson, H.B. 1974. *Democracy and the Work Place*. Montreal: Black Rose Books

Winpisinger, W. 1973. 'Job satisfaction: A union response.' *AFL-CIO Federationist* 80, 3–10

Work in America. 1973. Cambridge: M.I.T. Press

Wrege, C.D. and A.M. Stotka. 1978. 'Cooke creates a classic: The story behind F.W. Taylor's principles of Scientific Management.' *Academy of Management Review* 3, 736–49

Wren, D.A. 1979. *The Evolution of Management Thought*. New York: John Wiley and Sons

Yankelovich, D. 1974. 'The meaning of work.' In J.M. Rosow, ed., *The Worker and the Job: Coping With Change*. Englewood Cliffs, N.J. Prentice-Hall

Zakuta, L. 1964. *A Protest Movement Becalmed*. Toronto: University of Toronto Press

Index